Praise for

OVERDELIVER

'Nobody has paid closer attention to the world of direct response advertising than Brian Kurtz. His new book—his opus magnum—brings that world to you, in great detail. This is a must-have book for anyone in the business . . . and anyone seriously interested in how people decide what, when, and how to buy.'

— **Bill Bonner**, founder, The Agora

'In Overdeliver, Brian chronicles almost four decades of hard-core experience that comes with building an iconic $100 million direct marketing company (and then a multimillion-dollar business on his own)—and then committing to teaching all he has learned, condensing it down into something you can absorb in an afternoon. Brian Kurtz is a different kind of author. He's forgotten more about marketing and sales than most newcomers will ever discover.'

— **Frank Kern**

'I've known Brian Kurtz for over 20 years, and he is a direct marketing and direct mail genius. . . . In Overdeliver, Brian shares how you can use offers, copy, multichannel marketing, continuity and a lot more to be a better marketer, grow your business, make more money and make a big impact in your market. If you want to learn from one of the greatest marketing minds alive, read this book.'

— **Joe Polish**, founder, Genius Network and Genius Recovery

'Filled with more useful information and history than any other book I'm familiar with. . . . You should dramatically improve your results after reading this book.'

— **Joe Sugarman**, direct marketing legend

'Brian Kurtz was not only one of the wunderkinds who practically invented DM publishing in the 1980s, but he was also one of the elder statesmen of the industry who guided its transition from paper to electronics in the 2000s. [In this book he] assimilates the best insights and ideas of the industry's best and brightest business leaders. Overdeliver is a must-read.'

— **Mark Ford**, chief growth strategist, The Agora, and author of two dozen books, including the bestseller *Ready Fire Aim*

'Brian . . . delivers a career manual and strategy book that covers every major principle that will affect your bottom line. This book should be on every marketer's shelf and its case studies should be burned into every marketer's muscle memory.'

— **Perry Marshall**, author, *80/20 Sales & Marketing, Ultimate Guide to Google AdWords* and *Ultimate Guide to Facebook Advertising*

'There's a very small group of true direct response wizards out there . . . [and Brian is] one of the guys who can change your career and business in a heartbeat with just a casually tossed off piece of advice. . . . This book is your invitation to join that elite conversation. To finally learn the mind-sets, tactics, techniques, and habits of the best in the biz. Do NOT read this book. Instead, devour it. Insert it into your brain and make it part of your DNA. It's that tight.'

— **John Carlton**, copywriting know-it-all, grizzled consultant and author of *The Entrepreneur's Guide to Getting Your Shit Together*

'Brian Kurtz's Overdeliver *refreshes and reminds of the elemental and critical forces that drive response while providing us with all new ways of creating new opportunities in direct marketing. . . . Destined to be one of the classics.'*

— **Greg Renker**, co-founder, Guthy-Renker

'Overdeliver *is the bridge that connects the timeless fundamentals of direct response marketing to the state-of-the-art marketing strategies, tactics, and channels of today. . . . Brian Kurtz is a living legend . . . nobody but him could have written this book. I consider it to be among the must-read direct marketing books that should be on the bookshelf of every marketer, every copywriter, and every entrepreneur.'*

— **Ryan Levesque**, #1 national bestselling author of *Choose* and *Ask*

'Brian Kurtz knows real marketing better than almost anyone. This book is a must-read for marketers of all generations. From tried and true modern marketing tactics to pearls of 'old school' wisdom, Overdeliver *provides a roadmap for jump-starting any organization's marketing efforts.'*

— **Ryan Deiss**, founder and CEO, Digital Marketer

'People claim to be marketing experts when their actual results are never tracked or measured. That is exactly what Overdeliver *is not about. Brian has almost 40 years of obsessing, learning and mastering direct response marketing and now he's sharing those secrets in this brilliant book. Read it and implement as fast as humanly possible.'*

— **Dean Graziosi**, *New York Times* bestselling author of *Millionaire Success Habits* and serial entrepreneur

'Whatever you are paying for this book, you're paying too little. Marketing is the lifeblood of your business and this book should be required reading for everyone.'

— **Ryan Lee**, founder of REWIND

'Why do successful entrepreneurs pay Brian Kurtz $20,000 or more per year to be in his Titans Mastermind Group? You'll see for yourself when you read this book.'

— **Steve Dworman**, infomercial writer/producer and author of *$12 Billion of Inside Marketing Secrets Discovered Through DRTV*

'Brian has become one of the industry's leading mentors—sharing his knowledge of direct marketing and well-honed strategies with some of the fastest-growing companies in our space. Any event he puts on or book he writes will always be at the top of my list—and it should be at the top of yours too.'

— **Kim Krause Schwalm**, A-list copywriter and copy mentor

'If you want to succeed in marketing and DON'T buy this book, you'd better pray your competition can't read.'

— **Arthur P. Johnson**, copywriter, product developer and infomercial star

'Got a low-priced product that you're having trouble selling due to high media costs? Brian reveals how he sold $2 billion worth of products, $39 at a time. Do you think Facebook invented look-alike audiences? Look inside this book and you'll find out how Brian and his team were creating regression models (better than look-alikes) back when Zuck was still in diapers! Do yourself a favor and read this book.'

— **Parris Lampropoulos**, marketing strategist and copywriter

'For years, I've given to students of marketing a list of 14 must-read books— I've now added Brian's book to a new list of 15. *Overdeliver* is the best direct marketing book since his and my mentor Dick Benson's 1987 Secrets of Successful Direct Mail.'

— **Richard A. Viguerie**, pioneer of political direct mail and chairman of American Target Advertising, Inc.

'If the word 'marketing' makes you cringe, this book is for you. And if the word 'marketing' makes you salivate, this book is for you. *Overdeliver* is loaded with time-tested strategies and invaluable ideas . . . a marketing balm to the sore business soul.'

— **Victoria Labalme**, performing artist and performance strategist and member, Speaker Hall of Fame

'Over the years, I've paid Brian tens of thousands of dollars for his money-making, business-building, life-changing advice and insights. Now they can be yours for the price of this book.'

— **David Deutsch**, A-list copywriter and author of *Think Inside the Box!*

'If you want to make a lot of money in direct mail, e-commerce, TV, radio, consulting, yard sales, or lemonade, *Overdeliver* is the roadmap that can make you relentlessly richer. How can I be sure? Brian is directly responsible for generating millions of dollars in income for my business. He can do the same for you . . . all you have to do is listen.'

— **Eric Betuel**, copywriter, president of Imagination Inc.

'I just read a new 'classic' for direct response marketers! I learned— and relearned—so much. *Overdeliver* is a MUST READ for newbies—as well as experienced marketers and copywriters.'

— **Carline Anglade-Cole**, copywriter and consultant, Cole Marketing Solutions

'Brian Kurtz has put together a definitive presentation of direct marketing, as apart from all other marketing. . . . Pros will find it fascinating. Those new to the disciplines will find a vital crash course. Pin-head executives in big, dumb corporations wasting oceans of money on utterly unaccountable brand and image and ego advertising should be forced at gunpoint to read it. Ogilvy was right when he ranted to his own agency's staff that only the mail-order people knew what the hell they were doing, and were Ogilvy alive, he would applaud Brian's work here.'

— **Dan Kennedy**, multi-millionaire serial entrepreneur, professional direct-response copywriter and author of 23 books

'Brian Kurtz boils down the most powerful, proven direct response marketing principles into a single, destiny-changing word—*Overdeliver*. Make it your credo, and you and your company will succeed as never before.'

— **Gary Bencivenga**, MarketingBullets.com

'[Brian Kurtz's] knowledge of direct marketing is unparalleled, all of it earned through decades of work at the highest levels of the industry. This book is a distillation of Brian's hard-won lessons, and it should be required reading for anyone who does any marketing. But this book is also a lot more: hidden in plain sight in these pages is . . . a guide to living a life of service, and a life of passion, and ultimately a life well-lived.'

— **Jeff Walker**, #1 *New York Times* bestselling author of *Launch*

'Brian's spirit and wisdom burst forth in abundance from the pages of *Overdeliver*, making this book as enjoyable to read as it is essential to any entrepreneur or marketer. Its gift is to provide clear insight into the bedrock fundamentals of successful direct response marketing and an understanding of how these will continue to apply to new media going forward.'

— **Dan Sullivan, president**, The Strategic Coach Inc.

OVERDELIVER

ALSO BY BRIAN KURTZ

The Advertising Solution with Craig Simpson

∎

OVERDELIVER

Build a Business for
a Lifetime Playing
the Long Game in
Direct Response Marketing

BRIAN KURTZ

HAY HOUSE

Carlsbad, California • New York City
London • Sydney • New Delhi

Published in the United Kingdom by:
Hay House UK Ltd, The Sixth Floor, Watson House,
54 Baker Street, London W1U 7BU
Tel: +44 (0)20 3927 7290; Fax: +44 (0)20 3927 7291; www.hayhouse.co.uk

Published in the United States of America by:
Hay House Inc., PO Box 5100, Carlsbad, CA 92018-5100
Tel: (1) 760 431 7695 or (800) 654 5126
Fax: (1) 760 431 6948 or (800) 650 5115; www.hayhouse.com

Published in Australia by:
Hay House Australia Ltd, 18/36 Ralph St, Alexandria NSW 2015
Tel: (61) 2 9669 4299; Fax: (61) 2 9669 4144; www.hayhouse.com.au

Published in India by:
Hay House Publishers India, Muskaan Complex, Plot No.3, B-2,
Vasant Kunj, New Delhi 110 070
Tel: (91) 11 4176 1620; Fax: (91) 11 4176 1630; www.hayhouse.co.in

Indexer: Joan Shapiro
Cover design: Scott Breidenthal
Interior design: Nick C. Welch

A catalogue record for this book is available from the British Library.

Tradepaper ISBN: 978-1-78817-755-9
Hardback ISBN: 978-1-4019-5675-2
E-book ISBN: 978-1-4019-5676-9
Audiobook ISBN: 978-1-4019-5691-2

Printed and bound by CPI Group (UK) Ltd, Croydon CR0 4YY

No one can do anything valuable in life without a loving and supportive family, and without Robin, Alex, and Madeline, I'd be lost.

CONTENTS

Foreword by Jay Abraham   xiii

Introduction   xix

CHAPTER 1:   Overdeliver   1

CHAPTER 2:   Original Source   17

CHAPTER 3:   How Paying Postage Made Me a Better Marketer   33

CHAPTER 4:   List Building & RFM   57

CHAPTER 5:   Offers   83

CHAPTER 6:   Creative & Copy   117

CHAPTER 7:   Multichannel Marketing   147

CHAPTER 8:   Customer Service & Fulfillment   169

CHAPTER 9:   Continuity & LTV   191

CHAPTER 10:   Playing the Long Game   207

Further Reading   243

Index   255

Acknowledgments   265

About the Author   275

FOREWORD

I rarely endorse books, let alone write forewords. Why? Well, I don't want to sound brash, but I don't want my reputation for preeminence being associated with mediocre material. But writing a foreword for this book is an exception I'm ecstatic to make. I am putting the full force of my reputation and endorsement on the line for *Overdeliver* by my dear friend Brian Kurtz.

This book you are about to devour (and believe me, it's like that famous potato chip commercial—you won't be able to read just one chapter) is going to explode the market of mastery. What daily workouts are to your muscles or what nutrients are to your mind and body, this book will be to building businesses that last a lifetime.

Some time ago, Brian co-wrote a book about the greats of direct response advertising. It was very informative, but I felt it didn't scratch the surface of his knowledge, brilliance, and teaching ability. Brian possesses a fascinating and ever-evolving way of thinking and a truly original mind.

So I challenged Brian with an audacious reward if he could blow the roof off everything else that had been written to date about direct response marketing. I challenged him to painstakingly create a hybrid book that would encompass the countless real-life case studies from his own career as well as his world-class colleagues' success stories.

I wanted to see a unique integration of his vast, incredibly effective knowledge along with a clear identification of how readers of these success stories could apply these enduring, immutable principles (which no one talks about) to their marketing. If he could interweave these stories, examples, and case studies into a one-of-a-kind format—where every page contained a story, an analogy, or an action step—not only would I write one of the most compelling forewords ever, I would personally back the success of the book.

I knew unreservedly that he could do it, so I felt confident making perhaps the most outrageous guarantee ever offered in order to induce you to read and keep rereading this book until the message becomes ingrained permanently in your mind and guides all you do.

Brian, of course, outdid himself, so now I'm on the hook to make good on my promise. And so I personally guarantee you—everyone who purchases this book and reads it all the way through, with a notepad and pen to identify the most relevant ideas and concepts that apply directly to them—that I will personally write a check for the purchase price if Brian's ideas fail to propel a meaningful improvement in not one but *at least three* facets of your business.

Describing *Overdeliver* as a mere marketing book is a disservice both to Brian and to you as the reader. I don't want this groundbreaking compendium to be misperceived as something light or general or a regurgitation of anything written before it. Brian's approach, experience, and strategies for transforming theoretical material into actionable systems are stunningly unique.

In direct response marketing, a key action is to tell the prospect what they're going to learn, tell them how to learn it, and then tell them what they just learned—but to do it in different enough ways so that the power of the message cannot be missed or denied. Brian does this to perfection throughout the book. I found myself reveling in the way he shares a lifetime of lessons and a world of insights, perspectives, and updated and modified implementations in this fast-moving, nontheoretical world in such a way that we cannot help but see the tremendous value of each lesson.

You will be unimaginably changed as a strategist, a marketplace psychologist, and a consequential thinker after reading this book, and even better, become a far more masterful marketer than the person you were before. This is no mere brain dump. Brian has achieved a profound knowledge transfer by adroitly intertwining stories with principles, principles with applications, applications with implications of how it all directly applies to you. He ties together the principles of direct marketing in a cohesive way that will improve your business—no matter the type, size, or marketing methods used—and in so doing, he succeeds in achieving something rare indeed.

This book will be a true catalyst for your growth—with Brian acting as your measurable marketing alchemist, transforming knowledge into fuel that can power and propel enormous growth and prosperity for years to come. But the economic rewards you'll achieve are equaled only by the powerhouse of newfound understanding you will gain from this fresh new slant on direct response marketing.

It's probably best now to provide some teasers (or what Brian refers to as "fascinations" in his chapter on creative and copy) to stimulate your desire and forge your perception of what this book is and what it isn't. Here are a few of my favorite insights from this book:

- Why almost every marketer has a limited understanding of all that marketing really entails

- Where great ideas come from and how to generate more breakthrough concepts in your industry than all your competitors combined

- Why today's marketer almost always underperforms the capabilities of their marketplace and which activities they could pursue to precisely identify where the biggest underperforming opportunities lie

- A better formula for multiplying results by meeting prospects where their response buttons are red hot and always making it easier for them to say yes than no to your offers

- Where the maximum money is in your business and industry and how to mine the richest veins in a consistent, sustainable way

- A creativity switch for turning on (and up) your creative abilities—and those of your copywriters and creative partners

- Understanding markets: identifying who's got the most money to spend in your market and why

- Changing the game you play, making new rules your competition can't compete with or win at

Here's a factoid you might find interesting: One of my good friends followed the basic lessons Brian shares here and—taking only $100 but measuring and maximizing every element—turned it into over a billion dollars in sales. This is no exaggeration and should give you some food for thought regarding just how valuable this book could be to you!

There's a famous book both Brian and I love, *Reality in Advertising*, which Brian talks about in more depth in Chapter 2. It sets out some of the most important realizations and understanding and underrecognized truths about advertising ever discovered. I'd say that what *Reality in Advertising* is to that market, *Overdeliver* is to all forms of business marketing today. In summary, no one in any stage of marketing should fail to read Brian Kurtz's *Overdeliver* at least three times. It's a new classic.

I'm proud, thrilled, and thoroughly impressed at the outsize contribution Brian will make to your marketing mastery and business success in these pages. I feel privileged to have been able to write this foreword, and I'm excited for the impact this book is about to have on your marketing and business life. I could say much more—but you get that I love this book and the way it's written and presented. But even beyond that, I love the enormity of usable maxims it constantly and beautifully provides.

I hope these words encourage you to read *Overdeliver* carefully and often.

— Jay Abraham

INTRODUCTION

Those who did it have an obligation to teach it;
those who teach gain many riches.

On my first day as a direct marketer, a crazed movie buff with a revolver shot the president of the United States. Against the odds, President Reagan survived and saw his popularity rate rise to over 70 percent as a result. But I was also quite lucky that day. While it was far from a full day of work, with everyone glued to the TV set watching the news unfold, it was the day I started working for Marty Edelston and his scrappy little company, Boardroom Reports.

Over the next three decades, Boardroom went from being a fairly unknown publisher to an iconic brand and direct marketer, and I'm proud to say I had a direct hand in that exponential growth. I went from being a junior list manager to executive vice president of the company, working across the most competitive niches with the best copywriters and direct marketers the world has ever seen. Marty saw to it that my education was absolutely immersive and, as one of the titans of the industry, he set an incredible standard to live up to every day.

A few weeks before that pivotal day early in 1981, a headhunter called to ask me if I would like to interview for a job at this up-and-coming newsletter company called Boardroom Reports as an in-house list manager. Like I knew what that meant.

Having graduated with an English degree, I had been working at my first job with a company in the theater industry (mainly because they were the only ones who would hire me). I liked the sound of this cool young company. Marty seemed so entrepreneurial and creative that I decided to see where things would go, even though I had no idea what a list manager did. So I accepted the role, thinking that I would move over to editorial as soon as I had the chance, and started sponging up everything I could about lists in the meantime. The job felt like a good fit, and soon I was joking that I had been voted "most likely to become a list manager" in my high school yearbook.

The role was essentially to be a salesman. My job was to make sure everyone in the direct mail community was renting (and mailing to) the Boardroom lists, which were some of the most responsive lists in the industry.

A year after getting started, I went into Marty's office to apply for a junior editorial role that had opened up. Despite having taken to lists like a natural, enjoying myself, and starting to excel beyond people who had been at it much longer, I thought I "should" be in editorial, since it was closer to what I'd studied.

But Marty took a hard look at me and said, "I think you have a nose for marketing. I think that you should stay on the list side of the business and learn everything you can about direct marketing."

Little did I know at the time that following Marty's advice that day would lead to a career I never could have imagined. Like any great direct marketer, Marty understood the critical importance of lists. He was one of the best direct marketers in the business, and here he was telling me that he saw a career for me there. I had tremendous respect for Marty, so if he said I was good, then I was going to listen. I stayed put, and over the coming months, I learned what a list manager did and I learned all about what list brokers did as well. It was the list brokers who represented the mailers (i.e., marketers), and because they bought all the media (lists), they were among the most powerful and wealthy folks in the direct mail business. Many of them were making as much money as the stock brokers enjoying the boom on Wall Street at the same time.

Learning that a list broker was not a stock broker was an important early lesson. Every list manager was obsessed with getting their lists into the hands of the right brokers, and there's where I found an edge, because my obsession was a little different. The most important thing I did was to make time to talk and meet with other list managers—my "competitors"—and not just the list brokers. I felt like I could never get enough time talking with the other list managers. They all had something to teach me, and every time I picked up a bit of new information from one of them, selling Boardroom's lists got easier for me.

On the surface, these encounters took away from selling time with the list brokers (since it was the brokers, not the other managers, who were responsible for my livelihood). But I was playing a different game, and I was willing to give up some short-term income to spend time sizing up how our competitors were selling the lists in their portfolios. What I discovered changed everything for us at Boardroom and has stood me in good stead for the rest of my career—the lesson is what I now call competition as coexistence.

Over the next few years, I earned the reputation of being the best list manager in the country. It all started with talking to list managers more than list brokers to build my career.

Years later, as I adapted my list knowledge to all areas of marketing, I became Marty's partner in every aspect of the business. I had the freedom to think of new ideas daily, with phenomenal resources at my fingertips: the best copywriters, consultants, database experts, list mavens, and numbers gurus, and a database of customers and former customers that fluctuated between five and ten million names. Those names—real people—would become the cornerstone of our success.

Marty used to say that we were in the business of saving lives, that as a result of what we were selling, people were saved from financial ruin and health disasters. In the end, our success all came down to becoming experts on our lists, building deep empathy with our audience, and knowing the market better than anyone else—and doing all this long before we ever tried to figure out the best offers and the best copy. We learned that to create a company that was truly transformational, the list (again, we're talking about real people here) has to be an obsession.

■

As time went on and Boardroom became more and more successful, Marty and I talked a lot about the obligation we had to teach what we knew . . . so much so that our financial advisors would beg us to do a little less teaching and a little more selling. But everything we were doing was so powerful that we knew we had a unique opportunity to share the abundance with other people who were willing to do the work.

Eugene (Gene) M. Schwartz, who I'll be talking a lot about in this book, was one of the greatest copywriters and Renaissance men who ever lived, and he was a key figure in this resolution to teach as much as we could. His death inspired us to republish his lost classic, *Breakthrough Advertising*, for a new generation.

Marty was not a sentimental guy. A few days after Gene's funeral, instead of waxing poetic, Marty focused on the lessons Gene had left us. He wanted to bring those lessons to the marketers and copywriters coming up at the time, as quickly as possible, so we got to work on the new edition of Gene's book right away. Marty was all business, always driving forward.

So when Marty died in 2013, I knew I had to continue holding up my promise to teach everything we'd learned over the 32 years we worked together, from list selection and running campaigns to maximizing relationships with customers and competitors. This book is how I fulfill that commitment. I accept that some young marketers might look at me like I'm some dinosaur from a bygone era; but while I playfully include "T. rex" in my e-mail address, that doesn't mean this book is going to be a stroll down memory lane. Instead, it's a way to share everything I've learned over a long career in direct marketing and to help the next generation of marketers understand that the principles of direct response are both eternal and essential.

I would like this book to serve as the bridge between those principles and the state-of-the-art multichannel marketing world of today. I believe it's my responsibility to pass on the fundamental lessons of direct response marketing to today's marketers and entrepreneurs who are hungry to learn them and apply them. Other people have already written about many of the marketing concepts you'll find in this book: product development and market selection, recency-frequency-monetary (RFM) scores, list segmentation, lifetime value (LTV), continuity programs (i.e., membership programs with a renewal component). I'm not the first nor will I be the last to write and talk about any of that.

What I *am* first at is putting it all under the umbrella of my experience and combining the ideas in light of everything I've worked on throughout my career. I have a unique position among marketers, as my journey took me from building a large direct marketing company offline to moving online and bringing some of the biggest players in the industry along with me.

I've been in some form of the direct response business for nearly 40 years, seeing the same principles work across all channels, offline and online. I've been able to take a lot of previously disconnected ideas and connect them in ways that make 1 + 1 = 64. (This is a concept that originally came from Gene Schwartz—that when you get the right combination of ideas and experience, growth becomes exponential instead of staying linear.)

Maybe you're new to copywriting, marketing, and entrepreneurship and wanting to improve your skills; maybe you're a seasoned marketer who is looking for a few new ideas, confident that you'll be able to have a huge impact with what you find. Either way, you've probably run into quite a few entrepreneurs who are uncomfortable with the idea that marketing is critical to every kind of business. You might have even met a few people who view marketing as a necessary evil (this could even have been you!).

I often say that marketing isn't everything . . . it's the only thing. That might sound like I only care about selling and making money, but it's just the opposite. When marketers understand what they're doing at the deepest level and act with integrity and purpose, their work becomes a vehicle for bringing positive change into the lives of the people they serve.

But let me be clear: It doesn't matter if your product or service saves lives, transforms businesses, heals relationships, or just makes you outrageously wealthy. It cannot and will not make an ounce of difference to anyone until you decide to aggressively sell it (within the boundaries you determine are right for your business). Having a direct marketing focus was the key to that growth as we moved from direct mail and print to TV and the Internet. It's all about getting in front of the people who need you most. This book is going to teach you how to sell aggressively without ever losing sight of the people you are selling to or compromising the respect and care they deserve.

This book is about *direct marketing*, which is *measurable marketing* in any medium. While direct mail was the medium I cut my teeth on (and I'm proud of it), I cringe when marketers think that direct marketing is only about direct mail.

This book is *not* about general advertising, or what we call the Mad Men model: advertising that builds brand awareness, and maybe evokes an emotional response, but has no way for the potential customer to actually *respond* to the ad or for the marketer to track that response. With most general advertising, you can't measure how effective the ad was because there's no way to measure whether the customer takes an action as a result of the ad. Direct marketing, on the other hand, is all about measurability and therefore accountability. It doesn't matter what medium we are talking about, and it doesn't matter if we are talking about marketing offline (like direct mail) or online (like e-mail).

All the advertising you pay for, regardless of the medium, should be measurable, which is why direct marketing is so powerful. It's the only way to get a specific return on your investment—every time you run a campaign, there has to be some way to measure it. Whether it's including a phone number, an e-mail address, or a web address to respond to, there must be some way to measure the response to the ad. Having some kind of response device with every marketing message you send in any medium—one that enables you to measure effectiveness and profitability—is the only way to know if your marketing is really working for the people in your target audience.

Before we dive into the lessons and obsessions I gathered over a long career in direct marketing, here are nine fundamentals for you to keep in mind as you work through the book (whether you are directly involved in marketing products and services or are an entrepreneur who needs to hire marketing talent).

1. Be Involved in All Your Marketing Efforts, Even If You Outsource Everything

Most people with a background in direct response probably won't need more encouragement on this one—we're all data junkies who love getting our hands dirty on every kind of campaign. But if your role also demands that you focus on other things outside of marketing (product development, finances, hiring, etc.), make sure you never let go of the marketing reins completely. Keep an eye on everything that everyone is doing, both inside and outside your organization.

The best people I ever hired internally were the people in operations, analytics, and finance who understood and recognized the value of direct marketing. Being on the same page meant we could move so much faster than our competitors. When everyone on your team is on the same page, you don't get slowed down by red tape. It might sound like a big ask to be hands-on with marketing when it's not your core competency or to only hire people who love marketing, no matter their job title. But remember that every marketing message is a representation of you and your brand. Look after your marketing like you would your own child—it connects you to your customers, and that relationship must be protected at all costs.

2. Marketing Is Not Evil

I totally understand mission-based businesses and the need to be "elegant" or "classy" with all marketing and sales messages. But marketing your product, *especially* when it is mission based, is about serving your customers, not taking from them.

Always remember this important premise, drilled into me by one of my mentors, Jay Abraham (still one of the world's most influential thought leaders on business and marketing, and author of the foreword to this book): it is irresponsible to bring your product or service to the marketplace without the same passion with which you created it.

There's an ethical line each of us won't cross (which comes down to your personal perspective), and that's important to define clearly. But there's nothing to be ashamed of in bringing your life's work to as many people as possible if you are doing it in a way that's congruent with your ethics and overall philosophy. To do this may require copy platforms and creative that you consider aggressive; but as long as you are working in the spirit of making a big impact, sell hard. The more people you reach, the better.

3. No One Spends Enough Time on Lists

You're going to hear that no one spends enough time on lists a few times throughout this book. Take it to heart. Dick Benson (another mentor and the smartest man I ever met on the science and strategies of direct mail) said this to me the day I met him, circa 1985, when we were researching and comparing lists. I never forgot it, particularly since he later revised the comment to say that the team I led at Boardroom was the only exception.

I can't emphasize enough that you must pay close attention to your customer list, your prospect list, and how you approach list building at a very detailed level. The real live people who make up those lists are truly the lifeblood of any business driven by direct response (and even many businesses that wouldn't identify themselves as being in direct response).

Ignoring your lists is like ignoring your family. It's a pre-scription for disaster. Making sure you talk to different segments of your list based on their relationship with you is critical to maximize success, and we'll talk about this at length in the following chapters.

4. Customers Refund Transactions . . . Not Relationships

E-mail is probably the most prevalent sales and communication medium in the world today, and it is also the most effective and efficient way to market any product or service when used properly. But just because e-mail is cheap doesn't mean it should be used indiscriminately or without careful thought about every message you send. The care that you take with your e-mail list (what I would call your online family) might be the most important thing you do as a marketer, both now and in the future.

If someone recommends that you mail every day, don't take it as gospel . . . take it under advisement. But here's better advice: mail when you have something really worthwhile to say. Blogging every day with purpose is effective; throwing out random thoughts or sending pictures of last night's dinner might be counterproductive. You wouldn't want your own family to start ignoring you because you were sending stuff they didn't care about. Think of your online family the same way. If you are just throwing out whatever you can think of every morning, including unrelated or insignificant content, you run the risk of burning out your list, causing your online family to ignore you when you really want them to pay closer attention.

Always look to build relationships for a lifetime, and deliver huge amounts of valuable content before you ever try to sell something. Because e-mail is cost-efficient, this is so much easier than in the past, when we only had offline techniques. Understanding lifetime value (which has its own chapter later on) gives all marketers real leverage and the maximum chance for success in multiple channels. It's this focus on the long game that you need to develop in your customer relationships.

5. Credibility & Transparency Trump All

Respect your customers. If they're following you, don't insult them with anything but transparency. Showing proof of your approach through testimonials, case histories, and professional endorsements is about building your case, not bragging. And when you make a mistake or want to show vulnerability, people always appreciate transparency.

Isn't the cover-up always worse than the crime? There are countless stories in the world of marketing where a business confessed to something they were not proud of or failed at and came back stronger than ever. But once there's a cover-up, you're doomed.

6. Always Think *Direct Marketing*

Remember—direct marketing is *not* just direct mail. It's measurable marketing in any channel. Measurable and accountable advertising is always what you want, and don't let anyone sell you a brand and image advertising "campaign" without being able to show a clear return on your investment (ROI).

I've been saying for years that the Internet is the ultimate direct marketing medium . . . and while that won't change anytime soon, *all marketing is direct marketing* in my world. Expecting an acceptable ROI must always be standard operating procedure. Just because a lot of stuff is cheap to do online doesn't mean you should allow sloppy campaigns out the door or skimp on requiring tangible results.

7. Use Your Personal Brand in Your Marketing When Applicable

Many marketing superstars understand their personal brand deeply and always keep it totally in sync with their products and services. They're confident talking about their achievements and know that their information is valuable to their customers. However, many entrepreneurs and business owners are squeamish about putting themselves out there for fear of sounding boastful or disingenuous. In response to that, I will quote baseball pitcher Dizzy Dean (and I think John Wayne and others have used this one too): "It ain't bragging if you done it."

8. Advertising Opportunities Are Now Infinite

There are endless ways to market your products and services today. None of us can master them all, because there's simply too much to know. This is why now is the best time ever to be a marketer . . . but this is also what makes it dangerous.

Having spent my entire career buying à la carte from the best experts across multiple marketing niches, I can assure you this approach will pay for itself. I tell entrepreneurs to run—not walk—away from anyone who claims they can be your one-stop shop for all marketing, creative, and media buying.

Remember that when you have more choice across channels, you also see more specialization and therefore more experts. I don't think I have to convince you that experts are much better to work with than generalists—and certainly better than generalists posing as experts. In today's supercharged, multichannel and technology-rich marketing environment, no one can be an expert on everything. Make sure you're always searching for the expert who is the leading specialist in the channel you want to use.

9. SingleChannelMarketingIsSoBoring.com

Feel free to go to this website because it just redirects to my website, www.briankurtz.net. I really *do* own this URL, just to prove a point.

No business should rely on a single marketing channel, because you never know when the landscape might change. If Facebook shuts down your ad account, or Google changes its search algorithm, or your e-mail provider slaps you for an infringement, you must have other channels dialed in to keep your business solvent.

This is not about one channel being better than another channel. That is, it's not an "or" but an "and." Not only is buying your media on a single channel boring, it's also dangerous. And the danger is easily avoided when you've committed to working with the best of the best across the different marketing disciplines, as I mentioned in the last point. You would expect the people who manage your money to diversify your financial risk, and you should expect the people who manage your marketing to do the same.

Remember, you have to meet your customers where they are, and there's not a single industry where buyers use only one channel. Meet them everywhere they spend time. And you can only serve your customers if your business stays afloat, so diversify your marketing to ensure you can provide for them over the long haul.

■

With all the tools, case studies, and information at our disposal, today's marketers have more opportunity than ever to leave an indelible mark on the world. While I can't guarantee what the market will do or which platform will take off next, if you approach direct response marketing with a spirit of service and healthy competition, your business and marketing can be a force that changes countless lives for the better—and pays off for you too.

You also need to calculate everything on the basis of your business model. You need to know when you have your money back. If you're not a mature company, focus on the sources that have shorter bogeys. The return on your investment doesn't have to be immediate, but it may need to be faster based on your cash flow and overhead requirements. When you're established and have stable cash flow, you can go with the longer bogeys and tolerate more risk.

FOLLOW THE ANECDOTAL EVIDENCE

The most logical person I ever met was a man named Adolph Auerbacher. His name may not be familiar to you if you're under a certain age, but he was one of the most influential people in both magazine publishing and direct marketing. Adolph was a senior executive at Meredith Corporation when it was one of the largest magazine publishers in the world. He was the brains behind the tremendous growth of magazine brands such as *Better Homes and Gardens* and *Ladies' Home Journal.* If you haven't heard of those titles, go look them up. They were incredibly successful and case histories worth learning from.

Adolph spoke softly and gave sage advice in very few words. He was always on point, and something he said to me in the early 1980s has stuck with me for over 30 years: "Follow the anecdotal evidence."

What he meant was to look at what was happening out in the world, think critically about any current trends and what had happened previously in the market, and then measure it against our experiences, strengths, and weaknesses to find a good way to capitalize on the opportunities in front of us. No one *said* that Boardroom should go into infomercials (28-minute TV spots), but the anecdotal evidence told us that since we had a lot of information to share, we should take advantage of this new long-form medium. Long-form copy had drastically outperformed short-form copy for selling our books and information in print, so it made sense that a 28-minute TV spot would be more effective than a 2-minute spot. Following the anecdotal evidence (and a bout of insomnia) eventually led to a franchise that created sales well over $200 million employing a trifecta of media: direct mail, direct response television, and online display advertising.

The story begins in 1988, when every magazine seemed to be selling subscriptions on TV, using one-minute or two-minute ads. The *Sports Illustrated* team was pranking people in shoe stores with their sneaker phone campaign and turning the recordings into ads: They would mount the sneaker phone on the wall with all the other shoes, and it looked so much like an actual sneaker that customers would be startled when the shoe they were considering started ringing. The phone came free with a subscription to *Sports Illustrated*, and between the sneaker phone and the football phone that had preceded it, the magazine sold millions of dollars' worth of subscriptions on TV.

I was jealous—TV was one medium that we had not conquered. Unlike direct mail, it didn't have postage and printing costs, but there were still other huge up-front costs in producing spots that made it a risky medium . . . but one that was high risk with high reward.

In 1988, our most popular consumer newsletter was the aforementioned *Bottom Line/Personal (BL/P)*, and our best-selling book was called *The Book of Inside Information (BII)*, a compilation of Bottom Line's greatest hits (the best articles that had previously appeared in the newsletters). We had an incredibly loyal readership, and the information was very valuable, so we figured that if TV worked for *Sports Illustrated*, it could work for us.

But our short-form TV ads bombed spectacularly. Even with spots as "long" as two minutes—about four times as long as most other TV ads at the time—there was no way to adequately sell products like ours, covering complex subjects with an unknown brand behind them. That is, our product line was basically unknown (except to the "lucky millions" in our direct mail universe). The TV market was very broad and hard to segment (this was 1988, remember), and viewers needed a huge amount of education before they would be confident enough to pick up the phone and place an order for products like ours.

In the late 1980s, an "old media" was brought back to life after a hiatus due to Ronald Reagan deregulating it. TV infomercials were long form (28 minutes and 30 seconds). I started following the work of Guthy-Renker, who created and produced huge winners with this format, many of them with content that had some affinity to ours. The Guthy-Renker show "Personal Power" (with Tony Robbins) inspired me the most. By 1991, over 100 million Americans (in 200 media markets) had seen the ad—which is astounding given the infancy of the infomercial industry at the time. I keenly observed that 28 minutes and 30 seconds was a lot longer than 2 minutes and would give us enough time to tell a story that would educate people and make them want to buy. So Marty and I met with Bill Guthy and Greg Renker to tell them about our amazing Bottom Line franchise.

We knew we could help millions of consumers with life-changing information, and we wanted to explore creating a program for this brand that would reach beyond our existing customers. We wanted Guthy-Renker to do for us what they did with "Personal Power." (If this program was before your time, look it up on YouTube. It sold like crazy, and it's an incredible early direct-marketing case study, suitable for the swipe file I know you are building since reading Chapter 2.) Our logic seemed solid: "*Sports Illustrated* sells with simple envelope mailings in direct mail and complements that with 2-minute TV spots. We sell with long 12-page letters, 16- or 32-page magalogs, and even 64-page digests (bookalogs) in direct mail, so long-form direct mail should translate to around 28 minutes to sell via TV!"

Brilliant, right? Nope. We couldn't get it off the ground.

Our first attempt at a TV infomercial went absolutely nowhere. Not because of Guthy-Renker or because we didn't understand the audience, but where Tony Robbins had a whole suite of congruent products—tapes, CDs, and workbooks—we only had the one book, a newsletter, and other disparate pieces that didn't make sense to sell together.

It was clear we hadn't collected *all* the evidence on what made infomercials work and didn't understand at the time how to use our assets to make the medium successful for us, despite the logic that long-form TV would be more effective than short-form TV. Even though I knew there was a huge opportunity for us with infomercials, the prospect of spending the time and money to figure out how to make such an expensive medium work for us soon collapsed under its own weight. So we went back to doing what we knew best.

Fast-forward a decade or so. I was sitting up at 2:00 A.M. just after New Year's Eve with a nasty bout of indigestion (I am so glad to have given up sugar now). I flipped on the TV to see an incredible pitchman, Kevin Trudeau, sell a single book for 28 minutes and 30 seconds, at $29.95, without a recognizable company, without a known brand, and frankly, without much credibility. If you've never heard of Trudeau, look him up as a cautionary tale about what happens when you prioritize fast money over truly caring for your customers. I won't comment further on his business practices, how he sold, or what he delivered. The point here is that he was using the medium that had been taunting me all these years, and he was clearly having a lot of success as evidenced by how often his shows were running—direct marketers don't keep buying expensive media if it's not paying out. This is another rule of thumb I learned from doing direct mail: If you saw the same control mailing piece in your mailbox over a period of months (sometimes years), you knew it was a successful control and "swipe worthy." Connecting that rule to TV, when someone pays for pricey TV time (like they might pay for postage), they are not simply washing, rinsing, and repeating without reading results and determining profitability by some measure. What really bugged (and eventually inspired) me was that he was selling a product that did not compare with or meet the standards of all our legitimate, high-quality material and experts. I knew I needed to reengineer what he was doing to achieve similar success.

Adolph's advice popped into my brain, and once again I knew it was time to follow the anecdotal evidence. I called the number on the screen to order Kevin's book and was on the phone for what felt like *hours*. The rep on the other end of line tried to sell me every version of the book—CD, digital, one wrapped in a Snuggie (just kidding on that last one)—followed by a Walmart discount card, a travel club, and a host of other offers. There were upsells and downsells, cross-sells and discounts . . . and now I saw the model that would work for us. We wouldn't sell *everything* on the phone, but we could sell something else to raise the average order value far above the price listed in the infomercial.

This is a good example of a direct marketing principle that I love—that is, every company can ratchet up or ratchet down the aggression of the sales message and the offer as long as they are measuring everything every step of the way. So while we were following the Trudeau model, we only sold things that were congruent with our brand and that we felt comfortable selling to a new audience. We followed the anecdotal evidence on what was already working and stayed within the boundaries we were comfortable with.

Then I had my lightbulb moment. We already had a book that could be the lead offer: *The World's Greatest Treasury of Health Secrets*. I reached out to infomercial producer and direct marketing genius Steve Dworman to help us execute this idea. Steve had his own lightbulb moment when he realized that the doctors we worked with, who had material in the book, could all be interviewed for maximum credibility. This would help the audience know, like, and trust us, and would lead them to understand the offer.

For the first show, we chose well-known radio personality Barry Farber as the host. He interviewed one of our copywriters, Arthur Johnson, who (like all great copywriters) had insatiable curiosity in all things health. Johnson also served as the "medical editor" for the show, representing the doctors and the material they shared. We ran the rest of the campaign just like we did with direct mail—multiple entry points and plenty of back-end offers, upsells, and subscriptions—and everything came together in a perfect storm. That first show did incredibly well.

That gave us the confidence to up our game, so we decided to really aim high for our next show. We brought on Hugh Downs, a well-respected newsman, as the new interviewer. Hugh again interviewed Arthur Johnson, our copywriter/medical editor. This show outperformed the previous one, as we added many doctor guests to talk about their own article in the book. And we kept pushing. The show's next iteration was live at the Hugh Downs School of Communications at Arizona State. While the previous shows had doctors on a panel, this one was also attended by doctors—including a Nobel Prize winner—who contributed through audience participation, adding to the gravitas and credibility.

These progressive iterations inspired us to create new variations of health books with more variety and cutting edge health information than previous ones. *Treasury of Health Secrets* became *Ultimate Healing*, with a new format and refreshed content. We kept striving for new heights once we had the formula figured out, and it worked for quite a while. The moral of the story is that although we realized in 1989, when infomercials first became popular, that long-form TV would be much better for our products than short-form TV, it took until 2004 to find the right approach, over 15 years after we made the initial connection. Trusting the logic and the anecdotal evidence was step one; figuring out the model took some time.

And don't forget—once we found the model, we didn't just imitate it (i.e., follow Trudeau); we adapted it to our own image.

THE VALUE OF DISCIPLINE

It took us a long time to make television work for Boardroom's brand. I chewed on it for close to two decades, coming back to it over and over, every time I got new information or saw someone else having great success with the medium. Fortunately, the wait was worth it, and the lessons were profound. When we entered the world of infomercials, we were told that the success rate for new shows was something like 1 in 15. Some experts even told us it was more along the lines of 1 in 20. But lucky us! We had a blockbuster success right out of the gate with our first show and proceeded to have even bigger winners in our subsequent shows. We beat the odds by a wide margin, with four out of our first five shows becoming blockbusters.

However, on further review, maybe we weren't so lucky after all. Once we figured things out, we should have been extremely careful with TV after taking such a long time to reach success. But with our huge hits up front, we got sloppy. We started planning all kinds of shows in new categories and taking bigger risks with unproven products and formats. Not only that, but we took all these risks when a recession was looming.

Not everyone agreed that a financial crisis was about to hit, but we should have factored in the possibility as we planned our aggressive strategy, particularly since we knew TV was one of the riskiest mediums. Unfortunately, we had been reading our own press clippings and assumed we could do no wrong. And I was by far the biggest proponent of our aggressive approach to getting another big win; thus, I was also the biggest culprit when results were not good. This was about my own hubris and it was my call, not anyone else's.

Let me be clear that there is no fault in trying to build on momentum when you're achieving huge success in a particular channel, but you do need to stay grounded and objective. Plenty of people with years of experience in TV advertising told me to be careful. They told me that TV was more volatile than other channels and that there were a lot of ups and downs with it . . . but I became too overconfident to hear them. Folks internally told me the same thing. Lots of people were gushing about how incredible we were and how we were an exception to the rules of infomercial success . . . and I bought it. While we *were* seeing amazing results, and had come up with a unique formula, we just kept churning out ideas without doing our research or holding the campaigns to the kind of standards we did with our direct mail.

Coming straight off super-successful campaigns that defied the odds, I thought I had the Midas touch . . . and I then proceeded to produce a series of shows that were not winners.

While the excursion into TV was the most successful multichannel campaign in my career, we could have made many millions more if I had been more disciplined with the medium.

We learned a lot of valuable lessons from those shows that did not work. The biggest lesson is that if you don't approach every direct response campaign with discipline and objective standards, you're dead in the water. Having the privilege of working with the best marketers in the world at Boardroom (inside and outside) made it almost worthwhile to have some shows not be as successful or campaigns that fell short so that I (we) could learn from them and come out even better the next time.

Discipline is what made the direct mail generation of marketers so successful. Every single campaign sent through the United States Postal Service had to be meticulously researched and planned so that nothing was wasted. Every test had to mean something. Every test needed to light the path to a potential breakthrough and a new control package.

Direct mail marketers are always testing new approaches against the control to find the new winner. The best marketers online today think about testing the same way—that's why they are the best marketers online today. They know that selling so easily and cheaply online is an opportunity that should be used and not abused, given that it's unlikely you'll have to pay postage anytime soon. I remember an urban legend in the early days of the Internet that postage was going to be assessed for every e-mail—it was a made-up story—but I have to admit that creating a tougher barrier to entry for anyone and everyone to use e-mail kind of intrigued me as a marketer who knew how to pay postage and make money. My fantasy was that this would perhaps weed out the imposters. But as we know, this did not happen. But when they truly understand that there is a huge cost to sending marketing messages that are inappropriate, not targeted, and lack discipline, maybe they will see the light. Their sloppiness hurts all of us.

Simply put, the best marketers in any medium know that waste sucks. Discipline isn't just something for the folks paying postage. It benefits every marketer, no matter whether you're using e-mail, TV, radio, affiliates, or pay-per-click advertising. The fact that you don't have to pay for postage to send your online marketing messages is not a license to beat your list into submission until they buy.

In the spirit of online marketers learning from the discipline of direct mail, here are nine best practices that can be applied to all media.

1. Use Content Strategically

Everything you send doesn't have to *sell* something, but everything you send must *achieve* something. When you are marketing—in any medium—while everything is not a revenue event, everything is a relationship event. Familiarize yourself with what different types of strategic content look like and always be sure that it fits with the content and products you eventually sell. Another way to express this is that the ability to give away your best content for free has created its own marketing medium—and it should be completely consistent with the content you sell.

2. Deploy the Best Resources for Your Copy & Creative

Surround yourself with successful marketers who understand direct response and copy. And remember that developing breakthrough creative is not just about employing the newest techniques, although those are important. It's much more about paying a lot of attention to your messaging. In addition, it's imperative to develop a clear strategy first and then work with the best creative talent you can find to execute that strategy. Creative and copy is not an afterthought. Spend time and money on hiring the best. Just because it's inexpensive to launch a promotion online, it is not an excuse to be lazy with your copy and creative. Get those heavy hitters in your circle to sign up for all your messaging. Listen carefully to what they tell you about how your copy looks when it gets delivered and where you should be tweaking. If possible, hire those people to help you.

3. Find Out What's Missing

Find some secret shoppers to buy and experience your products; also, use focus groups to get information you cannot get anywhere else. Dan Kennedy calls this "marketing by walking around." Find people to buy, bend, and break your offerings without giving away who they are; and constantly talk to, and hang out with, people who represent your ideal audience. These aren't experts in direct response and advanced copy. They're the type of people who could potentially be your best prospects and customers. Several world-class copywriters use an innovative technique when writing copy to a particular audience. They pay a panel of people who seem like their target customer to read their work before they send it to the client. This gives them real-world opinions and reactions before the copy actually gets in front of a "live" audience.

Perry Marshall has his own version of how to "learn what you can't know." His idea is to get on Fiverr and hire people to read the material, then ask what they liked and hated, what they wanted more of and less of, whether or not they would pay for the product in a store, and why. Paying for this kind of feedback will give you accurate, useful insights that will help you improve your material. Listening to your customers, or people just like them, is always going to be the most powerful tool you can use to shape your products and marketing, no matter what you're selling or how you're selling it.

4. Sweat the Small Stuff

Invest the time and effort to agonize over every word in your copy. Even though copy has less impact on your campaign performance than list selection and the offer itself, why let it go out at any standard below perfection?

5. Look for Consequential Thinking in Your Messaging

I learned the term "consequential thinking" from Marty. It means putting yourself in the prospect's shoes and seeing how you would react to the elements of the copy. Does it take you through a sequence that makes sense? In direct mail, this is a science. How the mailing piece is received has a huge impact, and every element matters—the placement of the address, the order the recipient sees the pieces in the envelope . . . Online, of course, you have many more ways to guide your prospect through a sequence. Navigation and site order or page design play an important role here, and you should think about how your audience goes through your landing page (e.g., sales pages, opt-in pages, first screen on a home page, etc.). Does each page make sense based on what the audience has seen immediately before? Are you guiding them in a logical, comfortable way through your sequence?

Always ask, "Who is the audience that this will most appeal to?" Conversely, think about who your copy could possibly alienate. If your copy does have the potential to alienate, consider whether those people are a good fit to become your customers. If not, don't worry about it—it's okay to scare off the people who will never buy from you anyway.

6. What's the Logic Line?

This is another one I learned from Marty, and it takes the idea of consequential thinking to a more strategic level. Is there a "logic line" that flows through your marketing? Does each part of the story follow from what came before it? Is there a thread that runs through your argument, tying everything together in a logical, believable way? The logic line is closely related to being consistent with your brand identity. It might be helpful to think of it that way too.

The purpose of each sentence should be to make sure you can move the reader to the next sentence. You need a logic line within each marketing message you send, but you also need a logic line for your business as a whole. Is each message congruent with your marketing message overall? Will it resonate with what you've sent in the past, or does it contradict earlier messages? For folks working with affiliates, this is especially important. The affiliates you partner with are a reflection of you, so they need to meet your logic line too. If there is a contradiction in the message, you need to decide if you want to move in a different direction or if you want to rein a particular piece in (or not allow a particular affiliate into the mix) to better fit the overarching message of your business.

7. Do You Care?

No matter how hard-hitting the copy might be, it's crucial to be empathetic. Is there some element of care and concern for your end user? Do you actually care about the problem your offer is supposed to solve for your audience, and does the message you are sending communicate respect and care for those seeking help? People see straight through fake interest, so if you don't care about the customer or the outcome they get, don't send the message.

8. Give Them a Reason to Care about You

Audiences are basically selfish. It's not their job to care about your business or what you do. To that end, create your marketing assuming that nobody cares what you have to say. Instead, write in such a way that you *give* them a reason to care. No matter how much you believe your product, service, or message is a "need to have," always assume your customers think of it as a "nice to have." Your job is to convince your audience to shift their belief from one to the other.

9. Understand the Basic Rules of Language

You don't have to be obsessed with correct grammar or perfect punctuation—enjoyable content and copy often uses informal language. But if you are going to violate the rules and standards of a language, you really need to understand what you're doing. Any nonstandard usage must be in line with how your audience uses that language.

Gene Schwartz always said, "Grammar is overrated." I believe he was saying that communicating with your audience in their own style always trumps perfect grammar and usage—but *make sure you get it right.* Messing with the structures people understand can really trip them up if they don't get it on an intuitive level. If you're not sure, stick with simple language so that everyone in your audience will understand it immediately.

WHAT IF YOU HAD TO PAY POSTAGE?

As a marketer, the stakes are high. Maybe you don't have to pay for postage, but you depend on the opinion and respect of your audience. That puts your reputation and authority at stake every time you communicate with them. It's hard to measure the cost of every off-brand or incongruent message, even if the e-mail you use to send it is virtually free. I can assure you that you will find the hidden cost in the long run when your customers don't trust you and your prospects are turned off before they ever buy anything. If you can't be bothered to approach your online family with discipline and care in your communication, it's better not to contact them at all. Save yourself the hidden opportunity and goodwill costs until you have something really stellar to offer or something meaningful to say.

KEY TAKEAWAYS

- Direct mail (and other offline) success stories have left a lot of clues for all of us to learn from. Your numbers don't lie, and they will enable you to identify campaigns that aren't working (and should be killed) as clearly as they will show which campaigns are winners (and should be expanded).

- Take calculated risks and build off previous successes before you reinvent the wheel. Follow the anecdotal evidence and remember that consistency and discipline are *everything* in direct response marketing.

- A windfall of profit does not mean you have unlimited funds for testing. Pretend you have to pay drastically more than you actually pay if you feel yourself getting sloppy.

- Be disciplined. Don't waste any opportunity to build rapport or a deeper relationship when communicating with your potential or existing audience, and don't piss them off either.

- When campaigns are expensive, it forces you to be 100 percent sure that you have done everything you can to make the campaign a winner. If you act as if your campaigns are extremely expensive to send, that will ensure that you only send campaigns that have been crafted to be as effective and profitable as possible.

- Track the metrics that matter: the lifetime value (LTV) of customers, channels, and campaigns and your "bogey" (what you are willing to lose on an initial order) are critical numbers to measure over time.

- Don't read your own press clippings; listen when the experts give you advice; and don't let hubris or any unproven beliefs take you off course.

- There are nine best practices gathered from direct mail that can be applied to any kind of direct response marketing:

  1. Use content strategically.

  2. Deploy the best resources (e.g., copywriters and designers) for your copy and creative.

  3. Find out what's missing from your campaigns through constant questioning, testing, and research.

  4. Sweat the small stuff.

  5. Use consequential thinking (i.e., how will your prospect consume what you send?).

  6. What's the logic line? Can the prospect follow your logic throughout the promotion?

  7. Do you care about your customers?

  8. Give those customers and potential customers a reason to care about you.

  9. Understand the basic rules of language. And know the language your customers and potential customers use.

CHAPTER 4

LIST BUILDING & RFM

"No mailer [or marketer] spends enough time on lists."

—DICK BENSON

When you really think about it, the only thing that matters is who you're communicating with—and how you're communicating with them. It's always about the list. I've said this so many times that it's becoming a running joke about me, both in the marketing world and in my own house. My daughter gives me a hard time about my solution to nearly every problem being "It's always about the list!"

We joke around, but it's true: every business lives and dies by their list. I often worry that the word *list* objectifies what we're talking about, so I want to say this again because it's worth repeating: the list is real people. I'll be using the word "list" throughout this chapter, but please understand that every time you see the word *list*, I'm talking about people, your online family.

And when I say "the list" here, I mean anyone in your audience. The term came from direct mail, where there would be a huge database of names to pull from, but it also applies to your e-mail list, your social media followers, prospects who see your ads in other media—anyone that you are building a relationship with and promoting to.

I focus relentlessly on this because the majority of my career was spent in the highly competitive world of business-to-consumer (B2C) marketing. There it's critical to create a powerful connection with the people on your list. Your advantage is how you communicate with them. Over time we had millions of names on our list, buyers and nonbuyers (and having the records of who *hadn't* bought was just as important in how we sold to and communicated with each segment).

After going out on my own, I still concentrated on building my list, but now in the business-to-business (B2B) world. My list at the time of writing is at around nine thousand names. I think about these people the same way I thought about those nine million people I obsessed about at my old job. No matter how big your list is, it's your most valuable asset.

In this chapter, I'm going to share the strategies and tactics I used then and still use now for myself and for clients to build a responsive database, regardless of size.

WHEN 41 PERCENT IS A MAJORITY

A direct marketing rule of thumb is the formula 40/40/20. This says that 40 percent of the success of any direct response campaign is based on the targeting, segmentation, and quality of the list; 40 percent of the success is based on how relevant and irresistible the offer is; and 20 percent of the success is based on the quality of the creative material and the messaging.

But the list is the most important part. Over time, as I've worked with clients, this has become so apparent that I've changed the formula to 41/39/20, with the list taking the lead with 41 percent, followed by 39 percent for the offer and 20 percent for the creative.

If you have a perfectly targeted list, you are well on your way to success. I've seen many situations where the list selection or the audience the marketer was trying to reach was off. Then—even though the business ran the best creative from the best copywriters, all with a compelling offer—the campaigns got virtually zero response.

If you have a carefully selected list, populated with people who are perfectly suited to what you're offering, you can throw average creative at them (red box with a flashing arrow, anyone?) with a fairly unremarkable offer, and you'll still make some money.

I am not *recommending* average creative or unremarkable offers. If you are an online marketer using great affiliates (i.e., people with lists that are compatible with your offer) who endorse your product enthusiastically, even while using very basic creative and offers, many campaigns will still make a lot of money just because their lists are such a fit for your offer. But you can make a lot *more* money when you combine perfect list selection with an irresistible offer and some world-class creative. That's when you start building a business for a lifetime and when things really start exploding, whether you're offline or online.

I recently saw someone online saying the 40/40/20 rule is dead and touting a new "25/25/25/25" rule. Their theory: a campaign's success is based on 25 percent list, 25 percent offer, 25 percent creative, and 25 percent technology. This just doesn't make sense to me. I respect anyone who wants to debunk an old theory, but this one doesn't land. I believe wholeheartedly that technology makes us better marketers, but to quote advertising legend Bill Bernbach: "Never adapt your idea to the technique, adapt the technique to the idea."

You want to come up with the perfect offer to make to the perfect list with the perfect creative. But don't get attached to the medium, or to any one technology. The medium or technology you use is not what matters most—the list is what matters most. Maybe Facebook will be the right platform, maybe display advertising will be.

Maybe space advertising in print magazines or newspapers would be better, or even direct mail. It could be TV or radio or working with affiliates. These are all good channels—all of them work—but what is critical is knowing which medium is going to be the right place to find your audience and engage with them most deeply. Technology is an important tool however you market, but it is not a building block like the list, the offer, or the creative.

A CLASSIC APPROACH TO LIST BUILDING

When Marty first had the idea for his flagship newsletter, *Boardroom Reports,* he really wanted to launch it as a magazine. Marty came up in the golden age of print—he was a very successful space advertising salesman for magazines and was also fascinated with direct mail. Launching a magazine that could compete with the big, established titles at the time would have required an astronomical amount of money. So he decided to build up the idea as a newsletter instead. That meant that there would be no advertising (i.e., no revenue from outside advertisers). Launching *Boardroom Reports* as a newsletter would keep production costs down, because unlike a magazine, a newsletter could print on less expensive paper and there was no need for extravagant design. Newsletters were first and foremost about the content.

But Marty saw an opportunity to market his newsletter like most companies were marketing magazines at the time—sending what were called bill-me-later offers, which meant that he was willing to give away free trial issues before getting payment. At the time most newsletters were cash-with-order (the new subscriber had to send cash or credit card up front with their order, like we do online today). But because Marty wanted to grow his newsletter larger and more quickly, he used bill-me-later offers instead.

A lot of publications were sending two or three free issues (or what we call "grace issues") before they sent the reader a bill for the subscription. Because Marty couldn't hold out that long for cash flow, he went with a lower risk model: he would send the newsletter to potential customers with *one* free trial issue and a bill-me-later order form. While he carried some risk, he was committed to quality content that he knew people would pay for, and he was confident that enough people would pay to get *Boardroom Reports* once they sampled it. This model allowed us to get to critical mass much faster than requiring cash up front.

We were able to extend credit to prospects like this because of our deeply targeted list selection, *based on their previous buying behavior* (we mailed lists of customers who had previously paid for bill-me-later offers from other publishers). We also knew that the quality of the content we were producing was groundbreaking and that the offers we were making were congruent and valuable too. The recipients, we thought, would immediately see the value of paying up. Later on we were able to take advantage of new credit-screening technology to cross-reference prospects with credit reports to ensure that only people with good credit ratings would get the bill-me-later offer, removing anyone who had bad debt and was unlikely to pay up.

This was risky because the model was mostly used by publications (e.g., magazines) who had another revenue stream: advertising. Some newsletter marketers thought this was insane (and still do), but we took the risk, and it paid off massively. Marketers I meet today who sell digital products online have a hard time wrapping their heads around this idea—and for good reason. But this could be game-changing for anyone who can crack the code on a true bill-me-later offer using today's technology. It would help to build a larger list, more quickly and profitably, and open the way to all kinds of potential promotions. I leave it to you to think about all the possibilities. Some online marketers have experimented (and some have had success) giving away their product without a payment up front—but this online model for a bill-me-later usually still includes taking a credit card number which they charge 30 days later (or sometime in the near future). It's what I call a hard-bill-me, and it's a worthwhile test. But I am sure you can see that being able to do a bill-me-later offer without asking for any payment information up front would increase response considerably (i.e. totally risk free and hassle-free for the buyer . . . no need to think about the charge on the credit card that will be coming at the time of the order). The key to making a true bill-me-later offer work is to make sure the offer only goes to more creditworthy people (doable with technology) and that your product is everything you promise in the sales copy, so there is no remorse (i.e. little or no bad debt).

Back to the launch of *Boardroom Reports.* Marty knew that the list selection would be good and the offer would be irresistible, so now all we needed was world-class copy. Who else but Gene Schwartz could write that launch package? The package he wrote was, of course, incredible, and I'll share its details in Chapter 6.

Marty couldn't mail as much as he would have liked at the start, since he had to manage the cash flow so carefully, but he proved this list-building model. Advanced list selection and segmentation, an offer where we could give away great content up front for free, with copy and creative written by one of the best copywriters in the world . . . that's a prescription for success in any medium, past or present.

Of course, this only works if your content is actually good. If your product sucks, no one will pay for it—even if you *give it away* to targeted lists with a great sales letter. A lot of marketers miss this when they don't pay attention to the quality of their product, which leads to the 40/40/20 rule (or the 41/39/20 rule) falling apart.

Targeted list segmentation is the most important thing you can do with any marketing program . . . and then adding a great offer and the best creative is the formula for success. But if you are not delivering on what you promise, no execution of any kind of percentage rule will help you.

HOW TO FIND THE RIGHT 41 PERCENT

Most marketers agree that their list is their most important asset. This was true for the direct mail industry, and I believe that rule will continue to hold. If you think that the idea of mailing other people's lists (i.e., affiliate marketing) was invented by online marketers, let's talk about where it originated in the direct mail world.

Direct mail companies regularly used their lists to access other relevant lists through exchanges, and they frequently rented other people's lists. The primary tool of the list industry for marketers using direct mail was the data card. Every list that was available in direct mail had a data card with (supposedly) all the pertinent information any mailer or broker would need to make a decision on whether to mail the list or not. Assuming that the data cards were complete and accurate, list managers (the people who represented the lists in the marketplace) would simply mail data cards in big stacks to list brokers (the people who worked with the marketers on list selection).

Data cards and the dance that list managers and brokers created around them was how the list business worked. Looking at how the most successful direct mail companies worked within this system to find the most responsive lists for their products or services is instructive for anyone marketing today in any medium.

Most list managers were lazy and did not give all the compelling reasons for list brokers to recommend their lists to clients. They usually just threw numbers at the brokers, expecting the brokers to make sense of the data in a way that would allow them to do something interesting or innovative with the list on behalf of their client. Even when list managers met with list brokers and presented the data in person, they would only talk about the lists, but not about the offers and creative that had gone into building those lists . . . which really was the key to whether a list would work or not. Not only did that mediocre approach undercut a list manager's opportunity to build great partnerships, it also turned a specialty product—a unique list—into a commodity.

The reason I got so good at selling lists was that I saw this hole in the system. When I presented to list brokers, I not only presented the data cards on Boardroom's lists, but I also brought the promotions that got the names onto the lists in the first place. I went way beyond giving the broker a pile of statistics to digest—I profiled the psychology of the buyers and subscribers on that list based on the offers and creative they had responded to.

Being able to explain how and why the names on a particular list got there was far more valuable than being able to rattle off a bunch of demographic data. I could also explain the segmentation we had used to create our list—that is, the promotions our best customers had responded to before. I could make connections between the copywriter we used for our winning promotions and the copywriter (or approach) the client was using, highlighting where there was even more synergy.

All this presented a powerful picture of how our lists would perform based on data that could never be discovered on a data card. Digging deep into the psychology of the lists you promote (for example, when choosing affiliates and joint venture partners) is critical to success. Again, your list is the single most valuable asset in your business. Marketing to lists that will bring in new customers with high lifetime value and intense interest and loyalty toward your company is always the business you are in as a direct marketer.

LIST BUILDING TODAY

The marketers getting the best results online today are constantly giving away their best stuff, and their audiences love them for it. Giving away high-quality content to get people to opt in to an e-mail list or some kind of offer is the best way to build trust and authority, even in saturated markets.

List building for the long term goes way beyond finding your ideal customers—although that is a starting point. It's also about quality over quantity—and an ideal customer is someone who will stay with you beyond the first sale and hopefully for a long time into the future. But they have to be a good fit in the first place. Your responsibility is then to continue to deliver quality to them with those subsequent offers and the products and services you sell them. The material in your promotions should be super valuable, and the offers you make should be congruent with the content you gave away to get people on the list in the first place. If you sell a product that looks like the material you gave away, and you consistently add more value as you move your audience toward a sale, they'll pay for whatever is coming next.

I know this sounds really simple—because it is. We're a little spoiled online today, because we can distribute content (promotion and product) so cheaply. The danger is that people often send out whatever idea comes to them without really thinking through the congruency issues or the opportunity and goodwill costs that this offer could have on the future responsiveness of their list. Congruency is the most important thing you can build into your business—it's the glue that makes your audience stick with you. This goes back to the discipline I talked about in Chapter 3. If you acted as if you had to produce a physical product, pay for shipping, and cover the costs of failed payments, you would be much more careful about what you expose your list to. And it pains me to think about online marketers I've met who seem fine with 50 percent return rates (or more) when they promote what they say are their best products. Congruency has to be off when return rates are high.

Of course, no matter what your model is, you have to be working in a market where there is enough opportunity for you to make the economics work in your favor. Since that is a choice that's made long before you even start building a list, let's dig into that here.

TABLE SELECTION (OR, WHAT MARKETERS CAN LEARN FROM POKER PLAYERS)

In some businesses, the likelihood of success or failure is determined before you ever start building a list or sending a campaign. This is what poker players call "table selection." For our purposes, this means how you decide which industry to go into in order to make the economics of direct response work for you. It's about identifying big, motivated markets where your expertise and positioning will give you an edge on your competition. For example, a lot of direct mail businesses made fortunes because they selected the finance and health markets, which are both huge evergreen markets with a wide variety of niches to be developed. I'm a stickler for going deep as opposed to going wide, and choosing markets where we can go really deep and become a "category of one" leads to the biggest opportunities. For example, being a leader in general health and wellness is a tough place to start, but coming up with a unique diet for a specific ailment or disease, or developing a supplement that does one thing or solves one health issue with unique ingredients not found anywhere else seems like a much better place to start. Your list selection, offers, and copy can go a mile deep rather than a mile wide when you are a category of one . . . and you can capture a bigger slice of a small market first rather than trying to capture a large slice of a huge market. I'm not saying you shouldn't reach for the stars or want to go wide with your vision—but going narrow to wide is almost always the better path for a disciplined direct marketer.

While *Boardroom Reports* was Marty's first product and his passion, he didn't go into it because it was an obvious opportunity where no one else was doing anything but he had an angle to make it a category of one. He had a real frustration that while the big magazines such as *Forbes, Fortune, Businessweek,* and *The Wall Street Journal* would tell you what was happening at the big companies, they really didn't tell you how to run a business. He saw a void in the marketplace. *Boardroom Reports* was a passion project for him, a way to scratch his own itch, *but* he also thought it could be a big market, one relatively untapped and with a lot of potential. He knew he could go deep into that subject, even if he didn't know at the time where it would take the company.

Fortunately, as time went on, Marty stayed open to what the market wanted. *Boardroom Reports* was by then very successful, but this audience of executives eventually started telling him that there were other topics *they* were more passionate about, specifically health, personal finance, and issues affecting them as consumers. The audience told him where to focus, and in 1980, a year before I got to Boardroom, the company launched *Bottom Line/Personal*. This essentially appealed to the consumer side of the same executive who subscribed to *Boardroom Reports*.

BL/P focused on things like health, personal finance, auto, taxes, home improvement, personal development . . . practical and useful nonbusiness information that an affluent executive would want to have at their fingertips in order to create more abundance in all aspects of their life. For example, subscribers showed increased interest in articles such as how to prevent a heart attack at their desk (i.e., how to live another day and make more money in their business). The health angle was an obvious addition, and that market was really growing at the time, so it's not surprising that we had lots of success right out of the gate with the new publication. *BL/P* grew so rapidly that it soon eclipsed *Boardroom Reports* in circulation and overall responsiveness. That led us to create other offers in such consumer-interest areas, while abandoning the idea of more books in business-related categories.

Clearly this new consumer focus engaged a much wider audience, and it was also one that was easier to reach through direct mail, since there were many more responsive lists available to us on the consumer side. Furthermore, as we got into consumer publishing in a bigger way, we realized that the category of health was huge by itself, despite looking initially like a niche that would fit within *BL/P*. That led us to the creation of a new line of health books. Once again the audience told us how to segment.

We went on to have big wins in the finance and health categories, and in time in another market that our audience told us they were very interested in as well—taxes. Without listening carefully to our audience, we never would have figured out this intense interest in taxes, which was less obvious than such categories as health and personal finance. To meet this obsession, our third newsletter became *Tax Hotline*; and with the success of all our health books pointing the way, launching a health newsletter became the obvious next publication. After these, we launched *Bottom Line/Tomorrow*, focusing on another area of intense interest among our customers—retirement.

Making the transition from business to consumer interest, then adding taxes, health, and retirement as additional categories to cover, we kept going where our customers led us. And we did it with newsletters *and* books. We watched our competition carefully at the time, and we saw the most successful companies also build their lists in the niche categories that their audiences wanted the most information about. Choosing the right market is sometimes about letting the market choose you.

COMPILED LISTS VERSUS RESPONSE LISTS

In the direct mail world, all lists fall into two categories: compiled lists and response lists. Simply put, compiled lists are about quantity, while response lists are about quality. Compiled lists are about who the prospects are or where they live; response lists are about what they've done and how they did it.

A compiled list is based solely on demographic information, collated from census data. You can think of a compiled list as being like a phone book. A list compiler starts with names and addresses from public sources, collects data, and layers information onto the names. For example, you might buy or rent a list of names from a compiler with standard industrial classification (SIC) codes appended, which indicate which industry someone works in, allowing you to target people who work in that industry. Lists are not always completely accurate as much of the data compilers use may be "implied" from census data and geography . . . but it is always better than mailing names from the phone book. Speaking of geography, another big data point on compiled lists is zip code: where the people on the list live, from the state level all the way down to their neighborhood. Retail stores use compiled lists to attract people who live within a certain radius of their locations, since this kind of data is the most useful to them. A compiled list will tell you any number of facts about those names, but it has nothing to do with how those people *respond* to anything.

Put another way, the single biggest thing missing from a compiled list is response. That's not to say that people on a compiled list won't respond to an offer; it means that they are not being selected based on how they have behaved or have responded to an offer in the past. In the world of direct marketing that I grew up in—whether the offers were for newsletters, books, magazines, charities, or consumer goods—previous response to other offers was far more important in getting people to respond to our offers than any demographic data.

Response lists also have all kinds of categories. There are inquiries, free subscribers, active buyers, ex-buyers—and response lists are considered more valuable than compiled lists because there are three key elements at play, which I think you could have guessed by now: recency, frequency, and monetary (RFM), which we are about to take a deep dive into. For now, suffice it to say that if someone has recently interacted with you, has interacted with you frequently, or has spent money with you, they're far more likely to respond positively to an offer than they would if you came at them cold (as you often do with compiled lists).

Understanding compiled lists versus response lists, as we defined them in direct mail, has a huge application for people in the online marketing world today. List selection—and list building—begins and ends with response. It's all about tracking the behavior of every person on your list, from hitting a LIKE button to buying a $2,000 product.

Here's a simple example from the affiliate space: If you want to do an affiliate deal with someone and they will only promote your offer to the people on their list who inquired but didn't buy, or who bought over a year ago, that list is unlikely to be as valuable as the list of people who are *currently* buying from the affiliate. While a 50:50 split is the norm for an affiliate deal, you could make the case that certain segments of someone's list might be worth less than a 50 percent commission. You'll have to set your own parameters for the affiliate deals you make, but I hope you see that how we value names in direct mail is relevant to e-mail names too. . . . When valuing direct mail names, a list of people who inquired about an offer or who bought a year ago always costs less than a list of people who are current, active buyers. An e-mail list of similar "nonbuyers" should cost less too; the affiliate partner should give you more than a 50/50 split, as an example.

That brings us to the foundational direct marketing concept of recency, frequency, monetary (RFM). While we may not talk about it much today in the online world, it is relevant to every-thing we do in marketing and list development.

RECENCY, FREQUENCY, MONETARY (RFM)

I've been shocked by how many people practicing direct response marketing today are not aware of RFM. Analyzing the RFM data on your customer database might be the most critical, high-leverage thing you can do with your list. RFM is a pretty simple concept, accessible to anyone, and much of it can be done by observation and "tallying" (or tagging) your prospects and customers. But many people aren't using this method, even when they could be getting huge gains from it.

That said, RFM can be both simple and sophisticated. We used it on multimillion-name databases, and you may need a statistician to help calculate RFM formulas and models for you if you have a large list. Regardless, understanding this bedrock concept should get you thinking in different ways about the markets you promote to and the people who are already in your internal database.

R Is for "Recency"

"Recency" says that a prospect or customer who has interacted with you recently is more responsive (and immediately more valuable) than someone who responded less recently. When I started in the business, I remember that this didn't make sense to me. I thought that if someone just bought from you, they would have less money to buy something else right away. That seemed like a logical line of thought, but actually humans behave very differently.

When someone is in buying mode, *don't get in their way.* In that moment, they are looking for help with something, and you can present a sequence of high-quality solutions that can solve their problem. Make the appropriate offers early and often. The best online marketers today understand this concept of recency and striking while the iron is hot. Some do get a bit overzealous—and like anything else, selling should be done strategically and thoughtfully. It's not about selling them everything under the sun immediately because they just made a purchase.

When you start understanding the data on *when* people buy, *how* they buy, and *why* they buy, you can start segmenting names and predicting the best times to make them offers—and the best sequence for those offers. And the products don't all have to be yours. If you don't have anything else to offer, sell affiliate products.

I remember an old-time legacy publisher who would not rent their mailing list of book buyers to other mailers offering books in direct mail. They foolishly thought that every customer had a set budget to spend on books per year, and they wanted their customers to spend that budget only with them. It's no surprise that this company is no longer in business, since they failed to understand that all boats rise when we keep the folks on our list active and happy with all kinds of relevant offerings, even if it means recommending other people's products occasionally. Making an appropriate affiliate offer to your list can increase the responsiveness of your list if you do it strategically and in a way that capitalizes on the list's recency.

Fortunately, most marketers know the importance and value of recency. When you buy something online today, it can be a surprise when you *don't* get a cross-sell or upsell immediately after your purchase. If you cross-sell and upsell aggressively, right after the new customer just bought something, you already understand recency quite well.

In direct mail the segments of recent buyers are called hotlines, and list owners still charge a premium for those names. Over a few decades of mailing millions of names and almost always selecting hotlines from lists, I can tell you with certainty that choosing this segment is usually the make-or-break factor on whether a list pays out.

But marketers cannot live on recency alone.

F Is for "Frequency"

"Frequency" pushes us to combine the most recent buyers with the most frequent buyers. These customers, called multi-buyers, are always among the most valuable people on any list. But they don't have to *buy* frequently to be super valuable—they can also inquire or respond frequently and still be valuable. For example, if someone on my list buys a direct marketing book and then buys a second direct marketing book, they become a VIP on the basis of their purchase frequency. I'm confident they'll buy a third and fourth book sometime in the future. But I also had someone correspond with me—without buying anything—to ask very sophisticated questions based on information I had provided in blog posts. That frequency of communication led him to join one of my high-level mastermind groups. Because we had this frequent contact, he became hugely valuable in the long run. Frequency comes in all shapes and sizes. It's easy to recognize the value of frequent buyers; frequent contacts require you to pay more attention.

Recency and frequency give you a one-two punch that will enable you to segment any list, no matter what size, in order to focus on the people who will be your best customers for subsequent products or offerings. Now, if you're an experienced marketer, this might sound basic to you. *Of course* someone who bought from you multiple times is a better customer than someone who bought from you once (or never), right?

But let me add creative and copy into the mix here: Are you communicating with your multibuyers (or your "multiqueries") using tailored language, creative, and offers, based on their purchasing and interaction history with you? Or are you sending the same message to the multibuyer who bought their third product from you today as you are to the one-time buyer from six months ago? The first group is "family" . . . the second group are "guests." And to keep multibuyers coming back, you need to target each group differently. (The same is true of frequent contacts too.)

There are even cases where frequency trumps recency. Let's say you had a customer who bought multiple products and then disappeared six months ago. If you don't contact them again with messaging that speaks to them like family ("We want you back!") rather than messaging that speaks to them as a guest (like any other new prospect), you could be missing a huge opportunity to reengage them with your offers. And based on the direct marketing rule of thumb that previous buyers are your most valuable prospects, this would still apply if they stopped buying a year ago or even more. I remember mailing to expired subscribers, many of whom had subscribed multiple times to a newsletter—but not for five to ten years. We were able to revive many of them with the right offer and messaging. Direct mail also has an advantage here, since we can enlist the help of the United States Postal Service's extensive change of address file (COA), allowing us to update previous buyers with new addresses fairly easily. This is an extreme example of when frequency can trump recency and the point is to not look at anything in isolation when looking at real people (i.e., your list). And there is a further lesson for those of you who work exclusively online: Keeping track of as many previous buyers as possible with an accurate e-mail address could be money in the bank for a very long time.

You might know this instinctively, but I have consulted with too many marketers and heard too many horror stories from folks who use one-size-fits-all copy to all segments of their audience. Something as simple as "we want you back" to a segment of frequent former customers (who may not be recent) can increase your response rate significantly.

Frequency analysis is critical and should be done on any list of any size. The more frequently someone has bought from you in the past, the more frequently they are likely to buy from you in the future. If you can get someone who has bought multiple products, and they also exist within a hotline of recent buyers, now you've got the cream of the crop. And if the frequency has led to them spending a large amount of money with you, knowing that information could enable you to spend more on reselling that frequent buyer than others who have not spent as much.

That's why there is a third leg to the RFM stool that we need to be aware of, since the more your customer spends with you, the more you can invest in them for even more sales in the future.

M Is for "Monetary"

We round out this RFM formula by making sure you know the total amount of money every person on your list has spent with you. Creating tiers based on different spending levels will give you far more information about how much customers might spend with you in the future. However, the amount of money spent by each customer in isolation can be deceptive. Combining it with recency and frequency is the most powerful way to segment your list.

In my previous world of $39 newsletters, for example, monetary value was the least important element of the RFM selection criteria, except when the customer had also bought recently and frequently. That is, one $39 purchase alone is not very powerful, but the customer becomes more valuable as they buy more over time.

If you are selling a high-ticket item, one purchase could be a lot more significant in determining the future buying behavior of that customer. If a buyer has spent a high dollar amount in the past, they're likely to do so again in the future. As with recency and frequency, how we talk to people who have spent a lot of money with us, as opposed to people who have spent less money with us, can once again make our messaging more powerful to each segment.

RFM IS AS IMPORTANT ONLINE AS IT IS OFFLINE

RFM is a universal language for all marketers, and it is a cornerstone for list selection and segmentation. It is still the best way to analyze past behavior and how that past behavior will dictate future behavior. Again and again, over decades of use across multiple industries, it's obvious that these factors are worth paying extra for in the external lists we select, and it should guide how we communicate and market to the lists we own as well.

When you're working online, it's even more important to be slicing and dicing your list through an RFM formula according to how people are buying and behaving. Remember, make sure you don't have one-size-fits-all promotions. Talk to your customers based on their relationship with you, calculated through RFM. This approach can be a game changer and can turn up some unexpected results. Let me share a quick story to bring this home.

I have a friend and client who has something like 18 different related products, and she does a great job of cross-selling and upselling those products to existing customers who have bought some (but not all) of them. But when I saw a breakdown of her buyer list, the majority of buyers had only bought one product, and most of the others had bought two or three at most. It seemed that with some RFM segmenting tweaks, there would be huge potential to get more of those one- to three-time buyers to buy *much* more, given all the related offerings available. She immediately got on board with this when I noted that there was one person on the list who had bought all 18 products (and no, it was not a relative!) . . . and I asked the question, "When was the last time you invited this eighteen-time buyer to dinner?"

Of course, I was being a little sarcastic . . . but I was also trying to make an important point. It's easy to forget that lists are people too. We can lose sight of that when we spend all day sitting behind our computers and spreadsheets. What would my client have discovered if she had in fact taken that customer out for a meal? Imagine all the insight she would have gleaned—the buying motivation, the questions and doubts they had overcome, the language they used to describe the incredible value they were obviously getting from her products. So from that question, we started surveying the most recent, frequent, and high-dollar-spending customers, finding out why they bought multiple products and also in what order they bought the products, looking for trends in buying behavior. That led to a logical (and much more successful) contact strategy. We started offering products to previous buyers in a sequence that made more sense based on what the multibuyers had told us about their purchasing motivation and also by tracking their buying behavior over time rather than simply making random offerings. It was all based on RFM. We paired this with fresh copy and creative that spoke to why their recent purchase led perfectly to the next purchase, customizing the copy to different segments.

I have used this concept of contact strategy in the past too. I recall the exercise of going through the highest-value customers, figuring out the next best product to offer them, and creating a logical path for new subscribers and buyers. We looked at the transaction data on every customer we'd ever had, and after we tracked the purchase history on many of them, we would map out the most appropriate pathways. The path forward was based on how they initially got on the list and what promotions made them buy most often a second time. And then we would try to determine what the second, third, and fourth purchases would most likely be on the basis of each unique entry point to our funnel (though we weren't calling it a funnel back then).

We were trying to predict what their next purchase would be, and we would then automatically send them an inexpensive promotion for it. A simple and obvious example was when we discovered that the buyers of a health book were most inclined to subscribe to a health newsletter as their next purchase. Once we knew that, rather than wait until the next promotion went out for the health newsletter, we implemented a new contact strategy that every time a new customer bought a health book, we would send them a low-cost piece of direct mail offering them a free trial to the newsletter. The original book was sold as a bill-me-later offer, so when we received payment for the book, it would automatically trigger the bill-me-later offer for the newsletter, since the customer had proven they were interested *and* creditworthy. They became paid subscribers to the newsletter at a very high rate with a much lower promotion cost. Having been recent book buyers—specifically, creditworthy book buyers who were intensely interested in health—made them more likely to be frequent buyers.

GOING DEEPER: REGRESSION MODELLING & DEMOGRAPHIC SEGMENTATION

The key to RFM is being able to collect, understand, and use all the transaction data on your own list, and when appropriate, outside lists.

Every time someone on our database did something—bought a product, ordered a product and didn't pay, returned something, made an inquiry—we noted that action on their individual customer record, making what I call a tick on the file. Every name on our database had these ticks on them, showing everything each person did, so that our statistician could access all that information when running a model on the list each time we wanted to do a new promotion. These ticks enabled us to build models to find out who would be most likely to respond to our offers. It was almost always based first and foremost on RFM. If there was a combination of a customer being a recent buyer, buying something more than once, and spending a lot of money, those features would always rise to the top.

Our modelling technique, called regression modelling, starts with mailing a cross section of a large list (say 50,000 or 100,000 names out of a list of 2 million) to collect real, paid responses to a particular promotion. Because the selection on the cross section segment was not precise, we would lose money on this up-front mailing, but its purpose was research. (And while mailing this many names makes this technique sound like it's only for large mailers or marketers, there are ways to "tick your file" no matter how small your list is. The segments you create for promoting from that data might be slender, but I know of no better way to predict future response than by tracking, analyzing, and acting on past response and behavior.)

The statistician would then analyze the buying patterns (based on all the common ticks) across all the people who responded to the test mailing and then rank the remaining names on the larger list we hadn't mailed yet based on their commonalities with the names that responded. Then it was time to narrow the list selection. We would build a gains chart, which allows you to divide the whole list into deciles (10 percent segments) or demi-deciles (5 percent segments) in order to predict what the response rate would be in the top deciles or demi-deciles. That would determine how we would approach the wider list to make the mailing profitable. It gave us a clear cutoff point because a particular decile or demi-decile would show where profitability was likely to drop off.

While we were taking the names that responded and finding more names that "looked like" them from the bigger list, this was far from a look-alike model. This was much more sophisticated because it was all based on response and buying behavior (what we call transaction data)—not just demographics or some-body hitting a LIKE button.

I hope I didn't lose you with all that detail, because there is a reason I wanted to share this widely used and successful technique for modelling millions of names at a time. My intent in going so deep is to show how the same principles are at play when you create a model of any kind on any list based on RFM—and you don't need a huge computer or a statistician to do it. However, let me be clear that I was not doing this analysis myself. This *is* sophisticated stuff, and we hired a Ph.D. in statistics to handle this (although for smaller lists, you can probably simulate the same kind of analysis yourself). But it was all based on RFM at its core.

Once we had these models, we might consider overlaying additional demographic data, such as household income, but none of that data was ever as powerful as the transaction data.

A lot of marketers confuse the significance of RFM and demographic data and segment their lists based on demographics as much as on behavior. But always keep in mind that demographics are *not* reliable indicators of purchasing behavior, and in most campaigns, the demographic data did not have a material impact on who we would mail. Sometimes it would add a few names into the top deciles or demi-deciles, but ultimately our name selection was based on when they bought, what they bought, how often they bought, and how much they had spent.

This is critical for online marketers to understand because a lot of the segmentation tools available rely far too heavily on demographic data. Sometimes you have to do a bit of the heavy lifting yourself to get the RFM information you really need. For example, it's much more valuable to know that someone bought a course on copywriting than to know they live in a city where a lot of copywriters live. Knowing demographic data on the people we promote to (things like race, ethnicity, gender, age, education, profession, occupation, income level, and marital status) or getting access to psychographic data about them (attitudes, aspirations, and other psychological criteria) are not meaningless. Both can be valuable, but it's always going to be RFM that carries the day.

Understanding the dynamics and data of the lists you are working with is absolutely critical in direct response marketing, regardless of your channel of choice. The concepts of RFM, contact strategy, and regression modelling are critical in caring for your customers, delivering the value they need, and in so doing, building a business for a lifetime.

KEY TAKEAWAYS

- Your list is the most important asset in your business—but never forget that your list is made up of real people. Think of them like family members who deserve your love and respect.

- Follow the 40/40/20 rule, which says 40 percent of a campaign's success relies on the list selection, 40 percent on the offer, and 20 percent on the creative. Or if you really want to dial it in, make that 41 percent list—so that the list has the clear priority—39 percent offer, and 20 percent creative.

- Pick niches where you can go really deep instead of going shallow across a wide range of niches. Just as importantly, listen to your audience when they tell you they want to go deeper on a particular subject (whether they tell you explicitly or you can infer it from their buying behavior).

- There are two types of lists you can buy or create: compiled lists and response lists. While they are terms that originated in the world of direct mail, it's useful to look at the distinction whenever you look at lists. Compiled lists are built solely from demographic and possibly psychograhic data; response lists are built based on actual responses people have given to previous offers. Response lists are generally much more targeted than compiled lists, since those people have already indicated a specific interest in what you are offering.

- Analyzing the RFM data of your customer database might be the most high-leverage thing you can do with that list of names. RFM can be applied to tiny lists just as well as huge lists (though when you have a huge list, you might need to bring on a statistician to help you manage it all). Regardless of the list's size, RFM should always be used to determine the types of campaigns being sent to different segments.

CHAPTER 5

OFFERS

The right offer should be so attractive that
only a lunatic would say "no."

— CLAUDE HOPKINS

If I ruffled any feathers in the last chapter by stating that the list is more important than the offer, rest assured that the importance of the offer will not be shortchanged in any way. That is what we will explore in this chapter. And if you want to stick with 40/40/20 rather than 41/39/20, I'm fine with that too.

Plenty of other books will give you lists of different offers you can make or the exact process to follow to develop good offers. This chapter is about the *strategy* of offers—how to think about creating them in order to make them as effective as possible. Whether you are selling information, physical products, or experiences, your offer needs to appeal so deeply to your audience that it's irresistible to them. This is why it's so critical to get your list targeting right—once you know *who* you are marketing to, it's much easier to work out what you should be offering them. Whether 41/39 or 40/40, list and offer must be in sync all the time.

START WITH NICHE

The power of choosing a niche (sometimes referred to as a vertical) should never be underestimated when bringing products and services to the marketplace. Finding niches that fit with your superpowers and then going a mile deep rather than a mile wide is often the key to success . . . and it is way more satisfying to be a master of one thing than trying to be a master of everything. I also believe that owning a niche is easier, more practical, and enables you to make more impact in the area you are most proficient in than attempting to be all things to all people.

Sometimes you need someone to point out when you are going too wide with your idea for a new product or service. Sometimes the niche is obvious to you without much help from others. Regardless, the rewards for carving out a niche are always worth it. I want to share two stories that illustrate different approaches to niche:

1. Being far too ambitious with an initial offer
2. The "horizontal vertical" offer: how starting narrow and expanding gradually can create an incredible windfall

WHY SHOULD I LISTEN TO YOU?

This first story is about a driven entrepreneur who presented his big idea to a mastermind group we were in together in order to get some advice and feedback. Let's call him John. After exposing his offer-to-be to the harsh light of day and fielding some tough questions, John walked away with a much bigger idea—despite the revised idea being of interest to a much smaller audience. Because the new, smaller audience we identified was a much better fit for his business and mission, his list would be much hungrier for what he had to offer.

John's initial idea was to create an information product (and eventual coaching program) for men going through a midlife crisis. That's a *big* goal, and I was just one of many skeptics in the group regarding whether he could really pull it off. While I wasn't trying to be nasty or obnoxious, I had to hit him with an uncomfortable question: "Why are you qualified to teach and coach men going through a midlife crisis?" The implied question there was, "Why should I listen to you?" Be advised: This is a question all customers ask, whether consciously or not, and it's why establishing authority and credibility is so critical in any promotion. You have to be able to answer that question with integrity and experience, or no offer you can make will strike the right chord.

John's answer actually told me he might just be the guy to get this thing done. He had gone through a terrible time late in his career when he spiraled into an awful depression, went through a divorce, lost contact with his kids, went bankrupt, thankfully survived a suicide attempt—and came out the other side stronger and better than ever.

Obviously he had some lessons to share. But with *all* the men who go through a crisis? Millions of guys of all ages go through crises; I didn't think there would be a one-size-fits-all solution to such a big problem. Other skeptics in the room started throwing out more questions:

- What would be the entry point to his funnel (i.e. his initial offer)?

- What were the "hot buttons" that would get someone's interest?

- What did he know about different segments of the market?

Eventually, frustrated with how broad his focus was, I asked another question: "What did you do for a living at the time of your breakdown?" He answered that he was an attorney. Now I thought we were on to something. It immediately became clear that he could create his product or program specifically for lawyers going through midlife crises rather than all men. Wouldn't the relatability lead to more powerful promotion? Couldn't it also be more personalized? Even if what he delivered to self-described recovering attorneys was exactly what he had in mind for every man (no matter what they did for a living before their crisis), owning a bigger slice of a targeted market where he had deep understanding and empathy seemed like a much better path.

He could always break into new markets later on if he wanted to, but I had a feeling that once he dominated a niche where he could be a standout leader, he might be less interested in going wider. We concluded that it's much more effective to focus on a tight niche and avoid competing with other gurus who were trying to be all things to all people. This is one of the biggest mistakes most marketers make: they start too broad. It's better to start narrow, and widen your focus over time, than to start wide and try to gradually hone it down.

Sometimes it's obvious how to narrow down your market, like we were able to do with our lawyer friend here. And sometimes you need to poll the marketplace and find out where the need is and how you can uniquely fill it. In other cases, you can just talk to your best customers to see how deep you can go.

If you have a solution that can appeal to "anyone in any category," chances are that the marketing message is so broad that you will struggle to get new clients. Here's a question, in a shorthand version, to ask in order to narrow down the market: in your current business, which clients have cut you the biggest checks? Or, who has spent the most money with you over some specified period of time? You'll probably find that your biggest clients—those who pay you the most money—are in similar categories, and that knowledge will enable you to build a strategy that goes deep to appeal to prospects in that same category. It's almost like a miniature regression model: find the clients who have the most recency, frequency, and monetary value so you can go and look for more of those.

It's far better to create your best offer for people you understand the best and who understand you *or* to create offers for people that "look like" people who have loved your offers in the past.

A NICHE OF 30 MILLION

My second story relates to how I spent a good part of my career selling useful (and often lifesaving) health information to consumers. Although we had gotten started selling general health books that were more encyclopedic, when we niched down, we were able to tap into one of the most powerful niches in health.

Our successes early on were always thanks to careful research, since we knew there was a real and present danger that if we went too wide all the time, we would look like our competition and risk commoditizing our content. Of course, the temptation to stay broad and appeal to everyone was tantalizing. This story is about trusting your gut and collective experience in addition to using research appropriately . . . and it's about being able to break the rules of direct marketing because you know what the rules are in the first place. It's important to recognize when current circumstances are different, and then seize opportunities when they are staring you in the face. This epitomizes that quote, "Learn the rules like a pro so you can break them like an artist."

Over the early years of selling general health information, we started using a process that would be deployed before we launched any new niche book through direct mail: the Q test. Here Q stands for questionnaire, though I have also heard these referred to as concept tests or survey tests. Whatever you call them, it is a scientific way to predict tangible results using quantitative research. I learned this technique from direct marketers who had been using it for many years—even decades—before I discovered it, and before I had the good sense to use this kind of research too.

First step: write a blurb for a new book. We always made it exciting, but we also made sure it was a description that we could deliver on. That is, the book we would ultimately create or buy the rights to needed to match the blurb closely enough that the test would be reliable.

Second step: put together at least four to six new book blurbs to test against each other, sometimes doing as many as eight in a single Q test.

Third step: select a universe from our previous book buyers. We were looking for a cross section from our internal database. Then we would mail approximately 2,000 buyers in three waves. The participants in the survey were some of our best customers, based on our RFM analysis. This was all done with physical mail, since we were also looking for direct mail responsiveness, but these days Q tests are done online just as easily.

The Three Waves of Our Q Tests

Wave 1: A postcard told the folks a survey was coming and we wanted their help.

Wave 2: The survey itself was sent, usually with a $1 or $2 bill attached, which encouraged them to participate so we could continue to bring them the best books in the future. In the survey, after each blurb, there were only two possible responses for the respondent to check:

☐ Would Order.

☐ Would Not Order.

(There are many Q test formats that can have up to four responses: would definitely order, would probably order, might order, would definitely not order. It's much more effective to have only two options.)

Wave 3: A follow-up letter in an envelope reminding them to fill out the survey.

All waves were mailed first class, which, although costly, guarantees deliverability, and that is worth it. If you're Q testing by e-mail, make sure you take deliverability and open rates into account so that you get enough responses to read the results accurately.

Using this methodology, we received what was close to the industry standard for response rates when Q testing—between 40 percent and 50 percent. Yes, that's *40 percent to 50 percent,* not

.04 percent to .05 percent, or .004 percent to .005 percent. And after the mailing was complete, marketers would be armed with 800 to 1,000 responses (which is about the number you should look for when Q testing, offline or online) that showed the comparative interest between titles. Extrapolating that data, using some benchmarking from the past, meant we never launched a book unsuccessfully once we started Q testing. It's expensive and time consuming . . . and I know of no better technique to determine the best products and offers for your core audience.

Of course, we eventually moved a lot of our surveys online, but it is harder to send a dollar bill through a phone line. If you use this methodology online I suggest you use other incentives, like free reports or discount codes for future purchases. But I recommend that you still e-mail in three waves. There were very few things that would compel us *not* to do a Q test on a new potential book title. But like I said earlier, there are always exceptions to the rules.

In one case, the exception was the epidemic of diabetes and prediabetes in the United States, an ailment that affected upward of 30 million people at the time, and a book that landed on my desk unexpectedly at exactly the right moment. We were handed an opportunity (sugar-free, of course) on a silver platter from a world-class copywriter who had given up writing to build a company producing exercise and nutrition programs for type 2 diabetics and prediabetics.

The 30-Day Diabetes Cure was a wonderful book and program that we felt could help hundreds of thousands of people—*and* it came with the outline for a direct mail promotion package from a seasoned copywriter we knew and trusted, who was available to write it immediately. We also knew that diabetes was a topic of intense interest among our customers for general health books, and many diabetes-related headlines and lead materials were performing well in current promotions for many of those books.

However, despite being such a hot topic, we knew that if we Q tested a niche title on diabetes to a list of buyers who had only bought general health books in the past, there was a very good chance it would not get an acceptable response to make the cut and be developed as our next project. So now it was time to break the rules. I suggested that we should bypass putting this one into a Q test and just launch it.

I was willing to take this risk because our window of opportunity could close by the time we got our results. Not only could we lose the copywriter's availability, but being a niche product, the Q test results wouldn't necessarily give us an accurate picture of the market's attitude to the topic even though it was one of the scariest health trends in the market at the time, and consumers needed lots of information. This was a situation where understanding the history of the niche might have been more powerful than anything we could have learned from additional research. This was an offer we had to make immediately.

I have made many errors over the decades I've been doing this marketing stuff, and jumping into this project without Q testing was risky. Fortunately it paid off. We jumped on the opportunity by getting into the mail quickly, and we never looked back. Our friend and world-class copywriter gave us a gift with his diabetes book and eating program, and it proved to be one of the best launches ever in the category. The topic is still going strong for health marketers everywhere because, unfortunately, the epidemic has only gotten worse. We were doing our part to reverse that trend.

Looking back on this incredible success, I've often wondered if I would have broken the Q test rule had I not known how important this topic was to our audience. I doubt it. But isn't that one of the beauties of experience?

Direct marketing success comes from accumulated wisdom, perpetual curiosity, unbridled optimism . . . and, of course, being a slave to your numbers and measuring everything. We were lucky on that launch, but it was luck created by experience and having played by the rules enough to know when to break them. That's how the best offers are created.

I encourage you to go with your gut once in a while when you have strong anecdotal evidence or information you trust about a marketplace or topic. Even though direct marketing is such a numbers-driven business (which is what I love most about it), there is still room for logic, instinct, and courage. Horizontal verticals (i.e., big topics in niche areas) like the diabetes epidemic don't come along often. But I believe that if you are always thinking niche first, these opportunities have a much better chance of showing up. Even if you never get to have a horizontal vertical in your career, being number one in any niche— especially if it's a niche you are passionate about—will almost always beat being one of many in a crowded, noisy marketplace that also has many imposters.

In addition, with direct response marketing, where everything is measurable and containing your costs is always part of the equation (since everything has to eventually pay out), there is no such thing as a "failure." It's either a breakthrough or it's education. You win or you learn.

LET YOUR MARKET SHAPE YOUR OFFERS

One of the biggest offer breakthroughs in my career can be traced to a new branding strategy. As a serial direct marketer who relies on measurability all the time, talking about branding gives me hives, but while this next story has a branding component to it, it also teaches us to never throw advertising, marketing, or promotion dollars at any offer that doesn't have an expected, measurable return.

To review: Boardroom Inc. was launched in 1972 with *Boardroom Reports*, which taught small business owners how to run their businesses better. It was a publication filled with practical, useful information, and subscriptions were sold almost exclusively through direct mail.

In 1980, the company launched *Bottom Line/Personal*, which, as I mentioned earlier, essentially appealed to the consumer side of the same executive who subscribed to *Boardroom Reports*, covering health, personal finance, personal development, and so on. As you read earlier, the company exploded (in a good way) and *really* got busy: health, tax, and retirement newsletters followed, as did dozens of books in those categories too . . . and eventually we had a product line where a majority of our offers focused on health, personal finance, taxes, and consumer information.

Business information had taken a back seat. So what happened to poor *Boardroom Reports*? Well, the core audience interested in business information—while enthusiastic for the newsletter—had shrunk quite a bit due to attrition and lack of available outside lists. And of course, our house (internal) list was not responding all that well to the business-related newsletter with the new focus on consumer-related editorial. That is, attracting new subscribers to *Boardroom Reports* was hard, while new customer acquisition in our new consumer categories was easier and more lucrative. But it was difficult for the company to let go of its firstborn, and *Boardroom Reports* chugged along for a while, albeit marginally.

Then we had an innovative idea for a test, although it's sort of obvious in hindsight. Here was the logic: The database of existing customers (after the explosion of *BL/P*) had huge identification and affinity with the Bottom Line brand. So instead of giving up on the consumers who still might want business information, we met them where they identified with us the most. *Boardroom Reports* was renamed *Bottom Line/Business* and was redesigned to look like an affiliated publication with *BL/P*. We then created promotions that looked and sounded more like what our customers were used to seeing for our rapidly growing consumer publications.

The rebranding created a huge lift in response from the house audience to the newly renamed *Bottom Line/Business* and breathed new life into our original publication from customers we had paid to acquire a long time ago and from new subscribers to our consumer publications too. It allowed us to create a whole new line of products, which in turn kept the newsletter alive (and profitable) for a few more years. When we eventually folded *Bottom Line/Business*, it was done by choice and not as much by necessity—always a better way to go. At that point we realized that the subject area was an outlier; we had gotten so much better at marketing in the consumer categories and at that time they deserved 100 percent of our editorial focus.

But we learned valuable lessons we could take forward from this transition from *Boardroom Reports* to *Bottom Line/Business*:

- Our first health newsletter, *Health Confidential*, had a huge growth spurt when it was rebranded as *Bottom Line/Health*.

- Boardroom's tax newsletter, *Tax Hotline*, got some new life when it went wider as *Bottom Line/Wealth*.

- *Bottom Line/Tomorrow* (the retirement newsletter) and *Bottom Line's Natural Healing with Dr. Mark Stengler* were both launched with titles under the Bottom Line umbrella. We didn't even bother trying anything *but* Bottom Line branding at the outset of any new launches after seeing the power of the umbrella brand. We were fast learners, I guess.

- All the books we published became publications of Bottom Line Books rather than Boardroom Books.

This all might sound a bit simple now. But the fact that Boardroom was never a household name made it less obvious that the company was sitting on a killer brand with a pretty large audience and that this audience was just waiting for us to ask them what kind of products they wanted to see.

I'd also like to quote ice hockey legend Wayne Gretzky in this context: "Skate to where the puck is going to be, not where it has been." We didn't change the entire branding and offer strategy of our company on a whim or because some brand consultant said it would be cool, but because our audience told us that's where we should go. And who are we to argue with the folks who pay the rent and the electric bill?

CHOOSING THE RIGHT CAMPAIGN STRUCTURE FOR YOUR OFFER (OR, HOW YOU SELL PREDICTS HOW THEY WILL RESPOND)

How you present your offer to your lists, internally and externally, will often determine the kind of response you get. Not just the number of responses, but the kind of people that end up becoming your new customers. For example, if you sell your offer with a sweepstakes, the people who respond are likely to be impulsive and might not have a high lifetime value, being more interested in winning millions of dollars than actually investing in your products or services. Or they might not pay as much for a particular offer and they might only do free trials (and are therefore more likely to be tire kickers). While they may still be profitable, they will have a lower lifetime value than other segments. But if you sell with long-form copy, online or offline, lifetime value is likely to increase, because the customers are going to be more engaged with the offer from the outset. That's what I mean when I say that how you sell predicts how the list will respond.

Regardless of the offers you make and how you sell them, you have to track how the list buys and how (and if) they buy again later. I've seen this play out many times, whether I was renting the Boardroom list to other mailers or selling our own products to our house list. I was always very conscious of those different buyer profiles (i.e., what offers they had previously responded to) to segment the lists and ensure the right people were sent the most appropriate offer with the most appropriate type of campaign.

The Survey Package versus the Bookalog

Once upon a time, back in the dark ages called the 1990s, one of the greatest copywriters of all time, Gary Bencivenga, wrote a lucrative front-end promotion for *BL/P* that we called the survey package. By "front end" I mean it was to attract new customers who were mostly unfamiliar with the newsletter and the brand. The survey package was a fairly simple letter, in a standard envelope, with a gift certificate attached to the letter. The gift certificate was also the order device. The letter began:

> I need your honest opinion . . . and I'm willing to reward you handsomely for it. That's why I've enclosed the above gift certificate, which entitles you to two very valuable gifts in exchange for your opinion.

The goal was to have prospects send in the "survey" with the gift certificate to get a free trial subscription to the newsletter. It was a generous offer: six free issues and a premium book before they had to pay anything, a true "try it before you buy it," or what you now know as the bill-me-later approach.

Getting people to subscribe with a survey felt like a gimmick and not the best way to sell such high-quality information. Despite that, the campaign was incredibly successful. The survey package performed like a sweepstakes, in that people felt they would be missing out on something from us if they didn't participate.

As you might expect, since the trial subscribers came into the newsletter without a lot of selling or extensive background on how great *BL/P* really was, the number of people who actually paid us the $29.95 subscription price after the free trial period was lower than previous packages. That's what I meant when I said the survey was more of a gimmick rather than the most powerful way to sell such important consumer information. We had a great hook that led to an impulsive response, but the promotion did not reflect what the product was all about. Impulse gets people to respond . . . but it doesn't necessarily get them to stick around.

The bottom line (pun intended) was that the survey package was, net-net, a huge success since it added many new paying subscribers, despite the low pay-up rate. However, the low pay-up rate ultimately became a problem, and it didn't feel great that many of the trial subscribers were unresponsive to the material.

I really didn't like the survey package. There was nothing illegal or immoral about it, but it always felt like a less than admirable way to sell the best consumer newsletter in America. A rule of thumb to being a world-class direct marketer—at least in my playbook—is to believe that the control is your enemy. It may be the current winner, but it's there to be beaten too. Whether I liked it or not, the survey package would have to remain the control until it was beaten on the battlefield of statistical significance . . . so I was pretty motivated to create a new package to beat it. Lucky for me, I was working with the best copywriter on the planet at the time.

Gary Bencivenga also saw the flaws with selling this offer via the survey package, despite the success it had up front. He is the one who did the deep thinking (and heavy lifting) to then beat his own control. Gary wrote a masterpiece to test against the survey package: a 64-page bookalog (which looks like a digest magazine) titled *The Little Black Book of Secrets*. There was no survey or quick, impulsive gift certificate order device featured in those 64 pages. And, in fact, it wasn't all selling copy either.

There's an expression we used before longer formats became more prevalent in direct mail: selling the sizzle but not the steak. This meant that we didn't want to give away the "meat" of the product in our attempts to sell it. The intrigue and mystery was part of the selling process. However, longer direct mail at that time was trending toward giving away some steak along with the sizzle, and Gary's bookalog did that very well. You might even say that promotions like that bookalog were a precursor to the content marketing we see online today.

So what were the front-end results of the bookalog against the survey package? *Much* lower: it produced approximately half the number of new trial subscribers on the front end. But the back-end results were just the opposite. The percentage of people who actually paid for the newsletter after taking a trial subscription from the bookalog was close to double that of the survey package . . . and they paid *long* before they got all of their six free issues, which I think is a tribute to the "steak" included in the bookalog.

Put another way, the bookalog got lower numbers initially but more quality engagement in the long run, and that led to much higher profits when we analyzed the subscribers from the bookalog offer after the first sale. Tracking those subscribers who initially came in from the bookalog into their second year renewal (what we called conversions) showed us the true miracle. These subscribers were engaged in such a way from the initial promotion that their expectations were met in year one of their subscription . . . and then long into the future. They were worth so much more long term than the survey subscribers.

The LTV of subscribers who came in from the bookalog over those who originally came in from the survey package was a real game changer. The bookalog became the new control, and it inspired many packages like it in the future. We also sold all sorts of books to our subscriber list, and the response rate to all our book offers (also using longer promotional copy) was significantly higher among the subscribers who came in from the bookalog over the survey package subscribers. That is, new long-form copy promotions did better with people who came in from previous long-form copy promotions.

And there was one more way the subscribers from the bookalog added to the company's profit: when we rented our lists to the outside world (equivalent to folks using their list for revenue share or affiliate offers online today), outside mailers saw higher response rates when *they* mailed names derived from the bookalog. Quality over quantity indeed—how we sold (bookalog versus survey) had a statistically significant impact on how our audience responded to our offers.

The Paranoid Package versus the Happy-Go-Lucky-Package

This second example of "how you promote is how they will respond" is also an example of how you promote creating new list universes if you pay close attention.

Just after the dinosaurs became extinct, around 1986, we tested what we called a "paranoid package" for *BL/P* with the headline "The World Crisis of 1986." The control at the time was a package that sold a wonderful premium book, *How to Do Everything Right*—a promotion that was much more upbeat and optimistic. (I guess anything seems upbeat compared to a world crisis.)

On the surface, the test results were clear: *How to Do Everything Right* defended its position as the control by a wide margin when we looked at the mailing in its entirety. It looked like paranoia could be put to the side until the next world crisis. However, something strange happened on the way to burying that test: When we looked at how each package did on a list-by-list basis, we found that there were certain names who were less interested in the mainstream offers and fell more in the opportunity-seeker category. These people responded to the world crisis package at a much higher rate than they did to the control.

To cut to the chase, we discovered that we had two list universes—two different sets of names with two distinct interests. So we ended up with *two* controls—one upbeat and one paranoid—each mailing to the list universe most suited to the messaging.

Key lesson: if we could create multiple control offers for different audiences in the most expensive medium, direct mail—with extra printing, sorting, and postage costs—shouldn't you be thinking about multiple controls to various list segments in your online business all the time? While one-size-fits-all creative *can* be profitable, it is not the strategy for long-term business building. Just about everyone on your list will be on other people's lists too. But they come to you to meet a *particular* interest or need, so the makeup of your list is always going to be one of a kind. And sometimes selling in a different style can help you understand the makeup of your list(s) even more effectively. There are no unique names, only unique lists.

In the words of Jay Abraham, this is getting everything you can out of all you've got. Here are the main lessons from these examples:

- Read your numbers, listen to your audience, and look for the hidden offer opportunities—and then act on the opportunities that present themselves.

- Don't underestimate the impact of how you promote on the kind of customers you will attract.

- Make sure you can calculate the lifetime value of every new customer based on the promotion they came in on. The initial sale is only one metric—and LTV, not the first sale, may be the most important metric when deciding on your most profitable acquisition vehicle.

- If you think these concepts are only true for direct mail, think again. All these principles apply on any channel you decide to use.

SOME OF THE BEST OFFERS AREN'T ORIGINAL

During my first decade at Boardroom, creating offers and products—mainly for books and newsletters—was relatively easy. We were publishing some of the most useful newsletters in the world at the time, including *Boardroom Reports, Bottom Line/Personal, Tax Hotline,* and *Health Confidential.* We created best-selling books by taking the "greatest hits" of our newsletters and putting them into huge volumes, indexed and categorized, and sold millions of copies of those "new" books.

I never lost sleep over not being on the *New York Times* best-seller list ... we were much happier selling millions of books and helping millions of consumers without needing to get involved with bookstores or anything that resembled trade publishing. We had a wonderful formula for creating these books and then had the best copywriters at the time (including Gene Schwartz, Gary Bencivenga, Jim Rutz, Mel Martin, Clayton Makepeace, and others) work their magic on each one.

We priced our books higher than anything similar you would find in a bookstore; we also created higher value than anything we could have done in a traditional bookselling environment. It worked like crazy for years. But then we were faced with a moment of truth in the late 1980s: we started running out of content doing these greatest-hits volumes.

Our bestsellers were often over 500 pages. They were encyclopedic, and we joked that we sold books by the pound. These kind of books sold much better than our niche titles (although we had a lot of success with many big niches, like the horizontal vertical we discussed before—the diabetes book).

Simply put, books by the pound was what our core customers wanted . . . but it was getting tougher and tougher to deliver those kinds of books without duplicating content. *The Book of Inside Information*, or what I called *Bottom Line*'s Greatest Hits, sold vast numbers of hardcover copies over many years, at $30 a book. We had offshoots of that book, including *The Big Black Book* and *The Book of Secrets*, and they all sold well.

There was also our book *Healing Unlimited*, which sold over two million copies; our big tax books; and even a title on estate planning, which sold hundreds of thousands of copies (as you recall, this was partially thanks to Bill Jayme). Even "vertical" books, including the estate planning book and the diabetes book, became a little more "horizontal" when direct mail targeting was involved.

But how were we going to expand this formula? We had a hungry database waiting for more big books and nothing to sell them. Enter Gordon Grossman, the man who was the architect of *Reader's Digest* in the 1960s and 1970s, and who I hired as a consultant in the 1990s. He looked at what we were doing and said, "Brian, what makes you think that all the content for your books has to be your own stuff?"

That simple question changed everything for us. I realized at that moment that I could buy our new books instead of having to make them all. Gordon had been involved in the practice of buying trade books and converting them to direct mail books at *Reader's Digest* and also for his other big consulting client,

Rodale Press. I put this lightbulb idea, invented by others, into action—and added my own twist.

It started with a trip to Barnes and Noble when I asked to borrow a hand truck. Thus armed, I trundled around the store to every category that fit with the interests of the millions of names in our database. I got a good workout running all over the store, piling the hand truck higher and higher with books. I visited every category that made sense, including health, fitness, finance, investing, taxes, personal development, food and nutrition, retirement, and so on. There were so many amazing books in those categories, most of which had an inch of dust on them because no one was picking them up. I knew many of them just needed a marketing makeover.

I also realized that if any of those dusty volumes had sold 10,000 copies in their lifetime, they would have been considered bestsellers by the trade at that time. Although most of them had not hit anywhere near that level, I was confident we could change that with our direct mail formula. Thinking ahead, I knew I could propose a windfall opportunity to some old-school trade publishers, who knew we were better equipped to take their books from the store to the mail. My master plan was to approach those trade publishers and secure the direct marketing rights, then blow their minds with how many books we could sell with direct mail when the title was selling virtually nothing in bookstores.

Five or six trips to my car later, after purchasing 40 or 50 books and weighing down my 1985 Toyota Camry until my tailpipe was almost dragging on the ground, I had the candidates to rival our current direct mail bestsellers.

The next step was to go through the books to see which ones had the most useful information from the most credible sources. Many books got nixed by the editors: "We can't put our name on *that!*" Others got nixed by the copywriters: "There's not enough juicy information for compelling copy!" But the books that got through this gauntlet were put into the new product pipeline.

We also had to come up with an amazing pitch to the trade publishers for the direct marketing rights (which took some doing), and we had to create a system to reposition any appropriate trade books to direct mail. Now, this was before we had started doing Q tests, so fortunately our approach worked well.

The books we added to our direct mail lineup were often in paperback in the bookstore already, selling for less than $20. But our direct mail version of the book would always be hardcover (which has a higher perceived value), and we would add bonuses and premiums to make the new version drastically more appealing than the one in the bookstore. This repositioning made the offer for direct mail unrecognizable as what it had been before. It was this "apples to oranges" comparison of offers that also got all the trade publishers to give us the rights to sell the books, and justifiably so. They saw the book as a single title on the shelf at a bookstore; we saw the book as part of a treasury of information. Our price points, which started at $30, eventually rose to $40 plus shipping and handling. All the while the same book was still sitting on bookstore shelves at half the price and with none of the attention.

That's how we created a whole book division with content we didn't have to produce. I didn't invent the idea of buying the rights to books to sell in other channels. But without these direct mail offers, these books would have died on the vine (or shelf) without helping an enormous number of people who needed that information. The way we did it enabled us to both bring fantastic content to the world and have multiple outside titles that sold in the hundreds of thousands. A few even sold more than a million copies.

There are a few lessons here for any marketer, offline or online:

1. Look everywhere and anywhere for undersold or underutilized assets or products right under your nose that could be of interest to your audience. I'm not talking about doing another affiliate mailing—I'm talking about buying the rights to those products and making them your own. This same principle applies to digital products as well, not just books and physical products.

2. Know the power of your name and your brand to your audience and look for products that you would be proud to put your name on.

3. Nothing gets sold without a great sales message, regardless of your medium, but the offer has to have legs of its own. Think about whether it has real credibility before you fall in love with your new product idea. Have seasoned copywriters look at everything you are considering so you can get an objective view on it before you try to get them to write anything.

And of course, the offer has to be unique and compelling.

ASSESSING YOUR ASSETS

The first thing I do when I take on a new client (or onboard someone into one of my mastermind groups) is to have a conversation with them that begins with, "Where were you? Where are you now? And where would you like to go?" Since the people I like working with the most are always up to something bigger and better, the "where would you like to go" part always seems to include something about "exponential growth" or at least "significant" growth. And no one answers the question of where they want to go with "staying where I am now."

But it's the next set of questions and the inquiry that follows that is most interesting. Almost everyone I've worked with assumes that creating huge growth involves inventing something new or doing something completely different than what they have done in the past, with completely new people, assets, and resources. And that might be the case. But I maintain that it is never the starting point.

This is where I would start: Your next big idea might be right under your nose . . . or in a drawer somewhere . . . or tucked away in something called a file cabinet . . . or simply sitting on your hard drive. (This idea is summed up in the phrase "getting everything you can out of all you've got," which happens to be the title of one of my favorite books by one of my mentors, Jay

Abraham.) Another way to put this: When brainstorming (with yourself or others) about that next big idea, first think deeply about assets you already own and control before thinking about trying to attain new assets.

I think the biggest reason I am a "mastermind junkie" is that I love to surround myself all the time with people smarter than me and to have others I trust and admire tell me things I can't see (and will never see) about my life and my business. Having others making you aware of your overlooked assets from the outside looking in—and pushing you to go deep with what you have already rather than coveting something new and shiny—is another reason to surround yourself with smart people who will tell you the truth.

Having sat on many "hot seats" in masterminds over the years, and participated in the audience for hundreds more, helping myself and others seek the wisdom of the room, it's often shocking how obvious the answer becomes when someone else asks the right probing questions. A problem or opportunity that seemed so daunting at the outset usually becomes clearer and manageable to solve when someone else forces you to focus on resources that are right at your fingertips.

Again, the first step is to go deep on "assessing your assets." Start by asking, *What are all the things I have access to or own that have already been created, written, developed, or curated—and probably with a sunk cost?*

Of course we should all think big and look beyond where we have been and where we are presently, and I am by no means suggesting that exponential growth is only the result of rehashing, recycling, and never buying something brand new. But don't ignore everything you have built, created, and achieved just because you see it as the "past." In fact it is all that material in all forms that can propel you even further in the future.

By assessing your assets in this way, you will create the most innovative offers. I guarantee that there will be more than enough time for you to explore the exciting (and unknown)— but looking at what is already there is where I recommend you begin. I know this might sound simple. Hopefully it will be helpful to you if we focus on three areas and some questions you can ask yourself regarding the inventory you own before you go shopping outside.

1. Lists

How many active or previous customers do you have on a list somewhere (anywhere)? How many people can you reach who know you, your products, or your service who have not bought from you in the past but still might take your call (that is, open an e-mail from you because it's from you)?

Your first step is to take inventory of all the lists you already own. And that includes groups of people not in some sort of automated database (your Facebook friends, your LinkedIn contacts, and your e-mail contacts all count). I can't tell you how many times someone tells me about their next big idea and the first thing they do is talk about extravagant marketing plans that include promoting to *huge* audiences who have no idea who they are and know nothing about their history or track record.

I know you are well aware that "warm traffic" is more responsive than "cold traffic" . . . but you would be amazed how many people go after the shiny object (such as cold traffic from the millions on Facebook) before approaching the "boring" previous buyers and prospects who might know and love them already. I don't even like using the term "traffic" when looking at potential audiences, since traffic in a literal sense is unpredictable—and the last thing we want in direct response marketing is unpredictability if we have some ability to make the media we buy predictable.

Believe it or not, there are many marketers today that won't even test offers and concepts to their Facebook friends (for free) before they buy costly ads on Facebook. The reason most people justify going outside before looking inside is usually a version of this (which is a real quote from a somewhat experienced marketer launching a new product with a new offer): "I have 3,000 people who know me and love me (and some have even sent me a check) . . . but I want this new product to be *big!*"

I maintain that you will get bigger faster (and prove any concept with more confidence) by going a mile deep with those 3,000 first rather than going a mile wide in another medium. Whether you sell business-to-consumer like I did (selling millions of subscriptions and books $39 at a time) or whether you sell business-to-business at much higher prices, the philosophy is the same. Mining your "house list" first in as many ways as you can think of (different offers to different segments, special copy based on interest areas, etc.) will become the foundation of your business and fuel the creation of your most successful offers. And after you prove the new idea with those folks, there will be more than enough time (with a lot less risk) to go after the millions of new people who can't wait to hear from you too.

But take care of those who love you the most first. And by "love" I mean anyone you might have touched in the past, whether they bought from you or not. Also, always look at the economics of being big in a smaller, niche market where you are already a hero (and that will probably spend more with you) versus being small in a larger, broad market that has never heard of you. It's worth doing the math.

2. Content

What content do you own or have the ability to use on an unlimited basis? What products do you own or have access to that have relevance (or once had relevance)?

This is a resource we all take for granted. It's so easy to think that once it's been printed or sent in an e-mail, you can't use it again. The idea of "repurposing content" has nothing to do with selling or distributing the same stuff over and over again to people who can't remember if they bought it or consumed it. It has everything to do with the fact that good material is always worth repeating . . . and updating . . . and thereby transforming previously used information into new information. Simply put, before creating anything new from scratch, see what you have already that can be repurposed powerfully.

3. Promotions

What previous winners do you have in your swipe file that have been retired? What previous *almost* winners or winners in a different medium are currently sitting in that same swipe file? And what losers do you have that surprised you when they lost, but you never went back to try to turn them around?

Everything you have done in the past with your marketing efforts is an archive of educational materials, not just sales letters, order pages, and copy platforms that are "one and done." Furthermore, anything that has worked well in the past for you or someone else should never die. Even anything that was a total dog (i.e., didn't work well at all) for you or someone else is a building block for future promotions. While I had very little luck in my career taking a huge winner from years past and just reusing it after simply giving it a rest, I have had winner after winner by repeating copy platforms, headline structures, and some previously used promotional copy with new and restructured offers.

I've talked about the power of swipe files and why every successful copywriter and marketer has elaborate systems to catalog anything and everything they can build upon for their own future promotions. Remember, you can look at winners from others and "steal smart" (i.e., adapt winning formulas to whatever you might be working on yourself). I say this often, but it is worth repeating here: "Stealing is a felony; stealing smart is an art."

I know you have probably been taught the lesson of "being grateful for what you have" and its kissing cousin, "you don't know what you have until it's gone." The beauty of marketing today is that nothing you have done (or do) will ever be gone. Plus, we have more media choices than ever before, more content available than ever before, and access to more successful promotions to study in an instant than ever before.

There is a dark side to the fact that nothing you've done in the past is ever gone. Just ask the kid who put a picture of himself on Facebook at a frat party five years ago and hopes the person interviewing him for a job today doesn't see it. On the other hand, every person you have ever had a previous relationship with, everything you have ever written, and every sales approach you have ever used is also around forever—and it's all far more usable (and less embarrassing) than pictures from a frat party.

HOW TO USE PREMIUMS (OR, WHEN OVERDELIVERY & BEST OFFER COLLIDE)

Bonuses and premiums have always been among the most important tools in the direct response playbook and should be considered with every offer. They can turn a good offer into a great one and can be the difference between mediocre response and massive response. Many pioneers in the direct response business (magazines, for example) always emphasized premiums, such as free reports, books, and even hard goods (remember the sneaker phone from *Sports Illustrated*?).

One of the top copywriters I ever worked with, a master at maximizing the effectiveness of premiums, is Eric Betuel. He had been writing control after control, and we wanted him to tackle a hot new product for us called *The Bottom Line Yearbook*. The book was hot because it was made up of the best annual content created from multiple sources . . . and it was a continuity, updated every year and sold as a kind of subscription, which would add a lot to the profitability long term if a new offer could beat the control offer.

The control offer Eric was trying to beat gave away a bonus report with the book, and he suggested increasing that to four bonus reports that were related to some of the most important topics covered in the book. Four bonuses instead of one increased response to the offer significantly. So we upped our game and started offering 50 free reports. Once 50 became the control, of course we tested giving away 100 free reports. And while the increased *number* of bonuses obviously created higher perceived value, we got the most bang for our buck by choosing report headlines that covered the most salient interest areas, creating many more entry points for our audience.

Going from 1 premium to 4 to 50 to 100 actually didn't cost us a lot more money the way we produced the reports, and the value of this overdelivery (an irresistible offer addressing the hottest topics) made a huge difference to the offer's profitability. One thing we did to keep the costs down while being able to increase the number of premiums from 4 to 100 was by binding all the special reports into one volume for delivery. But the direct mail piece displayed the titles of all 100 reports individually; that way the customer could see exactly how much value they were getting by being able to read every topic of every report. Each report was only a few pages long, but the consumer advice was deeply impactful on a wide variety of topics.

This is a great example of getting the most out of a premium-driven offer. You can see the value added here—by offering 100 bonus reports, you get 100 extra entry points, any one of which could be the key reason someone will buy the book. A reader might buy the whole package on the basis of just one of these bonus reports. And our revenue and profit for *The Bottom Line Yearbook* rose significantly as a result of massively overdelivering high-quality information to our customers inside an irresistible and super-compelling offer. And very little was brand-new content, just great content from the archives that had been updated.

THE SIGNIFICANCE OF STATISTICAL SIGNIFICANCE

One of my favorite marketing cartoons (I have collected many over the years) shows three marketing people in weighted sacks at the bottom of a polluted river.

One says (from his sack), "I could sell this!" That's curiosity (and the importance of dreaming) about what makes a great offer.

One says, "It could work!" That's optimism that the offer is going to be great for the customers.

The last one says, "Numbers. I need numbers!" That's measuring how the offer performs to get real data.

I use those three geniuses to create my direct marketing offer success formula. Most companies that sell with direct response have plenty of curiosity and optimism, but without the final part of this formula, measurement, they spend much more time strategizing than implementing. Of course, you always have to assess the downside risks of doing faster tests (and more tests); but when there is a chance for a big winner, get it out there quickly.

Remember: curiosity + optimism + measurement = direct marketing offer success. What that really means is that you have to be disciplined with your testing. Test the first segment that you know *should* work for this offer. If they don't respond, kill the product. Don't even go to the next segments for testing—*you don't have a business with that product if your most targeted customers are not interested.* As Gordon Grossman always said, "First find out if you have a business." This is the first essential step.

If you have a brand-new product you're excited about, should you test 15 variations of it to see which one will perform best? No. You test whatever you need to test to prove that you have a business with that product first. Then get a critical mass of engagement from paying customers . . . and *then* you can test your variations.

This is why you should never walk out of a product development meeting without a clear idea of the tests you want to make—your only initial focus should be to find out if you have a business for that product. Most online marketers are pretty impulsive about testing many things at the outset, since they can roll out products very quickly. And on the surface, the cost of multiple tests (even in a launch) is not financially prohibitive. So why do they need to think through testing a new product so intently? For one thing, there is a massive hidden cost to rolling out products that aren't robust enough to stand up to basic testing. There might not be a monetary cost to you in the short term, but if you present an inappropriate offer to a list, those people are less likely to respond in the future, and you won't be able to track why their responsiveness declined. Put another way, you might have a success in terms of overall profit but the nonbuyers probably won't tell you why they didn't buy—and if the offer was a disconnect, you might end up losing those folks forever. You will have no chance of reviving them with your next offer because they will feel betrayed. And if you get in the habit of disconnected offers, this pattern will continue. There's opportunity cost, goodwill cost, time cost—you accumulate huge losses over time when you don't test properly.

Dick Benson was a stickler for proper testing methodology. I think if Dick were alive today, he would be excited that technology has enabled us to test more frequently, faster, and much more inexpensively than we ever could have dreamed in the days before the Internet. But with all that excitement, I think he would have identified a new problem. I can even hear him now: "Do you and all your clients understand statistical significance enough to accurately identify the winners of the tests you are doing?"

A quick primer on statistical significance: You must have enough data (and the right data) to take the results of a test and then roll a product out to a much larger universe of names with similar success and confidence. This requires large amounts of data so that your results are replicable.

A while back I was consulting with a marketer who didn't understand statistical significance. We were starting a test on a $97 offer, and just as we were getting the first results, he turned to me and said, "We've got a winner with test A over test B! Test A has 12 orders and test B has 8. This is great!"

On a $97 offer, I can *assure* you that 12 orders over 8 orders does not mean you have a statistically valid winner. Statistical significance requires many more orders. (If you don't have a list that allows for thousands of responses, you're probably better off focusing on finding more of the right people for your list and relying on the anecdotal evidence they give you rather than running tests that cannot reach true statistical significance.)

But not only do you need to test for statistical significance, *you also need to test the right things.* I like to combine Dick Benson's obsession with testing with another maxim from Gordon Grossman: "Don't make tiny tests." You need to test the things that can give you significant lifts in response, revenue, or profit (or a combination of all those), not just the things that make you feel good.

Here's a tip: Whenever you are in a brainstorming meeting discussing things to test, after you get all the possibilities written on a whiteboard, posted all over the room on sticky notes, or written in crayon on the wall, *look to test things that could give you at least a 30 percent lift in your key metric.* For example, changing the color of your guarantee box is unlikely to give you a 30 percent lift in front-end conversions, but testing the headline on that page might. Depending on your product, offer, and price, you could look for a little less than a 30 percent lift . . . but this is not a bad benchmark to hopefully help you make fewer "tiny tests."

THE POWER OF PYRAMIDING

The concept of pyramiding will prevent you from making big mistakes when rolling out a new offer, whether you think you have a big winner or not. When you test a small quantity and your results say it's a winner, you only roll out to an additional select set of names (that look like the names you initially tested) to prove the first result. If the results hold up there, you "pyramid" a little more, promoting to a larger set of people who look like the second group. Regardless of price point, you need a certain level of response that will be a good indicator of how a bigger portion of the list will perform.

For example, the rule of thumb in direct mail (if you could afford it) was to mail around 5,000 names from a particular list in the hope that you would get around 100 responses to the offer you were testing. In most cases with a winning result on 5,000 names from a specific list with a specific selection on that list, you would pyramid to 25,000, and if the 25,000 validated the initial test result, you might pyramid to 100,000.

There are many factors that can affect results as you go from smaller quantities to larger quantities, so the guiding principle is to have discipline and be cautious but continue to expand.

The most important thing to know about pyramiding is that at each step, as you move up the pyramid, the test needs to pay for itself. You don't move on to bigger quantities and take on more risk until you've consistently proven the method and the profitability.

OFFERS ARE CREATIVE

Even though the *next* chapter is about creative and copy, don't underestimate how much creativity is involved in coming up with your most compelling offers. In this chapter I didn't want to give you tactics on building offers, or to create a checklist of things to test, or give you lots of copy advice around offers. Many of the titles in the bibliography at the back of this book (see page 243) have lists of potential offers and tests you can consider that are based on decades of solid results and case histories. Here I want to lay out philosophies around offer testing that can be applied to many things you might be working on in your business today.

Having said that, offers and creative (copy) go hand in hand—the offers you make must be consistent with the messaging you use.

I remember a wonderful copywriter who wrote some very successful controls for me but didn't spend any significant time constructing the offers that went with his very well-written sales letters, headlines, brochures, and outer envelopes. Looking back on this now, I think we missed much bigger opportunities for success with this talented writer by not pushing him to be more holistic with the package, forcing him to think through the offers that went with his copy more deeply. Whether we could have done better or not with that copywriter, the lesson is that offers *are* creative . . . and this is a perfect segue into the next chapter. But before we leave the subject of offers, a reminder: Coming up with the best offers for your products and services is something that's personal and specific to your business; and after you create your most irresistible offers, make sure you test them and build on them using the bedrock principles we've covered here in Chapter 5.

KEY TAKEAWAYS

Making your best offers is another area in direct response that has a lot of moving parts. This chapter ranged far and wide, and I hope you will have a sense of everything that goes into delivering world-class offers to your carefully selected lists. Here's what you need to keep "top of mind":

- Choose niches where you can go a mile deep on your offers rather than a mile wide.

- When you choose your niche, make sure it fits with your "superpowers" and that there is ample reason for people in your audience to listen to you. Why are you uniquely positioned to give them what they need? How can you use that position to create innovative, powerful offers that will make them feel like you've been reading their mind?

- Survey your audience when developing your offers. Using the Q test methodology, you can collect hard evidence on the offers your ideal customers will be willing to pay for.

- Sometimes your audience will help you develop additional offerings over time. If your audience's interests evolve, evolve with them. Maximize the offers you have that are working, but don't stay so attached to them that you never innovate to meet the market where it's going.

- How you sell is how they will respond, that is, the structure of your campaigns and offers can have a huge impact on how your audience responds to them. Make sure the copy and creative package are congruent with the type of offer you are making and with the psychology of the ideal customer for that offer.

- Your offers don't all have to be original. Look at the assets you already have that could be repurposed, or look at buying the relevant assets if that makes sense for you. If you have an established brand, putting your name on an existing, proven asset can create some easy wins.

- Use bonuses and premiums to overdeliver even more on your best offers (and they should *all* be world-class).

- Make sure you test all your offers, provided you have the volume to generate statistically significant results. Remember, don't make "tiny tests." Once you have the results, you can roll out the offer using the pyramid structure throughout your list to validate the test results without risking your shirt.

CHAPTER 6

CREATIVE & COPY

"It's not the copywriter's job to create desire."

— GENE SCHWARTZ

Under the 41/39/20 rule, I hope it's clear that I am *not* suggesting that creative and copy (the design and the words you use in your marketing) are half as important as list or offer. In fact, creative and copy are just as important for effective campaigns as list selection and tailored offers. However, what I *am* suggesting is that you must have everything regarding your targeting and list selection buttoned up with your best offer *first* in order to make sure you don't waste precious creative dollars on expensive copywriters and designers.

It's a tragedy that so many marketers outsource their creative to amateurs when it's so vitally important. But many marketers don't pay as much attention to creative as they should because when you have a perfectly targeted list and an irresistible offer, sending mediocre creative can still create a profitable promotion. For example, an online marketer with a perfect affiliate partner ("perfect" meaning having an audience suited to the offer) will probably generate a decent number of orders and sales regardless of the messaging.

But even if it saves you money, there is no reason to coast along with mediocre messaging, since great creative will significantly increase your list's responsiveness to your offer and your overall success. When you can add killer copy to an irresistible offer and the tightest list selection you can manage, you've got the direct marketing formula that will create a business for a lifetime instead of creating a series of one-hit wonders.

Copywriting legend John Carlton made the brilliant observation that the next big things in marketing may not be in the areas of whizbang technology but rather in the nuts and bolts that career direct marketers are especially good at: building responsive lists, creating the right offers, and developing the right copy approaches.

That's not to say that technology won't continue to move at the speed of light. But when it comes to making sales, no one can argue that the right list—combined with the right offer and strong creative—still wins, every time. The marketers who spend their time building up these big three (and less time figuring out the next big quick win or ninja technique) will be the winners for the long haul. Great copy and creative approaches create sustainable, profitable businesses; ninja techniques create single revenue events. Now, this chapter is not about how to write copy. I am not a copywriter. There are many fantastic books available about how to write powerful copy (and you can go to my reading list at the back of this book for my recommendations), but this book is not one of them. That said, I know good copy when I see it. That's because I had the privilege of working with some of the best copywriters who have ever lived, which taught me a lot about what to look for in copywriters and the work they produce.

Whether you write copy yourself or you aspire to write copy, or even if you have no intention of ever writing copy, I believe that understanding seven key characteristics present in every great copywriter will give you a powerful perspective that will enable you to create the most successful campaigns possible. Interestingly, these seven characteristics have also been present in the makeup of every great *marketer* I have ever worked with as well—which tells me that to be a great copywriter is also to be a great marketer (and number five below talks about where the worlds of copywriters and marketers collide).

THE SEVEN CHARACTERISTICS OF WORLD-CLASS COPYWRITERS

"Do you know any good copywriters?"

This might be the single most asked question I get regularly—and I mean multiple times a week for decades. I guess I must look like a headhunter for copywriters. The question always frustrates me because I can never give someone a quick answer. I believe it is a disservice if I do. There are so many variables, and as you will read in this chapter, it's not "one size fits all" when it comes to matching a copywriter with a marketer. Copywriting is a specialty, not a commodity, and finding someone who is suited for your offer, products, or company is never a shot in the dark.

Of course I know good copywriters. I worked with—and still work with—the best of the best. But to find the copywriters who will have the most impact for your business, I believe it's critical to understand what makes the best of the best tick.

If you are hiring or looking for the best copywriters, or aspire to be one yourself, success leaves clues. What follows are the key factors to look for in a candidate's work and behavior, or your own. If you're a copywriter yourself, be prepared to internalize these ideas and cultivate these seven qualities so that you meet the standard when you're being hired by shrewd marketers who know what to look for; and if you are one of those shrewd marketers, go through the process of finding the right fit for your business and see if your best candidate(s) have what it takes *before* hiring.

1. Hunger

Spending thousands of hours researching and learning the craft of writing copy will make you one of the best in your field. Gary Halbert talked about how difficult it is to become a great copywriter as a type of "hard labor," and he suggested to writers working for him: "Do one hour's worth of road work every morning, right after you get up, for six days a week." Like road work, writing copy is hard labor and not everyone is cut out for it. You just sweat a little differently.

Marty Edelston's first pillar to becoming extraordinary was outworking everyone—and it's not only about working more hours. It's about showing dedication to the craft. If you accept that real expertise is developed over thousands of hours of deliberate practice, if you study and practice writing great copy without complaining and you keep a focused mind, you'll be well on your way to becoming one of the best in your field.

Every great copywriter is willing to do the work. They know this isn't easy, but their hunger drives them forward. Here's another maxim from Gary Halbert on this theme: "Get yourself a collection of good ads and DM pieces, and copy them in your own handwriting." Many of the greatest active copywriters who are now coaching young copywriters use this technique (and it has no resemblance to writing "I refuse to write crappy copy" 100 times on the blackboard).

Studies from around the world have found that handwriting (instead of typing) has a profound impact on our brains. It taps into what's called visual-motor memory, and it increases our ability to quickly recall information and execute commands and encourages higher order, abstract thinking (the free flow of creative ideas). Of course, copying out successful promotion packages from the past by hand requires patience and a particular mind-set—the hunger I am talking about to become the best. It's hard, it takes a long time, it's repetitive . . . but it has worked for the best copywriters who have ever lived. Who are we to argue?

Shortly after I republished and began selling Gene Schwartz's lost classic *Breakthrough Advertising*, a young copywriter who knew about this technique sent me a fat package in the mail that contained dozens of handwritten pages—the complete first three chapters of *Breakthrough Advertising*. Now, in every copy of that book, I enclose a letter welcoming and congratulating the buyer on purchasing what I think is the most important book ever written on copy, creative, and, dare I say, human behavior. I suggest that they read the first three chapters several times before moving on to the rest of the book.

While this book wasn't an ad or a direct mail piece, one young copywriter was listening, and he was clearly hungry . . . or maybe he was just trying to get on my good side (and he did). That was an unexpected package, but I will tell you that this copywriter got on my radar for the future—not because he showed any particular talent by copying three chapters from a book word for word, but because he copied three chapters from a book that will become his bible for a lifetime.

Hunger also frees you from the fear of a lousy first draft. Gary Halbert is so quotable when it comes to the drive it takes to become a great copywriter: "I don't exactly know what I am going to write about today, so what I am going to do is just keep putting words down on paper until I start to get some direction." Beware of the copywriter who complains about writer's block. The best writers I have worked with over almost 40 years all follow Gary's advice and understand that it won't be perfect on the first pass. And more importantly, they know they have to just keep writing to get each piece where it needs to be. (Hunger goes hand in hand with tons of patience.)

2. Curiosity

When it comes to being a great copywriter or marketer, nothing is more important than insatiable curiosity. As I mentioned earlier, a glowing example of this is Gene Schwartz, who read everything. His prolific consumption of media and information of every kind came from a need to know what made people tick—knowledge he wanted in order to be able to write to them at the deepest level. Remember his warning not to lose touch with the people in your audience, and his advice to spend two hours a week (at least) finding out where the market is.

Arthur Johnson, the star of our infomercials, became so immersed in every area of health and medicine he wrote about that he went from being a copywriter to being a medical writer and editor. Copywriter Parris Lampropoulos was almost as knowledgeable as my urologist on alternative prostate cancer treatments because of the hard work and insatiable curiosity he had for that topic and all the other health topics he ever got involved with.

Insatiable curiosity is also tied closely to being an expert researcher. The best direct marketing companies today who hire copywriters to work full time in their organizations sometimes don't have them write any significant copy for six months (or longer) while they deeply research the topics they will be writing about in the years ahead.

As David Ogilvy warned: "Advertising people who ignore research are as dangerous as generals who ignore decodes of enemy signals." Research (such as Q testing) is important to everyone in the marketing process, but especially to the copywriter. When assessing the level of curiosity of copywriters, it's a red flag when they show little interest in research. If they are not obsessed with knowing everything they can about their audience before writing a word of copy, they are copywriters to avoid.

The most prolific copywriters I have ever known and worked with are as interested in the "41 percent" as the marketers are— they know that understanding their audience (i.e., the list) at every level is the key to writing the most powerful copy. If a copywriter I'm considering hiring doesn't ask me for a "list history" (every list mailed for the product they are writing for— with the results—good and bad), I immediately write them off. The best of the best always come back to me to find out if I have any of the promotions that were used to create the lists that were being mailed most successfully for the product they are working on.

3. Smarts

Copywriting is seen as a very lonely profession; you really can't write copy by committee. On the other hand, every copywriter knows that if they don't have people around them to help them hone their craft and ideas, they will never get their copy to a world-class level. The best of the best understand this, and that's what makes them the best of the best.

A question I ask every copywriter—and a question I would ask myself if I wrote copy—is "Who do you hang out with professionally, and why?" I then ask, "How do you stay accountable to your craft, constantly improving your skills and insights, even when everybody is telling you how great you already are?" Even the most talented and confident copywriters understand how important it is to have constructive critics available to them 24/7. The communities you align yourself with may be the most critical career decision you will ever make . . . and there is not one copywriter or marketer I know who goes it alone.

Copywriting is a profession, like so many others, that lends itself to apprenticeship. Sometimes (though rarely) this will happen organically; other times, you will need to pay to play by joining private masterminds, attending high-leverage events, and paying for coaching from the greats who have come before you.

For example, many young copywriters paid Gary Halbert a huge (and nonrefundable) sum of money to work with him for a short time (but long enough for him to figure out if they had the right stuff to become a great copywriter). And from that group, successful and well-known copywriters are still working today, long after Gary Halbert's death, all trained by the master.

The sacrifice they made to get this education was partly due to hunger, partly to curiosity, and all about what I call "smarts"— they became great because they were accountable to someone smarter than themselves. They paid significantly in both time and money, and it set them apart from the pack for good.

But leave it to Halbert to be a contrarian on his own philosophy (he was quite a character): "A support system is like a garden, and you always need to be on the lookout for weeds to pull." I guess you have to be smart about who you get your smarts from too.

4. Passion

It's so much easier to write about something that you have passion for than something you care little about and are only doing for a payday. Almost all the greatest copywriters began their careers writing about material they knew a lot about and loved writing about as well.

Although not a copywriter, filmmaker Steven Spielberg is one of the greatest creative talents of all time. His three most successful early films—*Jaws, Close Encounters of the Third Kind,* and *E.T.*—on the surface simply look like blockbuster films about terror, science fiction, and special effects. What they are really about is family and loss, and they were expressions of Spielberg's childhood.

I bring this up because when you look at the early work of many great copywriters, it's often driven by something from their personal experience that made them go a mile deep before they went a mile wide. (When I speak publicly about this characteristic, the visual I use is an upside-down funnel: narrow to wide.) That's one expression of passion—copywriters starting their careers writing about something they already know and care about. Or at least, writing about things they *want* to know more about and taking a deep dive to discover everything there is to know.

When you look at the careers of the most successful copywriters, it looks like they could write about anything, any time. But it doesn't start that way. Whenever I interview a new copywriter, I really try to understand their journey and how they got to my office with an interest in writing about this kind of offer.

The deeper they've gone into subjects they were curious about or had some connection to in their past, the more confident I get that they will take those same deep dives in the present . . . and that they care enough about the topic to write me a winner.

There's another angle on passion: we should want to hire copywriters who think in terms of impact before there's ever a conversation about money (and we should hang out with other marketers who think that too). Don't get me wrong, making money is important—but impact with passion goes hand in hand with profit. We have a responsibility as marketers to teach and reach aggressively, and it is actually irresponsible to not sell hard when we know we've got the goods to change lives. That's the passion I want in my copywriters.

People who do not consider themselves marketers might say that we're just trying to justify our existence with this philosophy. But I implore you, whether you are a marketer or not, to look at your list, your customers, your community, your tribe, and your potential prospects as your most important asset. These assets will enable you to achieve everything you dream of creating over the course of your professional life.

Your copywriters must be in step with you here—passionate about the project, clear on how much impact it can have, and congruent with everything you believe. Of course you should aim to make a lot of money together. But if you both come from the perspective of making a difference, I guarantee you will leave a huge mark on the world—and build a more profitable business for the long term too.

Sometimes your passion won't be directly related to the subject matter of what you're writing about or marketing, but being passionate is always powerful, and the energy from your passion will often drive curiosity in other areas. For example, even though Gene Schwartz didn't write a lot of direct response copy about art, he was both one of the greatest copywriters who ever lived *and* one of the greatest modern art collectors and experts of his time. Art was his passion, and he used the energy and perspectives it gave him to take deep dives into all kinds of niches with his writing.

It's interesting to note that Gene's obituary only had one paragraph about his direct marketing and copywriting success; the rest was all about his impact on modern art. He may not have written any control packages for art products, but his passion showed up in everything he did. This quote hints at how his passion for art translated into his genius for copy: "The arts not only imbue our sense of sight, balance, movement, touch and hearing, they also lift our logical minds—the traditional focus of modern education—into the reaches of possibility, invention, and genius."

5. Understanding Direct Marketing Principles

The most successful copywriters are far more than just writers. They are true advisors and partners in every element of the client's marketing and business growth.

So how do you become an advisor? Simply put, you have to understand the direct marketing principles to which your copy is going to be applied. In writing my first book about six legends of advertising, all of whom wrote copy, I was astounded at how obsessed all of them were with lists and offers, and not just with the poetry they wrote.

Robert Collier, the father of the sales letter, said: "Study your reader first, your product second." The sales letter guy was thinking about lists. I love that. And while they were all obsessed with lists, they were obsessed with offers too. John Caples said: "Test everything. Doubt everything. Be interested in theories, but don't spend a large sum of money on a theory without spending a little money to test it first."

Every copywriter who has had a long career, or expects to have a long career, needs to know almost as much about lists and offers as they do about writing copy. At a minimum, they need to understand RFM and LTV. That's why if you can understand even the basics of direct marketing, you will have a huge advantage over other copywriters competing for the same assignments. And if you're a marketer, having a copywriter who can truly partner with you on all your marketing initiatives will also be a huge advantage. The best in the business know this and are constantly reading, studying, and learning, both from books and from experts.

6. Humility

Since everything we do in direct response marketing is measurable, there is very little room for arrogance and hubris. The most successful copywriters will tell you all about their winners, but they'll tell you even more about their losers. That's not to say that we don't want our copywriters to have supreme confidence in their work. But if we're working with partners who are always hungry, curious, smart, passionate, and well educated, then hopefully confidence will come naturally to them despite many failures.

Before I left Boardroom, a young copywriter wrote to me and said: "I will be the best copywriter who has ever walked in the door at Boardroom. We should talk about an assignment." (I didn't want to be outright rude, so I put the blame on myself: "Shame on me—I've been doing this for over 30 years, and I've never heard of you, so I'm glad you brought this to my attention.")

This guy's approach is exactly how not to do it. The hubris put me off immediately, especially since the quality of his work didn't back up his claim . . . and he apparently had no idea that some of the greatest copywriters of all time had walked through the doors at Boardroom previously. He didn't even do research on *that* . . . so you've probably guessed that he never got hired.

On the other side of the spectrum, in 2014 America's best living copywriter, Gary Bencivenga, and America's top TV infomercial producer, Greg Renker, both spoke at the Titans of Direct Response event. They were headline speakers, yet both thought that they should pay for their admission to the event because of the other people who were speaking. They came on my invitation—as keynote presenters—but saw themselves as humble students.

Of course, I didn't take their money . . . and I learned a valuable lesson about humility. These two giants would have been justified in throwing their weight around, making demands and expecting constant attention, but instead they behaved nothing like the prima donnas they could have been. If Greg and Gary can be so humble after such incredible careers, the rest of us can keep our pride and egos in check too.

7. How They Share Their Success

When hiring a copywriter, the first thing clients usually ask for is a portfolio of work. The portfolio is always important. But I purposely put this as the last of the seven characteristics to show that you won't get to a portfolio of success without prioritizing the other six characteristics. Clearly, the more you write (as a copywriter) or the more you test (as a marketer), the more lessons you will learn on the field of play, and the larger your portfolio will become. More proof is, of course, always better. Build up a portfolio you are proud of, and don't be scared to show it. But show who you are first and what you've done second. Hunger, curiosity, smarts, passion, direct marketing knowledge, and humility come first.

Based on the characteristics we've just discussed, it's obvious that a great copywriter is a secret weapon that should be deployed in every part of your business.

There were years when our highest-paid "employees" never showed up at the office. Gary, like so many other copywriters with a similar mind-set, was probably at home, not resting on his laurels. While he was collecting royalties for blockbuster winners he was also always thinking about how to beat them with even bigger winners. When people asked if paying huge royalties bothered us, Marty and I would simply say: "No! If our copywriters are making that much, can you imagine how much *we* are making?" This philosophy enabled us to mail millions of pieces, because Gary and all our top gun copywriters wrote packages that beat all comers by a wide margin, and then they followed them up by going back to the drawing board every time to make the next one even better.

Feeling bad because a copywriter makes too much money is shortsighted, because it shows you're not thinking about the growth of your business. I maintain that is scarcity thinking. A mediocre copywriter will hold you back. Despite all I said previously about being your own best copywriter, good copywriters have a unique talent, and it's one that should never be shortchanged.

Don't believe what you read about the toughest job for a copywriter being how long it takes them to count their money while hanging out at their beach house in the south of France. The best copywriters are relentlessly disciplined, and we can all take many lessons from them as we study how they work and what makes them tick; and if they are able to buy that château, it's because they deserve it.

Throughout the rest of this chapter, I'm going to share how you can best leverage copywriters and other creative talent across all your marketing to make the most of these incredible assets.

THE COPYWRITER IN THE COAL MINE

This expression refers to the old practice of sending canaries down into coal mines with miners. Any dangerous gasses would kill the birds before they would do any serious harm to the miners, giving them an early warning system and a chance to exit the tunnels before things got dicey.

Now, I don't want you to think my thesis is that we should actually sacrifice our copywriters for the sake of saving *other* humans (yes, copywriters are people too), but the best copywriters are always ahead of the curve. With their insatiable curiosity and need to research everything at the deepest level before putting pen to paper, they are in the best position to heed the warnings of what is happening in the marketplace and what will (and won't) move people to take action.

We can stop the metaphor here. No one needs to die (canary *or* copywriter), but I want to talk about some examples of why I think the top copywriters are the folks to watch (and lean on heavily) if you want to know the best route through your marketing tunnel.

Boardroom's four top copywriters, responsible for over *600 million pieces* of successful direct mail since 1995, are a Mount Rushmore of copywriters, and they are heroes to me: Eric Betuel, David Deutsch, Arthur Johnson, and Parris Lampropoulos. They consistently wrote winning promotions, and the company could never have made it through 40 years without their talent and persistence.

Marty was not the expert in any one area we wrote about, but he was the most inquisitive man on the planet. And he had a strong sense of justice that was central to what he wanted to achieve at Boardroom—he was a true bloodhound for our audience. He was always looking out for the little guy. However, Marty wasn't the only bloodhound in this partnership. The copywriters were equally aggressive in how they approached inside information and helping consumers get the edge whenever possible. These four writers (and others before them) were able to write in his voice, perfecting the bloodhound approach and tracking down vital knowledge for the average American. It was amazing to behold.

The bloodhound publisher only hired bloodhound copywriters. And even if you are not like Marty, you should hire like Marty. That is, even if you are not a bloodhound yourself, hire copywriters who understand this concept. The best copywriters plunge into one coal mine after another—often uncharted or controversial territory—and let themselves be completely immersed: they read, research, study, and then read and research and study some more. And sometimes they even do their research over dinner.

You should also hire copywriters who understand your vision and philosophy at a very deep level well before they write one word for you.

One of our trademarks for gathering information and content for our newsletters was bringing our experts together on a regular basis (more about this in Chapter 10). We would assemble experts from all the disciplines we covered to meet and debate to see what sparks might fly when they got together in a moderated discussion. Those sparks always turned into the best story ideas, and the best story ideas often turned into the best promotion copy.

So when Marty had a brainstorm to bring together experts from one discipline—taxes—he was smart enough to invite not only our tax editors, to get story ideas, but also one of our copywriters, Parris Lampropoulos, who was working on our tax newsletter promotion at the time. What came out of that meeting were dozens of great story ideas . . . and a blockbuster control package for our newsletter *Tax Hotline.*

Parris loved the content that came out of the discussions at the meeting, but he went even deeper—he saw something in the format and the idea behind the meeting as well. He set up his promotion around a "secret meeting of the country's top tax experts" spilling the beans on things they would not normally talk about in public and the reader having access to this inside information. This approach would convince readers that *Tax Hotline* was the most valuable publication of its kind. It wasn't just the content we got from the meeting that led to this winning package, but also the intrigue of who was in the room and what they knew that made this a blockbuster. Only a copywriter could have thought of that.

DON'T LEAVE YOUR COPYWRITERS ALONE IN THE COAL MINE

In the past, I have readily admitted that I am a copywriter wannabe. Despite the fact that this is never going to be my gift, I have come to believe that at some point, we will all be our own best copywriters. Put a different way, we all need to be a bigger part of the creative process for our campaigns whether we do the actual writing or not.

This refers back to what I said about passion—and not only the passion of the copywriter for the topic they are writing about, but also the passion of the marketer or entrepreneur for the product or service they are offering. Marketers and entrepreneurs make the mistake all the time of giving a copywriter an assignment without immersing themselves in the project right at the beginning.

I encourage you to hire the best copywriters you can find to push the envelope (pun intended) on your behalf—but it's not just about their writing talent. It's also about their gut instinct on what will make your audience respond and what will differentiate you from your competition.

Always allow your copywriters to probe your editors, your gurus, your experts (and you) to make sure there is not more material in those incredible brains that could create some of the most exciting and breakthrough articles or concepts. These can lead to more compelling promotion copy, and yes, more sales of your product or service. In the right hands, that information—even if it seems controversial, crazy, or weird—can become cutting-edge, transformative copy. So keep an open mind, spill your guts (to a seasoned professional), and search high and low for your next best idea.

I'm not recommending that you ever be irresponsible or push the envelope for the sake of pushing the envelope. But it reminds me of the classic Henry Kissinger story (which I will tell in my own words): A speech writer for Kissinger sent in his first draft of an upcoming speech, and Kissinger sent it back to him with a question written in the margin: "Is this the best you can do?" The speech writer went back to work. He sent in another draft, only to get the same response. This back-and-forth happened several more times until the speechwriter said: "This is the best I can do! I can't possibly improve one more word." To which Kissinger then replied: "In that case, now I will read it."

A-list copywriters would never dream of showing their early versions to a client. They only bring them the most complete version, after immersing themselves deep in the coal mine, getting down and dirty to turn up every piece of information they need to deliver the goods for that promotion. I knew that those copywriters had not only honed the copy on their own with multiple versions and approaches, but they had also bounced it off trusted colleagues for ideas, tweaks, and opinions (which I discussed earlier in this chapter under #3 of the seven characteristics all A-list writers possess). When you hire the best, you get a bonus—the wisdom and insight of the writers and thinkers *they* think are the best as well.

And don't forget: Before they write, while they are writing, and after they deliver a draft to you, don't leave them down there in the coal mine on their own. Get in there with them and make sure they have all the tools they need every step of the way so they can work their magic, but never forget your vision and passion too.

THE ART & SCIENCE OF COPY

Most people think one of two things about copy: that it's some mysterious art form, a panacea for every campaign problem, or that it's an extremely technical science—a plug-and-play system that works according to a formula. The truth is that it's somewhere between the two. The linchpin that brings both elements together is the list—and how the copywriter thinks about it.

I can't emphasize enough that the best copywriters I ever worked with (and I worked with nearly all of them) were obsessed with the list and the audience first. I know I am repeating myself, but I want to make sure you are obsessed with this relationship between copy and list too. Gene Schwartz, Gary Halbert, Gary Bencivenga—and every other super successful copywriter I have ever met and worked with—all of them wanted every scrap of information they could get on the list (or audience, or in today's jargon, avatar) before they ever wrote a word.

So what does that tell you?

It tells you that any copywriter worth their salt will be obsessed with the audience they're writing for—and they will be chomping at the bit to get into the research. I want to repeat this again too: my general rule of thumb is that if a copywriter doesn't ask me for a list history in our initial interview, I don't hire them. (While list history was documented list by list in the world of direct mail, compiling a list history in any medium you work in is doable, and you should consider it a requirement.)

In addition, any copywriter who does not do a deep-dive interview with their client about the new project and its target audience is a copywriter you don't want to hire. This might sound like I'm back to saying the list is more important than anything else . . . and while the list *is* the most important thing, that's not my point here. What I'm really saying now is that to write your best copy, and to get copy that's going to move your business forward consistently, you have to understand how your copy relates to the list.

ASKING "WHAT'S NOT HERE?"

One of the greatest lessons I learned from working with leading copywriters is to never be satisfied with a product as is—to always ask the question, What's not here that should be?

Whenever we handed Gene Schwartz a book and asked him to write a winning promotion for it, he would start by asking us what was *not* in the book. That's often what would inspire him to write the most compelling copy he could. One of my favorite Gene Schwartz-isms is, "Copy is not written. Copy is assembled." Gene had a voracious appetite to gather (assemble) everything in plain sight, and also those things that were not so obvious—which would then maximize the impact of what he eventually wrote. He wanted to know everything: what we had cut, what we had ignored, and what we thought was too out there to be included. He made an assumption that what we had was good but not great (yet) and that we had an opportunity at the start of each project to build marketing capital *into* the product as it was being created.

Gene's view was that even if the book was well done, there was huge upside (and no downside) in pushing our editors and marketers to find the material that no one else was talking about . . . which would then enable him to write much more compelling copy and teasers. Let me expand on this with some examples that came from copywriters who were dissatisfied with their assignments as given. Each time, we turned their dissatisfaction into unbridled enthusiasm by letting them ask a few simple questions of their clients with the purpose of uncovering the most impactful copy platforms.

My favorite is the story of Gene interviewing Marty about the new publication Marty wanted to launch in 1972, to be titled *Boardroom Reports*. Marty had a vision for a newsletter that would teach business owners and entrepreneurs what they really needed to know about running their businesses. He wanted to include only the most important information from leading experts, helpful and actionable information he felt the business magazines were missing. The goal of *Boardroom Reports* was to be useful and practical from cover to cover. Marty asked Gene to write the promotion to launch his big idea and gave him the premise above—but Gene was too smart to simply run off and start writing. He grilled Marty at length, digging deep into why Marty would put his life savings into launching this idea. They spent many hours together over many days before Gene wrote a single word of copy. The result was the headline that launched everything for Boardroom:

NOW!
READ 300 BUSINESS MAGAZINES IN 30 MINUTES!

And get the guts of every one of their most valuable ideas—in super condensed form you just can't forget!

Looking back, knowing that Boardroom eventually became one of the most successful direct marketers of newsletters in the decades that followed, we could assume it was Gene's brilliant copy that started it all. And of course Marty gave him all the credit.

However, talking with Gene some years later, I asked him about this headline (which was just the beginning of an incredibly engaging sales letter). He said to me: "You can give me all the credit you want but I didn't write it. Marty did." Gene's genius was not just in the writing . . . it was also in how he extracted what he needed from Marty's brain. According to Gene, all the best material in that sales letter was in Marty's head already and just needed to be brought up to the surface.

Gene's great ability was in how he questioned Marty and then created the story around his answers. He knew that Marty (his client, who was really his partner in this promotion) was also an experienced expert who was passionate about the topic and who was constantly researching how he could deliver a better product. Gene knew that gold (i.e., good copy) was just waiting to be mined. (Of course, there *was* genius in Gene's writing too . . . even if he was too humble to admit it.)

After leaving Boardroom, I had a similar experience with a client: I wasn't writing their copy from scratch, but we were brainstorming how to create a copy approach on a landing page that would get prospects to order (which was not happening with their current strategy). During a long interview process with the entrepreneur, all I did was ask questions around two themes:

1. "Why should I listen to you?"
2. "What's in it for me if I buy your product?"

What poured out of her was passion and copy that seemed to write itself.

It was her story of persistence and grit, how she got to where she is today, why she wants her tribe to have the same success, and why the product will be a game changer for their businesses. In the end, we had copy that captured her readers' attention at a whole new level. And even though she needed someone with copy experience to bring it up to the surface, she—not the copywriter—is the one who "wrote" it.

When I think about this process, perfected by the world's best copywriters, it reminds me of the services available today for thought leaders to write books quickly and efficiently. Even those who say they could never find the time (or have the discipline) to write a book can all "talk a book"—and a transcribed interview capturing what is in their brain becomes a book super fast. When I see so many folks being able to "write" books this way, I smile and think of the interview processes employed by the best copywriters of all time. After all, a great promotion is sort of like an authored book for many entrepreneurs and gurus selling their vision to a wide audience.

YOUR BEST STUFF MIGHT BE ON THE CUTTING ROOM FLOOR

Something you should always keep in mind is that your best material (and copy approach) might not be in the spec assignment but rather, as they say in film editing, what is on the cutting room floor. It might also be in a wastebasket or deleted file somewhere, waiting to be snatched back before it is lost forever.

I recall a time when I was working on an alternative health newsletter written by a naturopath (who was our guru for the newsletter), and we needed a new control badly. I approached one of our A-list copywriters and asked him if he would take on the assignment. When he started digging into the past issues of the newsletter and previous promotions, he was underwhelmed: "There's nothing new or groundbreaking here . . . and this is an area of health that should be all about new and groundbreaking. I don't think I can take this assignment. Based on this material, what I will write will be boring and not likely to be very successful."

After some begging and pleading on my part, the copywriter consented to dive in some more. He interviewed the guru, all the editors, and all the marketers who were working on the newsletter at the time.

What he found out was startling: There were all sorts of stories and ideas that never got past an initial idea meeting. The editors had vetoed lots of material and left it on the cutting room floor because it seemed too controversial. And I didn't blame them—they were only being super conscientious. However, that discovery became an incredible opportunity: could "controversial" become "new and groundbreaking"?

Rather than lament the fact that we couldn't cover the controversial material, we went back to the editors to see which of these potential stories could be researched further and resurrected. We knew there must be *something* there that we could share with our audience without taking any big risks. Our readers were hungry for brand-new health information they had never heard before, and we knew we could give them something useful and responsible without crossing the line into sharing incomplete or undocumented information.

Well, we didn't revive *all* those discarded ideas, stories, and research. But we were able to save a surprising amount, and this brought what we thought was dead material back to life, much of it becoming some of the most exciting articles the newsletter had ever published. And our copywriter had many new entry points into the promotion with leads, headlines, and stories—not risky, but super exciting. The result was a new control that beat the old control by a wide margin.

I'd like to leave you with two important takeaways from these stories:

1. While I always say that you should never leave your copy and creative to amateurs and to only hire the best copywriters and creative talent, I also think you are often your own best copywriter—that is, you are the best source of the most compelling information you can deliver. With the right copywriter guiding you, you might actually write your next great promotion simply by talking and thinking about your "big why."

2. Never assume that there isn't more to your product, service, or message. The more you can differentiate from what's out there already, the better. Search everywhere to find some of those differentiators that might have been dismissed before the proper research or hard work had been done.

TALK TO THEM LIKE YOU KNOW THEM . . . ESPECIALLY IF YOU DO

In 2016, Donald Trump won the U.S. presidential election. While political advertising is often boring and even irritating, the one thing we can say about the 2016 campaign is that it was a marketing case study for the ages. This is not a political book, and I won't tell you who I voted for; nonetheless, marketers can learn *a lot* from Trump's campaign about matching message to list.

Gene Schwartz also taught about this relationship between message and list. He said, "There is your audience. There is the language. There are the words that they use."

When writing my first book, I was surprised that all six men I was profiling were supremely interested in knowing their audience—despite all of them being known more as copywriters than anything else. When you read their work, and especially their quotes about audience and list, their writing sometimes seems almost secondary, a consequence of having gotten to know the people who would read it. Remember Gene Schwartz's warning: you cannot lose touch with the people of this country, no matter how successful or potent you are.

Gene and all the copywriters at his level knew that their best shot at connecting with almost any market was to know as much about them as possible, and the only way to do that was to read everything they were reading, to understand everything they were experiencing in modern culture, and truly live in their shoes.

It should be noted that the copywriters I knew and worked with rarely had much in common with or lived a similar life-style to the audiences they wrote for. . . but they did everything they could to be in their heads when they wrote to them. For example, Gene lived in New York City, in a penthouse on Park Avenue, and had one of the most impressive modern art collections in the country. He was a very sophisticated man with an incredible intellect, but that never stopped him from being a student of all types of people.

There is another secret all the greats focused on intensely: they learned how the audience communicated with each other. Every successful copywriter uses language that is in sync with the market they are writing for . . . and it takes a lot of time and effort to make sure they get every word and every sentence perfect.

Did Donald Trump spend the kind of time and effort researching his market and honing his language that Schwartz and Halbert did? Probably not. But he figured out the right words and the right tone to garner over 60 million votes, despite never having run for any office in his life.

I love what David Ogilvy said, to drive the point home even further on language: "Never use jargon words like reconceptualize, demassification, attitudinally, judgmentally; they are hallmarks of a pretentious ass." There are probably times (maybe in some academic journals) when you could get away with words like that—but only if your readers use those words too. As marketers and copywriters, use words and phrases that are unfamiliar to your reader at your peril. It only takes one pretentious word to ruin a sales letter.

I do the following exercise with clients to remove every word in their promotions that can't answer these two questions in the affirmative:

1. Would they know what this word or phrase means?

2. Would your customers use that word or phrase while talking with each other?

It seems like a pretty simple litmus test, yet if you read copy through this lens, you may be surprised by how little some copywriters and marketers seem to really know about their audience.

In short, know the language of your audience. Sometimes it will be simple, other times complex. Sometimes it will be clinical, other times emotional. Know your audience, know their language, know the words they use.

Some ideas to ensure you do this well:

- Hang out in online forums where your audience spends time to see how they talk and what words they use.

- Read reviews on Amazon for books that your audience is likely reading and see how they write about them.

- Create customer panels (paid groups of people who are typical of your audience and the kind of people you are trying to find more of). You can try out headlines, phrases, and copy platforms on them to see how they respond and react.

Someone in the Trump campaign knew something about this . . . or maybe they just got lucky. But I'd say it's more than luck. We know that when audience and language are aligned, big things happen.

THERE'S NO ONE-SIZE-FITS-ALL CREATIVE

Tailoring your creative and promotions to your different list segments is critical. It seems nuts that anyone would try to come up with one-size-fits-all creative, given how inexpensive e-mail and most online marketing is. We had different control packages for different segments in direct mail, where it was very expensive to do, so there's no excuse not to tailor your creative online to specific list segments.

There's never any reason to talk to everyone on your list the same way. You want to talk to former customers differently than you talk to current customers, who are both very different from prospects who have never bought, who are then also different from names acquired through joint ventures . . . and those are only the obvious segments.

First and foremost, you must segment your list on the basis of source and behavior, which is much of what we talked about previously regarding RFM. The next step is to create messaging for each segment that makes sense on the basis of source and behavior, using language and creative appropriate to each segment. The goal is always to maximize the response rate of each segment rather than trying to increase the overall response rate with one-size-fits-all creative.

That said, it's important not to segment to the point of diminishing returns. Keep your focus on building segments that have meaningful differences and will yield meaningful results as they respond. You might only have a couple of variations. But let your audience tell you how many segments make sense.

To make the economics work in direct mail, we couldn't afford too many segments with different promotions because we had the barrier of paying postage and printing—every time we had different creative for different list segments, that added a lot of costs. Regardless, we would still often have two or three controls for each product, which would be sent to different segments of our existing and potential audience, based on all the data we had collected on them.

While I believe no direct marketer should ever "go cheap" with copy and creative offline or online, taking out the cost of postage and printing should be an incentive for online marketers to get even *more* creative with their creative (to different list segments). Split testing in direct mail had additional costs because when you mailed smaller quantities of a particular piece of creative, postage and printing were more expensive too. Online you can split test much more inexpensively and efficiently, but of course, everything still needs to get measured and everything still needs to be meaningful (remember, no tiny tests).

UNDERSTANDING SEGMENT PSYCHOLOGY

Whenever you are building a promotion, you can run through lots of numbers—the total number of names on a list, the new names on a list, the multibuyers—but often, the more interesting piece of information is what type of content brought each group of names onto the list.

For example, we had entire segments on the Boardroom list that came in through fascination pieces, which were very curiosity-driven and were focused on the people we affectionately called mail-order junkies. These fascinations were the handiwork of the best copywriter you never heard of: Mel Martin. While Gene pioneered the use of interesting bullet points in copy, Mel turned fascinations into a true art form.

My friend and direct marketing historian Denny Hatch described fascinations like this:

> Fascinations. Teasers. Taking an old-fashioned teaser—usually found on an envelope—and stuffing an entire mailing full of them, nakedly appealing to the emotions that scare people and drive them to action.

Mel had so much success with fascinations that eventually they became a staple technique of copywriters everywhere and have even become commonplace in today's copy.

By knowing that a name (also a person!) had subscribed based on a deep need to satisfy some intellectual curiosity or to find answers to questions that had been plaguing him or her, we also knew that he or she would likely respond well to other fascination campaigns.

This also showed that when there is synergy between lists and offers, you can feel confident that their responses will be similar, if, for example, you are doing an affiliate deal with a complementary list and you know that they have used a similar creative approach to what you used to convert your own customers. More clues, such as if price points are in the same range, if bonuses and premiums are prevalent, and so on, tell you where synergies lie in the offers and the products and how they are promoted.

An obvious example is that if you're a guru in a particular field and an affiliate has done well with guru-driven offers in a similar space, then that will probably be a high-performing list for you to promote to. On the other hand, you may have affiliate partners who are not guru driven, and therefore talking to their lists will require a different approach and/or language.

All these elements—the source, the type of promotion, the piece of creative that got the name on the list—are subtleties that are rarely touched on when most people are doing list research. Yes, it's more demanding and requires more legwork than just throwing a one-size-fits-all campaign together, but that's why there is such an amazing opportunity in thinking this way: you basically have the strategy to yourself.

Here are some questions to help you dig down into the psychology of each list segment:

- What type of content brought someone onto the list?

- What was the tactic that got the person to opt in?

- What's the psychology of the buyer?

- What triggered the decision to buy?

- Who wrote the copy?

- Has that writer produced other packages or promotions that perform well with this list or lists like it? (And can you use that writer again for similar offers to similar lists?)

- How long was the copy?

- What was the format—long form, short form, free trial, sweepstakes?

- What was the conversion behavior? Did the person download something, opt in, mail something, make a purchase?

Note that there's a direct correlation between how much prospects engage with the initial promotion and how long they will stay with you. For example, if someone joins with long copy, is highly engaged, and buys promptly, you want to track what kind of promotion he or she came in on and how that differs from the people who came in on short copy. Usually people who buy with short copy are more likely to have made a more impulsive purchase and won't be as wedded to the product, because they haven't read as much about it and haven't engaged as much with your promotion piece.

In all of this, you are looking for the underlying motivation of the people on your lists. And the more you understand, the more you can segment intelligently and the more you can create precise copy and messaging to those segments.

KEY TAKEAWAYS

While this chapter didn't talk about how to write great copy (see the recommended reading at back of this book for that information), you now understand why the final 20 percent of the 41/39/20 rule is so critical. Your copy and creative shape how your list experiences your offers and are how you connect with them in a meaningful (and profitable) way.

- Don't outsource your copy and creative to amateurs. These are critical elements in getting your targeted lists to respond positively to your curated offers.
- World-class copywriters share seven characteristics:
    1. Hunger (their dedication to the craft)
    2. Curiosity (their obsession with learning about the audience and its history)
    3. Smarts (the way they surround themselves with people who know what they don't)
    4. Passion (their deep interest in the material they are writing about)
    5. Understanding direct marketing principles (to become true advisors and partners on their clients' campaigns and businesses)

6. Humility (they'll tell you about their winners, but even more about their losers)

7. How they share their success (their generosity)

- Copywriters are like canaries in the coal mines: they know what's happening in the market long before anyone else does.

- Support your copywriters any way you can. Don't leave them sweating in dirty coal mines if you already have the expertise they need to produce great creative.

- Copy is both an art and a science, and sometimes the best material for a campaign will have been left on the cutting room floor before the copywriter even arrived on the scene (so make sure you give them a chance to resurrect it).

- There's no such thing as one-size-fits-all creative. You need to communicate with your audience according to the relationship you already have with them and based on their previous behaviors.

CHAPTER 7

MULTICHANNEL MARKETING

"Never adapt your technique to the idea; adapt your idea to the technique."

—BILL BERNBACH

Many online businesses (and plenty of offline businesses too) default to marketing on one channel, whether out of convenience or because they know one channel above all others. This might be the most dangerous thing you can do in marketing, regardless of why you are doing it. This chapter is about why you should market across different channels and how to measure how each of those channels is performing for you.

I learned from Dan Kennedy a long time ago that the number to avoid in business is 1 (of anything)—and this lesson needs to be top of mind as we focus on the importance of marketing in multiple channels. This is not just a nice idea—it is the key to survival and, therefore, to being able to overdeliver today . . . and on into the future. It's understandable why many marketers will default to one big channel—many of the largest platforms have millions of users with multiple advertising opportunities and advanced reporting technology. Most businesses will find an active part of their audience on any given platform. But just because it's easy to use one huge channel doesn't mean it's your only option. It doesn't even mean it's your *best* option.

Size *might* matter—or it might not. Many marketers make the mistake of thinking that if they are not able to promote on the largest platforms (the ones with the most people on them), they will inevitably have trouble scaling their business. I am all for marketing to the biggest universes available, but if those universes are unresponsive to your offer, their size really doesn't matter. In fact, when we look at lifetime value (LTV), we see that it's often smaller, more targeted lists and audiences that are the key to long-term growth. Fewer orders at higher dollar amounts can often be much more profitable than more orders at lower dollar amounts. And you might achieve higher LTV in the process, making that profit even bigger in subsequent years with additional purchases.

When we looked at the differences between compiled lists and response lists in direct mail in Chapter 4, we saw firsthand how quality almost always beats quantity. This is a universal principle to keep in mind as we explore all the marketing channels that are available. For some businesses, the most popular channel at any given time, even if it's the biggest, might actually be a *bad* option. This may be particularly true if you're looking for quality over quantity (if, for example, you're selling a high-ticket item).

I often hear marketers lamenting that they can't convert prospects with similar profiles to the people who have become customers in the past. But those marketers are missing the point. Don't be fooled by what you think customers *should* do . . . it's all about what they *have done* in the past. Previous response is the best predictor of future response—which has nothing to do with whether the channel they come from is large or small. There are so many ways to build your list, so many channels to choose from, and putting all your eggs in one basket is never a good idea.

My good friend and marketing thought leader Michael Fishman says, "Never define yourself by a channel." I didn't call myself a direct mail marketer in the 1980s, and I recommend you don't call yourself an Internet marketer today. Instead, look at yourself as a direct marketer who chooses to market through various channels, offline and online, whatever is best for your products, services, and ideas, always thinking about measurability and profitability. You're not a social media marketer, you're not an e-mail marketer, you're not a direct mail marketer . . . you're a direct response marketer whose most effective channel is social media or e-mail or direct mail. Defining yourself by the channel you use most could prevent you from being open-minded about effective channels that you have not considered.

This is why diversity is key. As my financial planner once told me: "While you may not make a killing with my investment philosophy, you will never get killed." Of course I want you to make a killing with all your marketing efforts, but I want you to do it with discipline and a mind-set that always emphasizes multiple channels so you don't get killed. We've all heard the horror stories of people running their businesses exclusively on one channel or platform and then getting slapped (even shut down) by a change in a policy or an algorithm.

If, for example, you run anything that you get paid for on someone else's platform and you do not have complete control, it's always good to have a plan B. I heard one particular story of an entire online business vanishing *literally overnight* when the e-commerce platform the business was built on (the one and only platform the business was using) woke up one morning (assuming e-commerce platforms sleep) and decided that the online business advertising on their platform wasn't compliant with their rules. This online business had been running smoothly (and making millions) for years exclusively on this one huge e-commerce platform; after being cut off, this business had to start all over again, whether the reasons they got shut down were valid or not. Needless to say, this business now markets on multiple channels.

I'm not saying this happens every day, but again, diversification is key. It's critical to be aware all the time of what you do control and what you don't control as you are building your business. Given how passionate you are about your product or service, and how hard you've worked on it, don't risk it all by using just one channel. Your product deserves to live a long life on different platforms.

You will also find much greater reach, with a more robust and varied audience, when you don't restrict yourself to a single channel. The trick is in knowing *which* of those opportunities to focus on, because while you need to be diversified, you also can't chase every shiny "game-changing media opportunity." There is a delicate balance between exploring every potential channel and stretching yourself so thin you can't deliver effectively on any of them.

That's why meeting your customers where they want to be met is far more important than being on the hottest, most cutting-edge channel. Which, of course, goes back to knowing your list and testing everything with measurable results.

FINDING THE CHANNEL OF CHOICE FOR YOUR CUSTOMERS

Very few people—including the people who make up your lists—go to one place for all their information. For example, when it comes to news and current events, no one is *just* using Facebook or Twitter or CNN or Reuters or those things called newspapers. Everyone uses multiple sources to gather information, educate themselves, and seek entertainment. No matter what you're selling or who you're selling to, it's up to you to do the research on what approaches will be most effective. Remember the wise advice of Bill Bernbach that opened this chapter—adapt your idea to the technique, not the technique to your idea.

At the time of this writing, social media seems to be where everybody is hanging out the most. People want to keep up with their friends and to keep an eye on the various groups they've joined and the pages they've liked. Maybe they also use this medium to get their news and to find out about cool things to do or buy. Now, many of those same people will also check their e-mail and, believe it or not, walk out to the end of their driveway to check what's in the mailbox too (and that one is the least crowded inbox you could send to today). In addition, many of these people might read newspapers, magazines, and books.

And that's not all. They also watch TV, listen to the radio and podcasts, go to the movies, use apps on their phones . . . you get the idea. If you're trying to reach your future customers in only one place, I hope I've made the case that you might want to expand your thinking.

Key Questions (& Research to Consider) to Determine the Channels of Choice for Your Core Market

- What is the biggest pain or problem your core market is facing? Where do they talk about it? (And can you "eavesdrop" there or, even better, advertise there?)

- Where are your competitors advertising? And, from what you can tell, where are they receiving the highest engagement from their audience (which is also your audience)?

- On your competitors' best channels, can you find out anything about how those people got there in the first place?

- Where else does your audience get their information before they buy, and where else do they do their research?

- What's the demographic profile of the audience? How old are they? With what platforms are they most familiar and comfortable?

- What's the psychographic profile of the audience? What other things are they interested in, and how do they self-identify?

- How do they pass their time? How do they inform, educate, and entertain themselves?

Developing a profile like this for each customer segment can highlight the opportunities open to you across multiple channels.

Whether it's through launching ad campaigns on a different platform, building partnerships with complementary businesses, or moving into physical marketing (direct mail isn't dead!), building out this deep understanding is what will give you leverage.

Now, there is a lot to think about when you're diversifying, because the opportunities are, dare I say, infinite—and getting overwhelmed is a real threat here. It reminds me of a simple yet profound quote I heard from an investment banker addressing the increased value of companies that have diversified their media, and those that offer best in class and unique offerings in one medium: "Advertising opportunities are now infinite." Marketers are at risk of paralysis by analysis because of all the options in front of them. Don't let yourself fall into that trap. Do the deep dive on where and how your customers spend their time and attention, and then ignore everything else.

THE DANGERS OF ONE-STOP SHOPPING

In the interest of keeping yourself sane and using your energy in your unique zone of genius, hire the best people working on each of your chosen channels to ensure your business makes the most of each one. I've said before that this is the best time ever to be a marketer, but with all the new opportunities also comes additional risk—and not just from being overwhelmed. With greater specialization in every channel comes more opportunity for charlatans and imposters too. So while we want to dive in and test every new thing we hear about, we also need to be very careful.

Dick Benson once told me his simple strategy for mitigating these risks: "Never buy everything in one place." Back in the 1980s, with far fewer media choices, I still bought media and creative (and all marketing services) à la carte . . . and it's even more important to buy that way today when the choices are infinite. After spending my entire career knowing exactly where to find the experts I needed in every aspect of direct marketing, the fact that the choices are now more vast and more specialized than ever got me thinking even more about the dangers of one-stop shopping. I wouldn't do it then, and I certainly wouldn't do it now.

I don't want to make any advertising or marketing agency folks feel bad, but even in the prehistoric era of "finite" advertising opportunities, I never met an agency of any kind that I liked very much, because there was no way they could be that good at everything they said they offered. It wasn't about the people, just the model. Often there was one thing they specialized in that I could trust them to do, but there was no way I would put all my eggs in a basket labeled "full-service direct marketing agency."

I went to a specific source to rent lists for direct mail, to another source who knew more about space ads in newspapers than anyone else, to another who just placed inserts in outgoing packages from catalogers (what we called PIPs or package insert programs), and to yet another to buy broadcast (radio and TV). Even within something like broadcast, there were multiple specialists: remnant radio ads were different from other kinds of radio buys, and short-form TV was different from long-form infomercials. Buying broadcast could include four different vendors . . . or more. And don't get me started about buying copy and creative in one place or as part of a full-service model.

When it came to hiring the best copywriters, it was painfully obvious that any copywriter who was working in an agency (when they could be making 10 times their salary as a successful freelancer if they were really good) was not at the top of my list as a prospect to write for me. (Of course, if you found Gary Bencivenga while he was still a pup at the ad agency Ogilvy & Mather, that's a win.) As I hope became clear in Chapter 6, copywriting is not a commodity, it is a specialty, and it must be bought from specialists who are not claiming to be able to write everything for everybody.

À la carte buying was, and still should be, a rule of thumb for everything in marketing, not just media and creative. Database building, sophisticated modelling and list segmentation, purchasing, production, printing—every role requires experts. Some are more commoditized than others (e.g., printing) and some are super specialized (e.g., proprietary software to build a customer profile) . . . but why not always seek out best in class? Even the most commoditized functions are often differentiated by things like superior customer service or personalized solutions inside a basic offering.

Although this chapter is specifically about multichannel marketing, I want to stress the importance of choosing specialists over generalists. This is how you will maximize each channel—by bringing in an expert for each one. That was true when there were far fewer channels, and it's even more important today when marketing opportunities and technology are both confusing and dizzying. Anyone who tells you they can handle all your marketing needs in their "one-stop shop" is someone you should run away from fairly quickly.

And as technology gets even more sophisticated and makes us more efficient—and we see the arrival of new channels (i.e., new ways to reach people with our marketing messages), there will be even more specialization . . . which leads to even more niche areas of expertise. With so many people getting so smart in tighter and tighter niches, it would be a shame not to make the most of these categories of one—they've spent so much time becoming the world's best in their "thing," you should want them on your team.

I believe multichannel marketing is the "make or break" in terms of how you sell and market in a world that is as noisy as ever . . . and that demands excellence as much as ever too. It is the core premise I start with when I build the makeup and content for my mastermind groups and any consulting I do today. It's not *just* about being multichannel . . . I want you to be multichannel with the best experts working for you on every one of the channels you choose.

Begin with intelligent outsourcing, and then buy à la carte from specialists. Dick Benson, the man who mentored me in a world where advertising opportunities were still finite, drilled this into my head so I could share it with you today: "Do what you do best and buy everything else around the corner . . . and never settle for second best."

MULTICHANNEL METRICS

In case you haven't picked up on this yet, direct response marketing is all about measurement. John Wanamaker, considered a pioneer in advertising and marketing in the late 19th century and early 20th once said, "Half the money I spend on advertising is wasted; the trouble is, I don't know which half." If Wanamaker had the measurement tools and discipline we have at our disposal today, he could have made back some of that "wasted money." It's all about putting out a campaign, being able to track a specific response from it, and then determining your next move(s). You never want to be stuck wondering what's working.

This is why I have very little tolerance for general advertising or marketing that is not accountable and measurable, complete with metrics that indicate whether each campaign was actually successful. And success is not only in the eye of the beholder either. It also needs to hold up in the eye of other key players, such as your accountant and your analyst. It's up to you to figure out whether the media you're using is working for you—and that's what we want to explore together now.

For a campaign to be considered successful, or for any medium to be used continually, it needs to make money—enough money to justify its ongoing existence in your media mix. There's no way to know if a campaign or channel meets that criteria unless you are tracking some key metrics. Once you establish those key metrics for every campaign and every channel, it's time to scale.

Lifetime Value (LTV)

Lifetime value is, above every other metric, the one number I urge you to focus on most. The lifetime value of a customer is the dollar amount you can expect to sell to a single customer over the course of your entire relationship with them.

Let's talk about LTV with a real-life and fairly simple case history. I remember sitting in the audience at a mastermind meeting a few years ago, before everyone had made *funnel* the most important marketing term ever. It was also before Facebook had figured out how robust their advertising model could be, so it was still super cheap to run Facebook ads.

One of the young, dynamic marketers in my group diagrammed on a flip chart how he sold a $10 report on Facebook and then created a funnel to convert that $10 buyer into a raving fan (and multibuyer) over time—making Facebook a key component in his marketing media mix, way ahead of the curve. His competitors, offering a similar $10 product, would usually receive very few sales early on (not understanding the quantity versus quality argument we talked about earlier). When the initial revenue from those sales did not equal the total advertising spend for the Facebook ads, they would jump ship to find even cheaper media. Their inability to figure out a way to make this channel work simply eliminated them as competition, due to their failure to understand lifetime value.

So what was the difference? My guy figured out that with these low-ticket buyers, the key was to determine who would buy a second product related to the first (for a little higher price), and then create a third and a fourth offer in an intelligent ascension model with price increases that made sense.

He tested dozens of subsequent offers and price points, again showing he was a student of direct marketing. And while he never came close to getting his money back on the *first* sale (or even the second), through all his testing, he created a series of offers that eventually led to an average sale of over $70 from a new $10 buyer.

Because he tracked the average lifetime value of the new buyers well past their second order, he was able to make back enough money to pay for the advertising within a reasonable period of time and without making cash flow difficult. He was also able to buy a lot more media from Facebook with confidence that it would be profitable in an acceptable period of time for him. (Remember what I mentioned previously when we talked about bogeys—it's up to *you* to determine what is acceptable, and you can't do that without a firm command of your numbers and understanding LTV.)

More importantly, our young gun was building a *business*, not simply looking for a way to be a one-hit wonder, making quick cash on a single sale. While many of his competitors were lamenting that they couldn't make Facebook advertising work selling a $10 product, he was buying the ad space for his $10 product that could have been *their* ad space for *their* $10 product. He was continuing successfully while his competitors looked elsewhere for media that "worked."

His biggest competitive advantage was that he understood direct marketing principles while others who were advertising on Facebook at the time did not. But it wasn't just that—this guy understood that the first purchase is just the tip of the iceberg and that it's usually not the first sale that makes your money back, it's about all the sales you make throughout the lifetime of that customer.

Let me give you another example of creating serious upside by doing an accurate lifetime value calculation. A while ago, I started consulting with a company that was doing well selling almost exclusively through referrals. However, when I asked them about their existing customer base—people who paid between $10,000 and $20,000 to be in a specialized program—they told me that the average person stayed with them for three years.

I did some quick LTV math and showed them that they could project $30,000 to $60,000 of revenue for each new client. I told them it was fine to continue with their referrals strategy— it was clearly working—but I encouraged them to not make it a stand-alone strategy. With such a robust lifetime value, we started talking about and diving deeper into other channels that might not be as profitable initially but would be a way to bring in more $10,000 to $20,000 clients. And they realized they had some significant opportunities to grow.

The chances are that other channels might not yield new clients who stick around for three years; however, even if "inferior" media yielded new clients who didn't last that long, my guess is that they would still be very profitable. Of course, we would test and measure everything to confirm my hunch. But we were able to agree that referrals was not *the* marketing strategy but just one of many (once we understood the real and potential LTV of new clients).

The Real Cost to Acquire a New Customer

To keep your business afloat and each marketing channel profitable, you have to understand how much you need to spend to acquire a profitable customer on that channel. Think of it this way: whenever you spend money on a marketing channel, you are "buying" a new customer. When you calculate the price tag for each customer, you must include the cost of producing each unit you sell and ship to them if it's physical product, including materials, product development, storage, shipment, staff costs, taxes, and—if you really want to go deep and account for everything—depreciation and amortization of any debts. Failure to account for these costs of acquisition can kill your business slowly and painfully, and it will be difficult to identify the problem. The business will gradually bleed out because what you earn from your customers will not cover all your costs.

A successful entrepreneur once told me that the most important person in his organization, an organization that prided itself on being a world-class marketer, was his analyst, or "numbers guy." Without that person dissecting response rates, cost of acquisition, and lifetime value, he knew he could never grow. (And "dissecting" includes making recommendations on how to expand in each media channel intelligently.)

In my past life, mostly in the world of direct mail and physical product, accounting for every penny in terms of media, postage, printing, and cost of goods sold was one of the most important things we did. And while you might not be worried about these things if you only deliver digital products, I guarantee there are all sorts of costs that need to be loaded up before you determine whether a specific media channel is working.

Attribution

Being a great multichannel marketer can cause some headaches, and attribution is a big one. But if those headaches lead to increased profits, I always prefer to deposit more money in the bank and just take an extra aspirin.

Attribution is the way you track a customer's journey through their experience with you from the first time they interact with you until the point that they put down money to become a customer. This allows you to see the channel each customer comes from, the path they followed that influenced them to convert, and how each channel performs over time. Most businesses will have multiple touchpoints along the customer journey, often across different channels, so the variables in any campaign can become quite complex if you are trying to optimize across each touchpoint. Attribution ensures you're able to simplify that complex web of interactions into a list of steps to be addressed.

The real value in having clear attribution is that you can track the performance of each channel over time, including the performance when you introduce a new campaign or control. It can also show you the lifetime value of a customer based on the channel they came from—for example, you might find that customers from your e-mail list have a higher lifetime value than customers that come through affiliate offers. This lets you see where to spend more (or less) money and can highlight new opportunities for each channel. The extent that you can attribute every order or sale that you ever make to a particular channel will help you maximize the profitability of that channel.

In direct mail, we knew where just about every order was coming from by individual list. That enabled us to easily attribute orders to specific sources, and we could make media decisions with the utmost confidence. Even in an era when technology was less advanced than it is today, we always had a key code on each piece of return mail that told us which campaign it came from and what list the response came from too.

But as we expanded into new channels, such as our infomercial television program, the lines became more blurry. For example, how do we attribute the order of someone who saw our infomercial and decided not to call in an order from the 800 number on the screen but then received our direct mail piece for the same product three weeks later and ordered? This person would now be a direct mail buyer, not a TV buyer, but would they have bought had they not seen the infomercial? And my problems around attribution were not nearly as complicated as a $1.8 billion business (Guthy-Renker) in many more channels than I was playing in. When I interviewed Greg Renker at the Titans of Direct Response event, he shared his experience.

At the time, Guthy-Renker was running ads on TV, sending direct mail, and hosting kiosks in malls, as well as creating e-mail funnels, online display advertising, and more. Everything was working together to bring in orders, so trying to identify where an order really originated was very difficult, even if they had added an identifier indicating where every order came from (such as a specific 800 number, key code on a mailing label, or source code on a coupon). Even an enormous company struggled with this (although since that time, a few tools have been created that make at least the online part of attribution much easier).

Regardless, you need to at least *try* to attribute each order to a channel so that you can assess the effectiveness of your campaigns on each channel. And it's okay if you have to split the attribution—some channel (or combination of channels) need to get credit for the order, even if it's just a piece of the order. Put procedures in place across every channel with a way to track response to media. If the customer calls or sends an e-mail or signs up in person, they should get a specific type of order number. If they see a commercial on TV, an 800 number should be set up for that specific commercial.

Of course, you can't account for everything. If the customer saw an infomercial and was sold on the product, forgot to call in an order, and then remembered when they saw the kiosk at the mall, should the infomercial get the credit or the kiosk? You can train kiosk staff to ask customers where they first heard about the product, and so give you a chance to split the attribution, but this is far from a precise science. However, it's the best you can do, and some data here is better than none.

Do everything you can to get that attribution so you can stay within your channels with confidence, knowing they are paying out. Remember that this is the foundation of direct marketing, and everything has to be measurable—it's not enough just to have a good feeling. Far too often, attribution is the metric that gets missed. In fact, I speak to marketers all the time who have never even thought about attribution . . . but without it, all the other data they collect is flawed.

"Conversion" Defined & Why It's Your Best Friend

When I understood the power of conversions, I began to understand the true power of direct marketing. In the subscription world, the conversion was the first renewal, not the initial purchase. We started with a free trial offer to our newsletters and got a certain amount of those folks to pay us for a one-year subscription. And of those folks, those who "converted" to a second year (i.e., made their second purchase) became the gold in our business.

Today in marketing, the term "conversion" is thrown around too freely. It's often confused with acquisition—that is, when a marketer goes into a new channel and gets someone to pay them once, they consider it a conversion. But I don't want to get caught up in semantics, and if a conversion for you is your first sale, so be it. However, if that's the case, it's time to track the conversions on your conversions.

I can't emphasize enough how important it is to record all the activity of every new customer as soon as they enter your orbit. When you acquire a new customer, it's exhilarating. I've never met a marketer who doesn't get a thrill when someone sends them real money for a product or service they believe in. But all new customers are not alike . . . some will never buy a second product from you, some will buy anything you ever offer, and some will end up somewhere in between.

Knowing where every one of those new customers came from and then tracking their behavior over time will enable you to determine the sources that your best new customers came from, all based on conversion. And then track carefully the renewal (i.e., next order, or "conversion of conversion") and so on. In addition, as a marketer you will have a lot more fun by interacting and making attractive offers to the converted (the people who have bought from you more than once) than the nonconverted, although I know it sometimes feels more exciting to get that first sale.

Lifetime value is the key calculation to determine what media to buy and how much of it to buy. Your focus should always be on how long a customer stays with you and how much they spend with you. And that you are calculating *all* costs associated with acquiring and keeping (servicing) that customer. Remember, pay more attention to the people who already love you (existing customers, including conversions) versus those you are trying to attract for the first time (new customers, or acquisitions). When it comes to multichannel marketing and diversifying your portfolio, there is nothing more important than knowing all these numbers and having them at your fingertips all the time.

ONLINE TO OFFLINE TO ONLINE (O to O to O)

Despite all the challenges around attribution and calculating an accurate LTV for every new customer, the opportunities available to us in combining online and offline media are too rich to ignore. Online to offline to online (or offline to online to offline, or any combination that fits for your audience) is a concept that I believe not enough people are talking about.

To define O to O to O, let me state it this way: Always be aware of the life cycle of a new customer entering your world. They can start in either O (online or offline), then be directed to the alternate, and then pulled back to the original source (O) where they started.

The ability to combine today's technology with the fundamentals of direct marketing and direct response learned over decades of testing is exciting. For example, bringing a highly qualified buyer or prospect from a direct mail piece or a print ad into an online funnel will certainly create customers with higher lifetime value.

Many marketers who work online have told me that their customers originating in a variety of offline media have a higher LTV than those who first engaged with them online. And the marketers who have figured out that *starting* online doesn't mean they have to be *exclusively* online have had some incredible results by going offline.

For example, using direct mail on the back end of a winning offer from e-mail or the Web can create more intimacy and value with those customers, which is often a winning formula. Great examples of this can be found with numerous health offers geared toward an older audience who love direct mail but can be engaged initially in an online channel. They may then buy in the future from either channel, or both. Again, this is all about meeting the customer where they want to be met. And don't forget about direct response television, space advertising, or inbound and outbound telemarketing to weave in and out of different kinds of offers, whether they start online or offline.

The breakthrough really comes when you get consumers to transfer from one medium to another, regardless of whether the medium is online or offline. You then have command of all the different media, and you are in a better position to monetize in a variety of different ways. Many marketers who you would probably classify as "online"—that is, they send traffic to a landing page—offer a free copy of their book (plus shipping). They send that book all over the country and even overseas, probably losing money on that kind of an offer and even the first sale. But shipping a book means they now have a physical mailing address.

These savvy direct marketers initiate using an online offer to get into the direct mail business. Having the physical addresses of their customers means that they can make offers in the mail, where fewer competitors are probably making their offers. Those physical offers (in this case a real book) are so valuable that customers are often motivated to move through to other products and services offered by the marketer, many much higher priced. The marketer has the choice to meet the customer in the medium they are most comfortable with.

Having spent most of my career marketing to an "older demographic" (folks 55-plus in age and even 65-plus and 75-plus), I have heard hundreds of times from marketers and nonmarketers alike, "You better start marketing to a younger audience since your audience will die off soon." While I didn't ignore them, I looked at it a little differently (in the spirit of meeting customers where they want and need to be met): I love marketing to an older demographic—they have the two most important things a younger demographic doesn't have: time and money. I don't want my customer base to get younger . . . I just want to be prepared for the next group of 55-year-olds when they are ready for my products and services.

Remember the case histories I told you about estate planning and diabetes? While those are ostensibly topics for "older people," the 35-year-olds today will need the same information on those topics when they are 55 (and dare I say, they should be thinking about "pre-estate planning" and prediabetes long before that). But regardless, when your audience is ready for the information (whatever you might be selling), my opinion is that you then deliver it in the format and media they want to receive it. That's another take on multichannel and "O to O to O."

Thinking about how online and offline can work together, you can see how multichannel marketers work at an extremely high level. They know their initial costs and they know how much they are willing to invest to bring a long-term customer on board. And they can do it online or offline, or both, using techniques and strategies that truly give them an unfair advantage. They may even make their first offer on television or at a live event. No matter what, their initial sale (whether it's a book, a course, or something else) becomes the gateway into their ascension program, and they have the ability to use multiple channels and platforms, online and offline, as part of that program.

Multichannel marketing is really the wave of the future—it engages your customers in all the places that they spend their time (online and offline)—and protects your business against unpredictable events in the business environment. It makes you a more robust marketer and opens up all kinds of opportunities that you just can't access when you're only focused on a single channel.

KEY TAKEAWAYS

Multichannel marketing is a critical element in maximizing your business growth, protecting yourself from unexpected downturns, and getting the kind of payoff you really want to see for yourself and your customers.

- As Dan Kennedy says, the most dangerous number in business is 1. If you are only marketing on one channel, you are risking the long-term viability of your business.

- Diversifying the channels you use for your marketing—and the media mix you deploy across them—protects your downside. It guards against being wiped out by an unfavorable change in a law or algorithm by always having more than one way to get profitable customers.

- The biggest channels are not necessarily the most responsive or profitable—a smaller universe with a higher LTV is always preferable to a larger universe with a lower LTV.

- Your audience does not use just one channel to get all their information. Work out their chosen mix of channels, and market across all of them as appropriate.

- Avoid "one-stop shopping" for your marketing at all costs. There are so many different areas of expertise in direct marketing that no one can master them all; buy à la carte to ensure you are working with the best providers in every area.

- Key metrics to track across all parts of your multichannel marketing strategy include:

- o LTV
- o Cost to acquire customers (including cost of goods sold)
- o Attribution
- o Conversion (not to be confused with acquisition)
- Take your customers from online channels to offline channels and back again to maximize their engagement and LTV with you.

CHAPTER 8

CUSTOMER SERVICE & FULFILLMENT

"Marketing by walking around is a requirement, not a choice"

In the early 1980s, baseball writer Thomas Boswell wrote a book called *How Life Imitates the World Series.* As a lifelong, diehard baseball fan, I loved this title. Baseball, like direct marketing, is a big part of my life, and I often look for ways where my two passions collide. It happens surprisingly often.

I am not just a casual fan of the game (or of this direct marketing thing either). I was a pretty good catcher in Little League—a legend in my own mind at 12 years old. But in youth baseball, when you turn 13, you go from a miniature field to a much bigger one—the same size field major league players play on.

Being a fat kid ("husky" to my family), that big field was a problem for me. I was quite slow, and navigating all that real estate just to get on base was a problem. And while I could still catch, the distances to throw the ball were too far for me as well. But I still loved the game and wanted to be part of it even if my body type (and ability) was standing in the way of my future baseball career.

How could I get on the field competently? That's when I became an umpire, often the most hated man on the field, but in my mind, I could be the savior, creating order out of chaos, especially with little leaguers. I knew they needed me, even if *they* didn't know it. I loved the game, I knew the rules, I had a loud voice, and being a little husky and slow was not an issue. In fact, it seemed like all the umpires I ever saw on TV were fat.

But umpiring gave me much more than just a hobby (inside a passion) and, as it turned out, a way to avoid obesity—it is also related to my passion for direct marketing in more ways than I ever would have imagined.

HOW BASEBALL IMITATES DIRECT MARKETING

Back to why I love the title, *How Life Imitates the World Series*. I became an umpire at 16 years old and have done it my entire life: Little League, high school level, men's and women's softball. My dream is to umpire at the Little League World Series. You probably also have passions in your life that, on the surface, have no relationship to your "work" . . . however, ask anyone about their hobbies, interests, exercise routines, etc., and they will tell you how the things they do outside of work give them more focus when they are back at their desk. I maintain that—as it said on the back of Marty Edelston's business card—"the master in the art of living makes little distinction between his work and his play." But for this part of the discussion, let's assume there is a distinction. At least a little one.

As with all the activities in your life, the concentration required to do something well is demanding—whether it's being a lawyer, an accountant, or a dentist, or if it's mountain biking, skiing, or yoga—and in all cases and situations, distractions will lead to failure. In the case of your livelihood, you could lose a client, have a downturn in business, or even get fired from a job; in sports, it could lead to physical injury.

With umpiring, while you could get hit in the head with a baseball if you are daydreaming, the real injuries come when you get yelled at for missing a call. I know you might get a correction during an imperfect downward-facing dog in a yoga class, but missing an obvious call in a baseball game will have a coach loudly arguing with you—in your face and possibly kicking dirt at you—while the parent of the kid who was the victim of your awful call will be screaming from the stands about what a despicable person you are.

Maybe I should take up yoga.

A copywriter friend once asked me, "Why would *anyone* want to be an umpire?"

There had to be something motivating me to be abused so much, and I came up with three answers. The first two I have already touched on:

1. I love the focus required to do it well.

2. I love creating order from chaos by applying established principles (in this case to the game of baseball).

3. I love that underneath it all, umpiring is about customer service and fulfillment.

This chapter is about #3, and when I say fulfillment here, I am not talking about my personal fulfillment but rather fulfillment for the customer. No one comes to a baseball game to see the umpire, just as no one goes to any sporting event to see the referee or official of that game. The best an umpire can get at the end of the game is "Nice game, ump." But the moment an umpire makes a mistake, all hell breaks loose.

If you have ever worked in customer service, fulfillment, or any part of a business that is all about making the behind-the-scenes stuff seamless, I think you might be getting the connection. Most customers don't interact with a company just to experience their customer service and fulfillment. They are buying, receiving, and enjoying their product (sort of like playing in a baseball game on a beautiful spring day), but if something is not right with the experience, it will be time to get satisfaction for the wrong that has been inflicted upon them.

No one wants to feel wronged—and if you don't make it right for them (quickly), I guarantee that the lifetime value of this customer will decrease significantly, maybe even to nothing, or less than nothing. This is the marketing after the marketing—and when we screw up on delivering for our customers, it is absolutely the worst thing we can do in business. As I've said in other ways throughout this book already, it's much easier to keep a customer happy (and increase their lifetime value) than to get a new customer . . . although it does feel sexier to get new customers all the time.

Saving a loyal customer after they feel you have not fulfilled your promise (at any point in the relationship) is your most important sales function. You do this by making world-class customer service your highest priority. While I worried about the title of this book being *Overdeliver*, worried that potential readers might think it is only about delivering impeccable customer service, I decided to go with it because it is such a core principle of marketing. And now you know that overdelivering is also much more than this.

The fact that so many marketers today put up with 30 percent to 50 percent return rates on an initial sale (I guess because keeping 50 percent to 70 percent of new customers is good enough) makes me cringe. And even if accepting that return rate on the initial sale is the prevailing philosophy, these marketers still don't spend enough time caring for and nurturing the folks who *don't* return the product initially, losing them later by not being laser focused on doing everything to keep these customers happy and coming back for more.

Having a total commitment to the highest quality (and integrity) on the initial sale is the most important first step . . . but that same mind-set needs to be in place with all customers throughout the lifetime of their relationship with you. And when you are thinking about customer service and fulfillment, it's even more important to have this maxim front and center all the time, one that I made up and one that I try to live by (and which you have seen at the opening to Chapter 1): "Everything in business (and in life) is not a revenue event, but everything is a relationship event."

Here's another way I like to put this as it pertains to customer service: Lifetime value increases the longer someone loves you and wants to buy from you in the future like they have in the past, but this requires you to take care of them like they are family, even without any exchange of funds.

Unfortunately, too many entrepreneurs and business owners treat their customer service and fulfillment as afterthoughts, and not just the function but the people they hire for those jobs too. These shortsighted executives act as though the actual real-world interaction with real-life people who buy from them doesn't matter once a sale is made. This is a big mistake. Alas, the fulfillment manager or customer service rep, on their *best* day, will get the feedback equivalent of "Nice game, ump." If there are no problems, these folks remain invisible. But when they blow a call (i.e., make a mistake) they become the least popular employees in the company.

It takes a certain kind of personality to umpire . . . or to be a fulfillment manager or customer service representative. Taking pride in giving exquisite service—and being willing to do it without being noticed—is extremely rare. These are the people who overdeliver at the highest level. Pay close attention to people you hire for these roles, and pay them well too. They are your first line of defense in protecting against leakage of your existing and potential customers, and they are your last line of defense against customers leaving you forever.

The wonderful telephone operator who solves a customer's problem behind the scenes and saves an order or avoids a cancellation feels like they are part of sales and revenue creation (or what we can call revenue saving). And the delighted customer, who receives a positive outcome, will have their day made and might just become a customer for life. The folks I know who are the best at customer service receive satisfaction in saving the day, whether it's noticed by one or by many. But while they may not be looking for positive reinforcement, go out of your way to applaud them. Give them accolades for their excellent skill at keeping customers; they deserve this just as much as the sales rep or copywriter deserves praise for figuring out creative ways to add new customers.

Make sure you look after every part of your customer service and fulfillment, because the only way to stay in business for the long haul is to focus relentlessly on keeping your customers happy. And that includes keeping your employees happy too. Even if things go wrong, if you are committed to making things right and saving every customer with every interaction, no matter how negative or potentially damaging, you will build resilience into your business—because, as we know, all businesses thrive on repeat purchases.

You can even base your entire differentiation strategy as a company on how you treat your customers. Look at such well-known retail businesses as Nordstrom, Stew Leonard's, Ritz Carlton—they are differentiated in extremely competitive industries due to their unrivalled customer service. I love tracking what companies have done to create superior levels of service for their best customers, especially with commoditized products. Premium services such as Amazon Prime and the American Express Black Card overdeliver and create customer experiences like no one else.

Creating what is called a barrier to switch is critical and will be discussed later in this chapter. For now, I will just say that your product or service is only a commodity if you let it be a commodity. Now let's look at some examples that prove why customer service and fulfillment are marketing functions (although I hope I have made that case already).

IT'S EASIER TO KEEP A CUSTOMER THAN TO GET A NEW ONE

I don't mind repeating this tenet of direct marketing: it's easier to keep a customer than to get a new one. It really is that important. And I learned it by staying late at the office to field calls from angry customers.

My theory is that if you can overdeliver and transform a customer's bad experience into something positive, almost making it a game of sorts, you turn them into a loyal fan for life. The lessons you can learn about human behavior by going deep with one unhappy customer can teach you lessons you can apply to multiple customers with the same (or similar) issues. Never assume you are making only one mistake in the eyes of each angry customer; rather, assume that you are making many mistakes all the time and that learning what it will take to save each customer is research you can take to the bank.

As Claude Hopkins said in terms of attracting new customers, "We cannot go after thousands of men until we learn how to win one." This applies to *all* customers, including those we have gone after and won already. And about them, I like to say we cannot understand why thousands of customers stay with us until we learn why one would consider leaving us.

No problem, issue, or complaint is too small. All complaints are relevant, even if you think the customer is being unreasonable or trying to take advantage of you. And there's always an opportunity to learn about your audience and to spot the holes in your process that are leaving you exposed.

I used to stay late at the office to answer the phone. The only people who called after 8:00 P.M. were angry customers, and I heard every complaint under the sun—from missing issues of a newsletter to irritation that a book had not arrived yet. There was one person whose dog ate pages 17 and 18 of the special bonus that contained the most important secret regarding treatment of their type 2 diabetes, and I recall a sad story about the postman who left a much anticipated book in the snow.

Everything our customer service folks hear needs to be heard and documented and shared with everyone on our marketing teams. Even things that on the surface seem to be beyond our control. Listening and interacting with your customers will give you far deeper insights than any spreadsheet or report on the makeup of your database. This is what I mean by "marketing by walking around." It could also be "marketing by listening more to your customers," or "marketing by talking more to your customers" or even "marketing by eavesdropping on your customers"—but only in the most ethical way and always with the goal to become more valuable to them.

As an owner, there are so many things that are not in your direct line of vision. Yes, you should read reports from customer service and monitor complaints regularly, but there is nothing like talking to someone who gave you their money (and their trust) when they might want you to give them their money back. Issues that look like minutia on the customer service side can end up having big implications for how you make decisions in the future.

I learned this by accident, staying late. But that experience led me to making it mandatory for marketing personnel to sit in on customer service calls on a regular basis. The valuable firsthand lessons you learn by paying attention to the bad news (which you will hate hearing at the time) will very often lead to making positive changes in your business.

One obvious thing I learned through my experience taking calls late at night was that what starts as confrontational can quickly be diffused through generosity of speech and spirit (i.e., not arguing but just listening and acknowledging their position). This can be followed up with giving away bonuses and unexpected extras as a thank-you for bringing the issue to your attention.

As you may recall from the example of going from 4 bonuses to 100, I believe this generosity mind-set that was part of both the front-end marketing and the back-end marketing enabled us to create more premiums and bonuses in our acquisition packages and then always encouraged us to give as much as possible later on if there was any dissatisfaction. This cut down on many kinds of complaints. Customers were always getting more than they ever would have expected up front. If they were dissatisfied later on, they were far less confrontational and their problems were easier to resolve. And we still overdelivered on the back end too.

Whenever I picked up the phone and heard an angry customer, I was ready to play the game that every direct marketer must master: to overdeliver and give the customer more than they would ever expect. It's an opportunity for you to discover the unanswered questions, to see their unexpected perspectives, and to shine a light on the unmet fears and desires of your audience.

The key then is to react quickly and to just keep saying yes until the customer is satisfied. This is how you learn what holes need to be plugged for *all* your customers, some of whom are too timid to make the call and are suffering in silence. Always assume that there are many more people with the same problem as the person who was bold enough to make an issue of it. There will always be a silent group waiting for a solution. This exercise can give you insight you cannot easily get anywhere else. And if your evening automated attendant doesn't allow you to talk to real people, or if all your customer service is outsourced, make it a practice to spend some time listening in to what your customers are telling the folks you have entrusted to be on your front lines.

All this ties in to that critical direct marketing rule of thumb: it is always easier to keep a customer than to get a new one. Remember the adage that marketers sell subscriptions, but editors sell renewals. Remember that this applies way beyond subscription offers—this lesson is universal. Another way to express this concept beyond subscription marketing: Marketers sell the first order; product developers, content creators, *and customer service and fulfillment people* sell renewals.

If you don't truly deliver the product or service you sell in the initial promotion, you can resell later until you are blue in the face and you won't get a renewal or repeat order. And even if you deliver what you promised on the front end, remember that the relationship is just beginning. Make sure the customer loves that first product, and continue offering the same quality when you sell them subsequent products. In between all that selling, however, the communication channels have to stay open all the time in order to satisfy every customer who, for example, doesn't get the bonus you promised or receives one of your amazing products three weeks later than you said you would deliver it.

It's all connected. And of course, be ready to answer the phone when they call and need something more.

THE SECRETS OF SECRET SHOPPERS

As I mentioned earlier, many insightful entrepreneurs hire secret shoppers (people on the payroll *outside* the company to go through every aspect of their sales and marketing operation) to find out where there might be a broken link or a hole in the operation that no one would ever see without this anonymous monitored buying. One brilliant entrepreneur had his secret shopper answer one question—and one question only—at every step of the process as they experienced the organization's sales funnel: "How does that make me feel?" This secret shopper bought everything, returned a lot, complained a lot, got on the phone with customer service people, sent e-mails—basically everything they could possibly do to stress the system as much as possible. Whenever the answer to the "how did they feel" question was anything short of thrilled (or at the least very satisfied), there were tweaks to be made in the system.

As soon as the customer feels like you're not interested in them, they are gone. They will take their money and go elsewhere. And in a world where people spend time sharing pictures of their dinner on social media, they certainly will make their displeasure known to many more people than just your customer service rep if things go wrong. Technology and the ability to share a lot more with a lot more people has quickly made impeccable customer service even more of a requirement for every business today. In our interconnected world, bad news travels faster than ever before. I don't have to emphasize how damaging bad word-of-mouth can be—it obviously brings your LTV way down, it makes the job tougher for your front-end/acquisition marketers and copywriters to sell to new customers, and it compromises your ability to deliver on what you've promised, assuming the bad news about the customer experience you deliver becomes more widespread.

One secret shopper story I heard reminds me to add that you must put your ego on the back burner to get information you can use and apply. This entrepreneur heard that after his expert sales people ascended customers at a live event into a high-priced coaching program (at $15,000 a year)—after they had only bought much lower-priced products and services previously—it was often four full days after the event before someone from his company would contact this new VIP customer.

He asked his sales staff, "If someone paid you $15,000, would you ignore them for four days? Or would you make them your highest priority?" This entrepreneur immediately saw that shortening the time between the sale and the onboarding, consultation, and simply getting the client started would immediately take away potential buyer's remorse (especially since they just spent so much money) and likely increase their LTV too.

While that might at first feel like overdelivering, this kind of thing is just the right thing to do, particularly since these are the customers you dream about. And if they start coming into your business, you must nurture them proactively and promptly. No matter how high up the food chain you are at your company—including being the owner—the responsibility of keeping your customers happy is ultimately yours.

CONTROL THE DISTRACTIONS YOU CAN CONTROL (WITH YOUR CONTROL)

There's another important area of customer service that has less to do with solving problems, fielding complaints, or satisfying customers. It's about being present with your audience—being conscious of what your prospects and customers might be going through in other aspects of their lives.

Unfortunately, many game-changing entrepreneurs and inventors have their best stuff ignored because of world events and things beyond their control that decrease interest in their offer. Major distractions in the marketplace can negatively affect the results you see for the products and services you are promoting. Some are predictable and can be avoided. Some are less predictable, but even in those cases, there may be ways to make lemonade from lemons. And some are just plain bummers all the way around, things that are unpredictable and unavoidable, leading to terrible results beyond your control.

Let's explore all three in the context of customer service.

Predictable & Avoidable Market Distractions

I heard from many people in late 2016 that their marketing results (i.e., response, revenue, and profit) just before and after that year's U.S. presidential election were lower than expected. While people were probably paying far more attention to this election than most, the point is that we need to recognize anything we know is coming down the pike that can be distracting to our potential audience.

These marketers should have known better—*every* presidential election is worth avoiding as a launch date, mail date, or promotion period. And I'm sure there are parallel events in countries outside the U.S. that could lead to distraction in the marketplace and diminished results. During my days doing large direct mail programs, we always avoided the time immediately before and after the vote, and this is a good practice no matter which channels you use.

In direct mail, it was a lot harder to predict when the mail would land (which we called the in-home date). You couldn't always rely on the mailman to deliver at the same pace. Today, although it's even easier to predict in-home dates with most forms of online media, we never mailed or advertised near any major event due to what we called the distraction factor. We always wanted to reduce risk whenever we could.

A presidential election is one distraction you can work around . . . unlike war, horrific world events, weather disasters, or just unexpected news. I recommend that you make planning for predictable and avoidable events part of your standard operating procedure. The example of the 2016 election is an obvious case, but there are many others (and this is not just an American phenomenon). In my years of planning promotions in various media—direct mail, print, inserts, TV, radio, e-mail—we mapped out our mailing and promotion schedule at the beginning of each year and took as many planned major world events into account as we could, such as the Olympics, The World Cup, elections, and so on.

In the 1980s and 1990s, we had mailings going out every week. We never had fewer than 40 mailings a year, all of which were over a million pieces—sometimes over five million pieces. There was even one year when we had over 52 mailings and had to double up a couple of weeks (while not mailing the same names more than once on the same mail date). Note: In the world of direct mail, if you rented names for a one-time mailing but names appeared on more than one list, you were allowed to mail duplicates on a future date using the same offer. And there were some weeks we simply avoided in every calendar year, since we kept accurate records on periods when responsiveness was very low for certain kinds of offers. Simply put, so many mailings with not enough mail dates.

No matter how often you send out promotions, online or offline, I recommend that you map out your promotion schedule at the beginning of the year and work around any events that are predictable distractions, as well as dates when your potential audience will be uninterested in hearing from you, such as a tax newsletter arriving in late April, right after the filing deadline.

Predictable distractions and potential irrelevance are both marketing issues and customer service issues. It's marketing since you don't want your campaigns to bomb because of events and circumstances that are in your power to plan around. There is also an important yet overlooked aspect of customer service at work here: if your offer is ignored because you didn't plan for potential distractions or seasonal relevance, you could lose a customer forever, or never get one in the first place, simply because they felt disrespected or annoyed.

Less Predictable, but Still Avoidable

Do you remember Operation Desert Shield in 1990 and 1991? In August of 1990, Iraq's invasion of Kuwait took everyone by surprise. If you look back at that very tense period, America had troops in Saudi Arabia, literally waiting for their marching orders, while everyone at home in the U.S. was anxiously watching the news, waiting to see how the situation would unfold.

Not that anyone cared (nor should they have), but during the troop buildup, we had a huge quantity of direct mail ready to go out. They were in mail bags, sitting at a "lettershop" (a warehouse where the mailing was being staged), and I remember meeting with my staff and with key consultants every day regarding what to do. We wanted to time the mailing as best we could without diminishing the responsiveness and recency of the lists we had rented—that is, we tried to find the sweet spot of making the mailing successful while avoiding having the promotion hit mailboxes just as our troops invaded Kuwait (a big distraction).

We had recency issues, since the names were getting older by the day (remember the R from RFM?), and that was colliding with a severe distraction factor. We wanted to be sensitive to what our potential customers were going through at the time. We waited a while during the troop buildup in Saudi Arabia and eventually timed the mailing when the distraction slowed down, early in 1991. We traded off some responsiveness (because the names aged a bit) to avoid mailing into total distraction.

We generated less revenue on that promotion than we had planned, but the waiting period also gave us time to revise our budgets, since we figured we would probably not do as well once we held the mail for so many weeks. But the mailing was far from a disaster, and thankfully the United States avoided a war at that time as well.

While everyone likes to make as much money as possible, giving up a little bit of profit by giving up a little recency and not marketing into a period where your audience is distracted (assuming you can wait a little while until the distraction is diminished) is a trade-off that is worth it. You won't completely write off the promotion—and you won't compromise the goodwill of your audience either.

A quick side note on how situations like this became an advertising opportunity for some: I heard from industry sources during Desert Shield that CNN was able to increase their advertising rates significantly, because the number of eyeballs looking at the TV matters, and at times like these, that number goes up. One medium's distraction is another medium's attraction.

There are always ways to try to use a distraction to your advantage, of course. This was something we experienced first-hand once we got into TV advertising, although this one is hard to recommend broadly. In different periods of the mid-2000s, I believe we were spending as much as any marketer advertising with infomercials at that time. At times we experimented with timing some ad buys week to week, trying to calculate when we could get the most eyeballs on a particular promotion based on the news cycle. It was kind of like day trading, which gave me a lot of anxiety, and like I said, I don't recommend it. Not only did the risk outweigh the reward, it also felt a bit exploitative.

When something unpredictable happens, you have to take care of yourself and your business, and at the same time, you can look for ways to help others too. This hit home for me in September of 1989 when the devastation of Hurricane Hugo led to the deaths of at least 60 people. Hugo was a category-five storm and was responsible for an estimated $10 billion in damage, mostly in the Southeastern United States and the Caribbean. It was one of the worst storms ever to hit the United States.

It seemed meaningless to send the millions of pieces of mail we had ready to go out that week as we watched homes in South Carolina swept away and lives destroyed. I remember watching a news report where there was a mailbox floating down a street and feeling so impacted by it . . . it emphasized to me that despite being my livelihood, direct mail was pretty insignificant at that moment.

But we had a business to run and our team's livelihoods to protect as well. So after a restless night, I called the mailing facility where we had that huge campaign ready to go out and had them resort the mail. We had time before it went out, so I asked them to remove all the mailing pieces set to go out within a 100 mile radius around Hugo's path as it came up the southeastern coast of the U.S. (it was easy to omit by zip codes). My logic was that if someone's mailbox was floating down the street, the odds that they would want to buy a copy of *The Book of Inside Information* were pretty low. To my mind, it was wasteful and disrespectful to the folks who were suffering to try to send them mail, and it seemed ridiculous that the postal workers in the affected region would also have to handle and store all that extra mail. Selling a book was not a high priority for me in light of the awful situation, and buying it was not relevant to them—staying safe and working out how to rebuild their lives was going to be the only focus for those people.

After the decision not to mail them, I decided it wasn't enough, and that we could do more. We reached out to every charitable fundraiser who had used our lists over the years. The subscriber and buyer lists we owned were some of the most responsive names for fundraisers, and I told every one of them (including the American Red Cross, Save the Children, Habitat for Humanity, and others) that they could have as many of our "best names" as they wanted—for free—for any fundraising effort related to Hurricane Hugo.

At the time, our lists sold for over $100 per thousand names, so this was a big donation—and we made an additional monetary donation to each of those charities who took free names from us (as long as our money would be targeted to Hugo) to help with their mailing costs. We ended up shipping hundreds of thousands of names to a variety of fundraisers and donated a significant amount of cash too. Those mailing efforts raised much needed funds for people who needed it most; later we made this standard procedure for any disaster where direct mail (and our responsive lists) could be used to help.

All this is to say that even when things go wrong—and you have some warning—you can protect yourself more than you think, while making a difference and turning a disaster into a positive experience for both your company and your customers.

Bummers You Just Can't Predict

On Labor Day weekend in the United States, response rates for many kinds of space advertising are traditionally very high, and in 1997, we had scheduled a large newspaper advertising campaign in anticipation. There was no way we could have predicted that Princess Diana would die tragically, in highly publicized circumstances, just days before. People were devastated by the news and glued to their TV sets. Everyone's Labor Day campaigns tanked that year. There was no time to pull the advertising like we did with the natural and (manmade) disasters where we had some warning, which meant that our newspaper campaign received less than 50 percent of the responses expected on a million-dollar media buy. Sometimes you just have to be prepared to take a hit when everything is out of your control. This is another reason to have your media buys diversified and to never be reliant on just one medium for the lion's share of your revenue and profit. Multichannel marketing is not just a neat sounding term, it should be your mantra.

But I believe situations like this made us even more sensitive to what we could control and what we couldn't. We were already pretty good at planning for distractions where we had some control, as indicated by our actions around Desert Shield and Hurricane Hugo. And we were always on our guard and encouraged others to do the same, and also to be extremely proactive in how we all approach our customers in volatile times. It's much better to be paranoid and proactively try to control as much you can with your campaigns than to leave things to chance and let the chips fall where they may—especially in situations where people are just not as interested in what you have to offer as you are.

Marty, my partner on all these adventures in marketing, once had T-shirts made up quoting the venture capitalist Frederick Adler: "Paranoia is not a psychosis . . . it's survival."

THE BARRIER TO SWITCH

Let's talk about one final element in building out customer service and fulfillment as functions of your marketing strategy: creating a barrier to switch. The barrier to switch is one of the most important things you can build into your business. It's about making it almost impossible for your customers to leave you because you give them such great service or a unique experience that would be hard to duplicate if they moved to a competitor.

Making it difficult (even painful) for your customers to leave you sounds like the antithesis of loving your audience and providing the highest level of customer service. But keeping customers for life is all about your deepest commitment to your audience and has nothing to do with holding them captive. If you have the better solution, I maintain that it is your duty (Jay Abraham might say it's your moral responsibility) to keep them with you, rather than have them leave you for an inferior competitor.

I hinted at this earlier when I gave examples of commodity businesses that make customer service their differentiator. Lifetime relationships and customers who never want to leave you happen when you create a shared history and a shared vision of your future together. It doesn't matter whether your business sells $5 widgets or $20,000 masterminds . . . there is always a way to create a deep connection and loyalty with your customers. And yes, the loyalty has to go both ways—when customers know that you will go to any length for them, they'll be yours for life.

In my own life, three brands have created a barrier to switch that keep me going back to them again and again. At one end of the cost scale, there's a barrier to switch from my dry cleaner. They gave me a beautiful garment bag with my name embossed on it, along with a barcode that contains all the details they need to never lose my pants and how I like my shirts done. All I have to do is bring my dirty clothes in the garment bag, then they scan the code and they instantly know who I am, how I want everything done, and when I want to pick them up. I don't have to fill anything out, and when I return to pick up my clothes, they are neatly hung in the garment bag and my credit card has already been charged. Sure, I can go to the next dry cleaner who has embossed bags, but as long as my current dry cleaner has exquisite customer service, and the quality is as good as any other dry cleaner, a barrier to switch has been established. They created differentiation inside of a commoditized service.

At a higher point on the cost scale, Ritz-Carlton records my preferences from every stay, so my experience with them gets better every time I book one of their hotels. When I get to the hotel in San Francisco, they have arranged my stay with all the little details passed on from what I wanted during my stay with them in Chicago. They know what kind of room I want, the type of food I order, the requests I'm likely to make. This makes Ritz-Carlton my first preference every time I travel (and no, they're not comping me for the endorsement). I don't want to stay anywhere else, because the other hotels don't know me, and I don't want to go back to being just another name getting another average experience in another impersonal hotel. (Loyalty points with other hotels I stay at also create a barrier to switch . . . but when The Ritz knew the kind of pillows I preferred as I checked in, it put them in a different category).

In the case of my car, Infiniti has also created a barrier to switch, again through differentiated customer service. I'm not a big car guy, and since I only buy a new car every eight or nine years, I'm not a great customer for the dealer either. At the time of writing this book, my 2008 Infiniti—which is a really nice car—might be due for a replacement any day. But I also might have it until 2028. However, it's going to be really hard for me to buy any car other than an Infiniti because of the barrier to switch they have built in, even with a terrible customer like me.

I have lifetime oil changes and services, I get first access to all their new models whenever I want, I will get a discount as a previous owner, and the dealer knows me by name when I walk onto the lot, as do the service people when I go for those free oil changes. They still treat me like a king *even though I buy so rarely*, because they know it's going to make it very hard for me to go buy an Acura or a Lexus. They are focused on the LTV of their customer, always thinking about the long-term, cumulative monetary value as much as high frequency purchasing. And although they are still waiting for me to buy my one car a decade, my wife bought an Infiniti during the period they were waiting on me. They can add that second sale to my LTV, I guess.

Creating a barrier to switch is about knowing what your customers want on a tactical level. The more you know the specific details they love, the easier it will be for you to create that barrier, and your entire business can be built around increasing lifetime value. For me, the barrier to switch is just another spin on customer service and fulfillment being critical marketing functions.

KEY TAKEAWAYS

Your customers are the most important people in your business. Keeping them happy—serving them, creating world-class experiences, overdelivering on what you promise, and always innovating for their benefit—is your primary role.

- Customer service and fulfilment are critical marketing functions. It's the "marketing after the marketing" that shows your customers that you do really care about them.

- It's much easier to keep existing customers and to increase their LTV—through overdelivering on customer service and fulfilment—than to acquire new customers.

- People who can deliver exquisite customer service and fulfilment are extremely rare, so if you find someone who excels at this, do everything you can to make them a permanent part of your team. They should be compensated, developed, and involved just as well as the other important players in your organization.

- Customer service and fulfilment can provide the basis for your entire differentiation strategy (as it has for Ritz-Carlton, Amex Black, and Amazon Prime—all premium experiences that create unshakeable customer loyalty).

- Listening to your customers and actually interacting with them will give you deeper, more actionable insights on improving your company than any spreadsheet or report could ever do.

- Use secret shoppers to help you identify where you can improve your customer experience—check your ego at the door, listen hard to what they find, plug any gaping holes immediately, and then get to work fine-tuning.

- Cultivating a spirit of generosity and overdelivery throughout your company makes it far easier to meet the demands of customer service and fulfilment.

- Don't forget that customer service and fulfillment extends to when, where, and how your customers receive your marketing campaigns. Always consider their context: plan your campaigns so that you don't send them into predictable and avoidable distractions, and do everything you can to mitigate situations that are less predictable (or that are completely out of left field).

- Always create a barrier to switch if you possibly can. Make it extremely difficult for your customers to leave you by giving them powerful, positive experiences every time they interact with your company.

CHAPTER 9

CONTINUITY & LTV

"No direct marketing business can survive without repeat business."

—BOB STONE

Some years ago, I attended a presentation given by a well-known marketer who mostly works online. He opened with a slide that said, "A product is not a business."

I can't tell you how much that warmed my heart. It made me realize that there were top marketers today who understand that it is not the first order that will be the key to their success, but rather that they need to develop a suite of products to ensure a foundation of future success. Copywriting legend John Carlton gave me another spin on this (from the creative side) when he said, "A promotion is not a business." Put those two quotes together and you actually have your direct marketing philosophy.

As you are figuring out your first product to offer to a select marketplace, think—even at that early stage—about products two, three, and four that you can offer to those buyers. Don't be fooled into thinking that when your first promotion does extremely well that your work is done or that you can ride on that successful promotion for any significant length of time.

Once you have a first-time buyer, what would they expect from you as the next offer? I love the idea of creating new products, but I like creating a franchise or suite of products rather than one breakthrough product even more.

I have engaged in many lengthy discussions over the years, whether in my own business or consulting on other businesses, about what the audience we were selling to would want next, coupled with what we would be proud to put our name on. Sometimes the conclusion was to *make* the product, and sometimes it was to *buy* (i.e., partner on) the product. But in all cases, this line of thinking is the key to creating raving fans that will stick with you for a very long time.

We've established that list selection is the most important element of a successful direct marketing campaign—and when you combine careful segmentation with powerful offers and compelling promotions, you create an intense focus on maximizing the lifetime value of every new customer you bring into the fold. But as you can see here, we've added the element of always thinking about multiple products and offers that are natural extensions for your audience—before you even launch the first winning product or promotion.

Target the right people, have multiple offerings from the outset, and never rely on one winning promotion for a significant length of time. This "business plan," while simple, is not easy. One of my favorite authors on the subject of personal finance and money is my friend David Bach. David's books have a consistent theme of "finishing rich," which I love, considering so much marketing advice we receive on a regular basis is about getting rich quick.

In this chapter, I want to make sure you have a keen understanding of LTV as the key metric in your business above all others, because it's this number that will give you the best possible chance of finishing rich. We have talked quite a bit already about LTV, because it is such an important principle and it influences every part of direct response—but we're going to go really deep in this chapter. The reason it's so important is that it helps you take the long view of any channel you test.

Many people jump to conclusions about particular channels when they don't understand LTV. They give up on a channel that they might think doesn't pay out, while their better informed competitors, as a result of *their* understanding of LTV, stay in the same channel with acceptable returns and an ability to scale. Three things can happen if you don't track the lifetime value of the customers that come through a particular channel:

1. You give up on the channel too soon.

2. You stick with the channel too long.

3. You experience a fluke and misattribute your success.

In the first instance, because you don't have command of your numbers, on the surface it looks like you're spending way too much to justify acquiring customers on that channel. This is what happened to all those guys competing with my friend advertising on Facebook with their $10 offers. They couldn't stomach not breaking even on the first purchase—because they weren't thinking about a second, third, or fourth purchase. This is why my friend ended up with the channel all to himself and was making back nearly *eight times* his ad spend on Facebook while everyone else in the space thought the channel didn't work for their offer.

In the second instance, it looks like you're making good money from each customer that comes through the given channel, but in actual fact you're losing money on them in the long run. For example, let's say you spend $15 to acquire a customer through ads on a big platform and make $30 on their first purchase—you've made $15 per sale (assuming you're incorporating your cost of goods into your acquisition cost). So on the surface, this platform looks like a winner. But when you start looking at the LTV of these new customers, you might discover that they never buy again . . . or buy infrequently . . . and that your $15 of net profit is short-lived and a one-time revenue event with no chance to add additional profit in the future.

You get this false positive because you didn't track the lifetime value of the new customer. And then you end up distracted from looking at other channels where you might add many more repeat purchases (leading to a higher LTV) that would justify the acquisition cost. You are not building for the future.

Note that original list selection and segmentation is critical here too. That is, if you are prospecting for new customers who are less qualified to buy repeat products in the first place, you are setting yourself up to be a one-hit wonder rather than a lifetime value hero.

In the third instance—and this happens a lot —you stumble onto a winner but neglect to calculate the LTV of any of your channels, which, if calculated, would identify the most profitable ones and lead to greater expansion (with confidence) in those channels. That is, you get something right, but you can't explain it. You misattribute your success to your own genius and never learn the underlying principle. This means you can't reproduce the success but keep expecting you will be able to. And you won't invest as much in a valuable channel since you don't know all your numbers. There may also be additional profits that you could attribute to initial buyers once they are intertwined in your multichannel marketing strategy, and if you can calculate that into their lifetime value, you may be able to go back and "lose more" on the first sale. (We'll dive deeper on that in a moment.)

Not recognizing the full lifetime value of every new buyer across every channel they buy from is the most dangerous of the three scenarios. In the first scenario, you'll abandon a profitable channel and jump to something else that seems to work better. In the second, you'll be running in place—and hopefully that won't lead to anything fatal. In the third scenario, however, you'll assume that you're doing everything right and applying the same thinking to every channel—not realizing that the expected value of a new channel may be inaccurate.

Understanding LTV allows you to simply sidestep these problems. The power of direct response is that it's marketing by numbers. Yes, you have to know which numbers to track (and you have to actually *do* the tracking), but once you have them, you'll be able to model out the trajectory of the business for the months and years ahead. It's a superpower that saves you the uncertainty and volatility that can so easily kill a business.

LTV is the linchpin in those calculations. When you know the LTV of a set of customers, you can then develop "the bogey"—a simple calculation that answers the question, "How much are you willing to *lose* on your initial order to make it all back (and more) in subsequent years?"

THE BOGEY MAN

Under the supervision of my mentor Dick Benson and a team of best-in-class direct marketers, Boardroom's flagship consumer newsletter, *Bottom Line/Personal*, reached a million paid subscribers at its height. This was quite a feat, since the newsletter took no advertising and had to exist (and profit) based solely on subscription revenue (and a little bit from list rental income). Getting to a million subscribers profitably was even more daunting because the subscription revenue was based on a very low price point (between $30 and $40 per year).

Enter Dick Benson, the smartest man who ever lived when it came to direct mail. (By the way, Benson's 31 "Rules of Thumb" in his classic book *Secrets of Successful Direct Mail* still apply, at least conceptually, to everything we do online today.) Dick told us that the way to grow *BL/P* was to establish the bogey, and I can safely say that calculating this number and basing all our marketing decisions on it was the single biggest reason Boardroom became as large as it did.

We calculated on a list-by-list basis how much we were willing to lose on the initial subscription. That calculation took into account the average renewal rates of those initial subscribers, list rental income we could derive from those subscribers for as long as they were on file as active, and what the average new subscriber would buy from us after the first sale (such as subscriptions to other newsletters and books in similar subject areas).

Despite the fact that *BL/P* was by far the most profitable product in the company's stable, it was certainly not stand-alone.

Lifetime value is always about the interaction of multiple channels, multiple products, and every way a new customer contributes to your bottom line.

The end result was that we got rich slowly. That is, the money in our bank accounts steadily increased and over time made us less concerned about monthly cash flow. This slow and steady process started with a one-year bogey (making a new subscription profitable a year after we sold it); then we moved to a two-year bogey, and eventually a three-year bogey. Who would have believed when we launched the publication that we would be willing and able to wait until year three to break even on a new subscriber?

The day Marty and I realized we were in the business of *renewals* was the day I believe we really understood LTV. We looked at all the sources of revenue for the company: subscription income, book sales, list rental. And as we studied it all, the *BL/P* renewals was by far the most significant number and accounted for the highest margins (since it was always cheaper to renew a subscriber than to get a new one). The cross-selling and upselling associated with the newsletter was the whipped cream on the sundae, and it was important too. The renewal revenue (plus the related revenue streams) allowed us to be much more aggressive with our marketing for new subscribers, given what we could lose in the first years of a customer's relationship with us.

Knowing that renewals and multiple product sales rule the day, the emphasis on editorial excellence takes on even more significance. We were committed to making sure that subscribers to any of our newsletters would renew at 50 percent to 70 percent after the first year. We wanted them to be so satisfied that they would trust us implicitly when we offered them additional editorial products (other newsletters and books). This strategy—getting renewals as high as possible and creating subsequent products of only the highest quality—enabled us to mail more names at an upfront loss to get new subscribers for a long-term profit.

We eventually reached a million paid subscribers. It took a long time . . . but it was worth it.

YOU CAN SPEND MORE MONEY ON YOUR UP-FRONT MARKETING THAN YOU THINK

Earlier I mentioned a client who offered a high-priced coaching program which cost $20,000 per year. They weren't spending much money on acquisition marketing to new, outside lists, and I wondered why, with such a high price point. Even a one-year buyer was worth a lot to them.

And when I asked what their average renewal rate was for the program, I was blown away. They said it was three times—that is, their best customers were $60,000 buyers, which *screamed* to me that we could devote a lot more dollars to marketing. I suggested all kinds of high-priced acquisition efforts (expensive three-dimensional direct mail, radio, TV, live events . . .). They were doing some of this already, but the real progress started happening once we understood the lifetime value of a new customer and, with that number at our fingertips, realized we could invest a lot more in our marketing. (Yes, LTV calculations can be made—and must be made—whether your offer is priced at $10, $30, or $20,000.)

This situation taught me to ask this as my first question when entering a company for a consultation of any kind: What is the lifetime value of a new customer worth, and are you willing to lose money short term to make a lot more money long term? It's an updated version of the question Dick Benson asked Marty and me when he knew that developing a bogey was critical to our future success.

If the marketer can't invest more in first-time buyers because of financial limitations, that's one thing, but if they *won't* do it because they don't want to play a long game and are only focused on short-term revenue and profit, that will be the biggest impediment to their growth. One of the main things to remember with LTV is that every dollar you spend on marketing and media does not need to be made back immediately. I understand that marketing isn't free, but if you intend to stick around for a long time, and you believe in what you are doing at the deepest level, you will embrace this notion of getting rich slowly.

Dan Sullivan, the world's top coach for entrepreneurs, says this when he talks about abundance: "Never spend less when you can spend more." He was not talking about spending more on marketing specifically, but the principle still applies, particularly if we factor in a proper understanding of LTV. Spend as much as you can on up-front marketing as long as you know exactly when you will make back your investment because you have calculated lifetime value of every new customer or client.

We tried to embody this as much as possible. Depending on the product, we would extend our bogey out two or three years. On *BL/P*, we were willing to be in the negative until the second annual renewal (i.e., the third year) because we knew those customers were so valuable in the long run. On other products, we would want to break even on the first conversion, because we knew those lists were more impulsive and less likely to become loyal repeat buyers.

When we started the book division, we had to be really disciplined. We could have had a bogey there as well, even though the books were based on a one-shot model—rather than a renewal model—but people who bought a book from us would often buy other books and newsletters, so we would see an increased lifetime value even in these one-time buyers. Without the renewal stream, we were more cautious—however, that didn't mean we weren't calculating lifetime value.

All lifetime values are not created equal. You must look at the potential revenue streams by product and channel and calculate accordingly. Being less aggressive with our book marketing than we were with our newsletter marketing was difficult because we had seen such incredible results by investing deeper in media with a higher lifetime value. But with books, we stuck to our guns—we had to make money on the first sale. This prevented us from mailing a lot more names for the books, but having the books make at least some money up front allowed us to have a much more aggressive bogey for *BL/P* and never got us into trouble from a cash-flow perspective.

Simply put, we stayed super aggressive without being greedy . . . and we stayed committed to the lifetime value calculation that we knew would be most profitable across all products. In today's marketplace, you might have certain "hero products" that are worth extending the bogey on because they are the most profitable based on lifetime value.

But to make the model work, you have to make sure there are other products in your business where the cash-flow cycle is tighter but just as predictable. This keeps you solvent—you want to make sure you're not extending out so far on every product that you run into cash-flow problems. For example, if we had extended a three-year bogey on all our products, we would not have been able to scale, and we probably would have gone broke. Once you have millions in the bank, it is much easier, but that doesn't mean you can ever afford to get sloppy. You can't afford to be complacent just because you've got a lot of money in the bank.

Rich Schefren, a marketing thought leader once told me, simply and eloquently: "You don't have a real business until you can profitably buy customers consistently from cold sources" (not JVs, affiliates, etc.). What he meant was once you can spend real money on media that pays out and you are not reliant on media that is some kind of "revenue share" (with affiliates), you are taking that leap from a "product" or a "promotion" and into a business. In the context of this chapter, it applies in that if you can buy customers consistently *at a loss initially*, knowing exactly when they become profitable, you have a real (and *big*) business for the long run.

Direct marketing is all about the numbers—not just the numbers coming in, but the numbers going out too. Good money management is *critical* if you're going to scale your business because you have to be able to service the increasing volume of customers, continue producing and fulfilling your product at a high standard, and often start working with consultants and partners that come in to handle areas outside your competency. To do all that, you always want to put some money aside that you're not going to reinvest, which becomes your cushion. This rainy day fund protects your assets and allows you to take a few risks too.

PROTECTING YOUR LTV WITH CONGRUENT MARKETING

Everything you do in your business needs to be congruent. While we've spent this chapter so far talking about lifetime value as a number, staying in business for a lifetime combines knowing your numbers with knowing who you want to be in the world and what you want your business to represent. That means building a culture into your business that reflects who you are and what you value most.

If you have a strong foundation that is congruent with your purpose, it's easy to attract the right audience and to develop offers and creative that are congruent and appropriate for them. And not surprisingly, when you focus on congruence, the number that you calculated in lifetime value per customer tends to increase exponentially. Whether you make the subsequent products yourself or buy them from someone else in some kind of partnership, whatever you put your name (brand) on has to be congruent—to you as a company and to your customers.

Creative is also an area where congruence can be at risk: what might work best to bring in new customers may be inconsistent with how you really want to sell. I have seen many thought leaders struggle when they begin marketing aggressively for the first time. Unfortunately, they start with the premise that marketing is evil—and then my job is to show them how to sell congruently yet still remain aggressive. It's a sweet spot that we can all get to, and it's different for everyone. But I maintain that being as aggressive as possible, while being as congruent as possible, is the formula for the highest lifetime value.

Since we're talking about marketing, and money is always involved, things can get tricky when your desire to be congruent collides with paying the electric bill. If you have a good reputation and a solid bank of goodwill with your customers, and therefore with your prospects too, it's easier to recover from a "congruence fail," but you can't count on it. I made one of these congruence fails, and thankfully survived, learning a valuable lesson that I refer to these days as "the moose on the table."

THE MOOSE ON THE TABLE

I once received a card from a business associate that gave this sage advice about meetings: "None of us is as dumb as all of us." Have you ever made decisions in your life, business or personal, where you look back and wonder why no one suggested you do the opposite . . . or simply do nothing at all? It's critical for someone to always call out "the moose on the table" . . . the thing no one wants to say, the thing everyone is afraid to suggest. (In my mind, the phrase conjures up an image of a dead, decaying moose right in the middle of a meeting room table . . . while everyone talks around the carcass, refusing to acknowledge that it's even there.)

That's how I felt after I made the second biggest mistake of my career (the biggest, as you recall, was reading our press clippings and assuming our quick and unexpected success in long-form infomercials was something easily reproduced). No one likes sharing their failures, but as Marty always said, the only things worth talking about are the things you can't talk about. So here's how I nearly tanked our LTV with an incongruent offer.

In the early 1990s, list rental was lucrative for the company. But we didn't accept advertising, and we were aggressive marketers, reinvesting most of our profits back into the business in order to mail as many millions of names as we could to grow circulation and to create long-term revenue. Direct mail was (and still is) very expensive because it scales and because it works. But that expense can be very stressful to manage.

One day, we were sent a request from a mailer to use our lists for an offer that, simply put, we would never have thought to expose our list to. Not surprisingly, this mailer often had trouble getting list owners to give them names for list rental. For me as the list manager, this seemed like an easy rejection: it wasn't something I felt comfortable approving for our customers. However, before I rejected the order, I turned the envelope upside down to see if there was anything else in it, and out came a check from the list broker who sent the request . . . for $100,000.

That was *a lot* of money for a list rental, since it was basically for a one-time use of the list. It was roughly the same amount we would receive for over two weeks in list rental income at the time, across *all* mailers using our list.

In direct mail, the recipient of the mailing rarely knew which list was used to rent their name. I went to a couple of my mentors at the time outside the company to get their opinion. The general feeling was that there probably wouldn't be any harm in it.

Looking back I should never have asked anyone who didn't have skin in the game with our customers for their advice. I should have followed my gut and sent the check back with a rejection.

I knew that was the right thing to do . . . but I didn't do it.

Even though none of our customers traced the mailing to us, one of our most trusted exchange partners (a huge publisher we exchanged millions of names with) got a complaint from one of *their* subscribers. At first, they couldn't figure out where this rogue campaign had come from . . . but eventually they realized that this person was subscribed to their publication *and* ours. Soon enough, all the evidence pointed to me. I had to confess to our exchange partner to renting names to that campaign. I would never do anything like this again, and it was a lesson for a lifetime. Simply put, your LTV on all channels will go to zero if you gamble with the respect of the most important people to your business—your customers.

You might read this story and think you would never do something like that. And I hope that's the case. But it's hard to know ahead of time what lines you might cross if you need cash and it seems like your business depends on you making a distasteful deal. Before you make your final decision, think long and hard about congruency and how being incongruent can affect the lifetime value of your customers . . . and of your business.

These are the critical lessons I took from this situation:

- Never make decisions when the need for money can take precedence over your core principles and what you know is right.

- Never forget that as marketers we are all connected. This is more true today than ever, since we mail for other people under our own names (as affiliates). But even on channels where you can hide for the most part (exchanging names in direct mail was more anonymous), we found out the hard way that everything comes to light eventually. Every action you take can have repercussions that you can't predict, given how interwoven marketing communities are and how much overlap many lists have.

- Always consult with multiple people with a variety of viewpoints who will tell you when there might be a moose on the table.

Of course, whether an offer is questionable is often in the eyes of the beholder . . . but always think about the perspective of your core customers before you send something that could be incongruent. I've seen offers sent to lists online today that are so disconnected to the audience that it's obvious the mailing was done for a quick cash injection or fulfilling a commitment to mail (reciprocation) or some other reason that has little to do with serving the customers.

I know of one online guru who had nearly half his list unsubscribe—a list that took years to build based on trust and integrity—because he sent an offer that had no congruence for his audience. In fact, it was a subject they had disdain for. Not only did he not make any money on the mailing, but he lost half his customers in the process. Ouch.

If you are playing a long game, there is no reciprocation for another marketer that should ever compromise how you want to treat your best customers. Or prospects. Or even suspects (people you eventually want to turn into prospects and then customers).

All in all, you can't create value for a lifetime without a total commitment to delivering exquisite products, value, integrity, congruency, and consistency.

Lifetime value is way more than a number.

KEY TAKEAWAYS

We've talked about LTV a lot in this book, and I hope you see that I've beat that drum so relentlessly because it's such a fundamental part of building a thriving business.

- A product is not a business. A promotion is not a business either.

- LTV is much more than just a number. Keeping LTV top of mind all the time will save you from making damaging decisions, show you major growth opportunities, and give you the best chance of "finishing rich."

- LTV allows you to accurately predict your bogey— how much you can afford to lose on your initial sales or cost of acquisition in order to make it back (and more) over time.

- Knowing your LTV and bogey allows you to spend aggressively (and strategically) on marketing because you know exactly when you will make your money back.

- Renewals and multiple product orders rule the day, which means that you must develop editorial excellence throughout your company. Remember, marketers sell subscriptions, but editors sell renewals; or, more broadly, product sellers sell subscriptions but product producers sell renewals.

- Be aggressive but disciplined in how you spend on customer acquisition. Don't extend your bogey out so far that you run into cash-flow problems. If you can, vary the bogey across your different product lines to ensure that you have regular cash flow regardless of the different product sales cycles.

- Staying in business for a lifetime requires knowing your numbers and doing everything you can to maintain a congruent message and approach that connects deeply with your customers.

- Be incongruent at your own risk. And when the decision comes down to needing the money, make sure there's no moose on the table.

CHAPTER 10

PLAYING THE LONG GAME

"Life is long."

—MARTIN EDELSTON

I hate the word *networking*. And that is despite having a reputation as someone who connects the dots as well as anyone once I know the superpowers of the people I interact with.

I guess networking and making valuable connections is one of my own superpowers—but I still hate the term. My distaste for the word (and the idea behind it) stems from my late 20s, when I was featured in a trade magazine in one of those "30 under 30" profile pieces, which on the one hand I was very proud of, though on the other hand, I was a bit embarrassed. The profile dubbed me a "strategic schmoozer," which to me implied that I was more fluff than substance . . . or that I had some secret agenda when I met people or added them to my network. Because of that article, I was concerned that people might perceive me as disingenuous. I believe it is the reason why I am so uninterested in superficial networking today—and why my take on this important area has evolved into something much more.

I'm glad I picked up on this before I was all grown up. I realized that it was not enough to simply *tell* everyone about my motivation to help as many people as possible by connecting them to others who could help them. I needed to *show* everyone that I was much more than a strategic schmoozer. I became intensely driven to create synergistic partnerships and relationships . . . but I needed to come up with different ways to do it than simply accumulating people and being the life of the party.

After that article, I thought more deeply about this concept. I remember attending a multiday personal development seminar and when I arrived, they asked us to define who we were—and I defined my core motivations as "Know everyone. Do the right thing."

At the end of the seminar, after lots of discussion and hard work on myself, they asked me to answer the same question, phrasing it, "I am the possibility of _____." The word that filled in the blank for me was, and still is, "contribution." I wanted to be a strategic *contributor* first, with the connection flowing naturally from there. Networking for me had now become contributing in order to connect, and a much longer (and more meaningful) game had begun.

LEARNING FROM GIANTS

This chapter is a collection of lessons accumulated over my career, both during my time at Boardroom and since. I've been privileged to know and learn from some of the best minds covering three generations of direct marketers; and while there is strategic and tactical brilliance at play, it's the intangibles that have made all of them so remarkable.

And I didn't ask these folks to write blurbs for this book simply to sell more books. I approached them because they have been the biggest influencers throughout my career. In every case, the relationship began with how I could first contribute to them . . . and then letting things take their course. Having Jay Abraham write the foreword to this book is indicative of how much I stand on the shoulders of giants and how important it is for me to recognize as many of them as I can. This is directly related to Adam Grant's "givers, takers, and matchers" concept . . . and now I can share examples with you of how this played out for me over almost 40 years in direct marketing and how I believe you can apply these principles to your life too.

I didn't want this to be a personal development book, not because the world doesn't need more personal development, but again, because there are better people than me to write those books. However, it would be a disservice to you, your career, and your business if we didn't take a deep dive into these intangibles. They will help make overdelivery, humility, and curiosity a way of life, and they will make you a better direct marketer too.

THE REAL VITAMIN C (IT'S NOT IN YOUR OJ)

Not only do I hate the word "networking," but I also think it's one of the most overused terms in the business world today. And given the omnipresence of social media, and that these powerful connection tools are often in the hands of amateurs, the idea of creating a network by pinging anyone and everyone with a smartphone makes me hate the term more than ever.

Accepting a request from every stranger who sends you one on Facebook or LinkedIn is far from the gold standard. In fact, I wouldn't really even call that networking; it's just screensucking (as ADHD expert Ned Hallowell calls it) . . . with little or no chance for true connection. Clicking a button is never going to build a genuine relationship with anyone.

I would like to share some observations and techniques I use to establish real connection with people, even in a world where relationship building has been reduced to clicking on a face (Facebook) or a one-sentence introduction supplied by someone else (LinkedIn).

To truly connect with people, you must contribute to them first with no expectation of a return (even though you'll probably get a return if you're investing in high-quality people). Ned

Hallowell, who I just referred to as one of the world's leading experts on ADHD, was also a frequent contributor to the Boardroom newsletters and a brilliant author of close to 20 books (my favorites are *Crazy Busy* and *Driven to Distraction*). He sent me a beautiful note some years ago in response to a blog post I wrote about the notion of "contributing to connect" replacing the notion of networking:

> You are a master of what this world needs most, and what has been the cornerstone of all my books: the power of connection. I call it the other Vitamin C, Vitamin Connect, and we live in a world where most people suffer from a deficiency of it. Glued to their electronics, they get massive doses of electronic connection, which in no way imparts the life-enhancing, indeed life-saving, power of the true Vitamin Connect . . . and the beauty of it is that it is free, and infinite in supply.

I know it sounds old-fashioned, but face-to-face connection trumps all. The fastest way to become deficient in Vitamin C(onnect) is to stare at your computer all day, screensucking and pretending that you have real relationships with people on the other end of an algorithm.

While there is obviously lots of utility—and convenience—in connecting electronically, that doesn't mean you should be taking shortcuts if your first interaction with someone is online. For example, I send dozens of personal e-mails every week to folks who send me LinkedIn requests—that is, before I simply accept the invitation, I look at their profile and shared connections and acknowledge what kind of overlap we have in our respective worlds.

I also encourage them to look at some of my writing and to opt into my list (in addition to scoping out my profile) for the purpose of staying in touch and starting a real relationship. I am so far away from thinking about selling them anything at this point—or trying to figure out what the benefit might be. However, I know that the odds of creating any kind of mutual benefit are much lower if I simply hit ACCEPT.

It's also what happens after this that matters. If they opt in to my list and they e-mail me, even in response to an automated e-mail blast or blog post, I answer the e-mail one-on-one; and of course, if there is ever any chance to meet them face-to-face sometime in the future, I would look for that opportunity when it makes sense.

Whatever you do, do something that creates a *real* connection with that person—even at the earliest stages of what could be a lifelong relationship. This philosophy needs to be consistent everywhere in your life in how you contribute to connect. I guarantee that you will find this kind of networking far more rewarding than just hitting ACCEPT without finding out more about the people you come into contact with.

It's sort of ironic that the guy who mailed close to two billion pieces of direct mail (not exactly an intimate form of communication) is talking to you about how to create a personal relationship with everyone you come in contact with . . . but I really mean it.

Being a mass marketer has not stopped me—in fact, it has only fueled me—to connect more deeply whenever possible and appropriate. That's why I loved answering customer service calls; it's why I return every e-mail that comes into my inbox; and it's why I meet as many folks as I can if I think I can contribute to them in some way.

I understand that sometimes you can't be that personal. But here is what I want to stress: never connect at a superficial level when connecting at a deeper level will only take a little more time and effort. It's worth it. Start as you want to finish. Develop a deeper relationship in the long term by avoiding shallow communication in the short term. And always put something special (and personal) into all your communications.

If you start with what you can contribute to the other person first, you are guaranteed to inject the maximum amount of "Vitamin C" into your bloodstream. It's so simple, yet so powerful. Another way to dose up on "Vitamin C" is differentiation: do something different to stick out—and not just for the sake of sticking out. Stick out because it really matters to create something extra special with every person you interact with.

I speak often to recent college graduates about opportunities in direct marketing. I ask them how many of them send an e-mail after they interview for a job or meet someone new who might be able to help them with their career. Just about everyone raises their hand. Then I ask, "How many of you actually send a handwritten card or a formal business letter as follow-up?" After I explain how you actually do that using the old artifacts of pen and paper, maybe a third of the room raise their hands. Sometimes I'm happy to see any hands at all. Then I suggest a different approach with my final question: "And how many of you look for areas of common interest with the person interviewing you—an author, a magazine, a subject area—and then use that in your follow-up, beyond just mentioning something in an e-mail? For example, sending a handwritten note or letter and maybe an article about something you discussed?"

Of course, no one raises their hand for that one.

At that point, I always whisper loudly into my microphone to really emphasize the point: "If you do something like that, no one else will be doing it, and that's a good thing. Even if you don't get the job, you will be remembered, which is always better than being forgotten."

This applies to anyone in business looking to find common ground and to connect beyond a superficial level. Whether you're at the beginning of your career or established in your career, contributing to connect should always be part of your playbook.

Marty always sent what he called "nice notes" all year round rather than just sending the important people in his world a card during holidays and milestones with everyone else. He believed that you should connect with people as the mood hits you, as things come across your desk that would create connection.

These are just a couple of tactics you can put your own stamp on. The ingenuity you use in how you contribute—and then connect—needs to be congruent with who you are and what you are comfortable with—but don't just do what everyone else does.

Bottom line: get your daily dose of Vitamin C(onnect) and avoid being a strategic schmoozer at all costs. When you invest intentionally in relationships with remarkable people, the return you get far outweighs any financial investment you could make. But I'm not naive. Being in business and creating relationships is also about making money. Contributing to connect might actually be your biggest moneymaker in the long run too (since many successful people want to partner with people they know, like, and trust).

However, this is a chapter about playing the long game and creating not just a network but rather "relationship capital"— the account that will have the biggest impact on your life and business, because it's worth a lot more than cash.

THE COMPOUND INTEREST ON RELATIONSHIP CAPITAL

My love for contributing and connecting has turned me into a mastermind junkie and a people junkie. I can never get enough great content from great people, and most of the other world-class marketers I know are the same way. It's impossible to calculate the value of being a lifelong student. The friendships and relationships I've developed this way mean the world to me and have been incredibly powerful forces in every part of my life. (Not to mention all the frequent flier miles I've accumulated.)

Moving from strategic schmoozer to "contributing to connect" and eventually learning how to invest deeply in relationship capital has been a lifelong journey. It started with that uncomfortable article, which motivated me to do a lot of work on myself. When it started having a big impact on my life, I kept at it. And it culminated in a huge way in 2014 with the Titans of Direct Response event . . . and shortly after the event and retiring from Boardroom, I started my blog. One of my first posts was about how I got all those huge names to speak at the Titans event (and, even more impressive, got some of them to come out of retirement and/or seclusion). From

Dan Kennedy and Jay Abraham to Gary Bencivenga and Greg Renker, the biggest living legends in direct marketing graced the event . . . and I can admit to you here that making those requests was painless (and gratifying).

Now, I could simply chalk up their willingness to appear to the fact that I'm a nice guy and that I always try to be appreciative and respectful. But it was more than that. The event was a tribute to Marty, who had died the year before. His stature in the industry as a legendary contributor didn't hurt in getting folks to step up, and at the time, I actually thought it was mostly that aspect that made the event such an easy sell to all these powerful speakers.

But since then, I have brought together more amazing direct response marketers and copywriters in my two mastermind groups, along with guests to regularly speak to those groups. These guests are all titans in their specialties, so I knew there was something more here. It's the relationship capital I had built with all of them.

You may find this hard to believe, but relationship capital is far more valuable than any asset in your financial portfolio. It has nothing to do with getting rich quick. It travels well, and it is accepted everywhere. This kind of capital is forever, and what you can "buy" with it doesn't take up storage space or require heavy management fees from a financial planner (although it does need to be watched very closely).

RELATIONSHIP CAPITAL IS AN INVESTMENT FOR A LIFETIME

So how does the special currency of relationship capital get deposited into your personal account and accumulate compound interest over time? Well, we can start with why all those icons in direct response marketing said yes so quickly to speak at Titans, why they continue to say yes, and why it was easy and natural for me to make the request of each of them. As I said, politeness and my connection to Marty has a lot to do with it . . . but building up my personal account had been a long time in the making.

I know how it *didn't* happen. It had nothing to do with trying to build the largest LinkedIn or Facebook account . . . and it didn't happen by contacting people only when I wanted or needed something. It also didn't happen by accident—it happened by being committed to consistent communication and always thinking about how I could contribute to the other person first. But even more important, it also happened because I truly care about these people and have consistently let them know how much I appreciate them, sincerely, and never just as a way to ask them for something.

Without playing a long game of contributing first and always caring, any "new deposits" into your account might as well be Monopoly money. There's no "interest" accumulated when you are simply playing a numbers game with your contacts, only going a mile wide and not thinking about how you can go a mile deep.

Someone said to me a while ago that it is far more gratifying and powerful to be interested than interesting. That doesn't mean you should sit on your butt all day not creating stuff that others find interesting . . . but try to notice when your conversations are all about you. At that point, turn the conversations around to focus on the people around you and the people you want to connect with.

I've been accused many times of writing too much about myself instead of focusing exclusively on *you*, and I accept that I'm not perfect at this. And there are certainly a lot of I's in this book. It takes a lot of practice and a lot of humility to get the balance right. If this is a new concept for you, it can be hard to even make a start, given the conversations going on in our heads all day about the most important person in our lives: ourselves. Those are the voices we hear all day telling us how interesting we are—the "legends in our own minds" thing. That's why I recommend that you have people around you all the time who will make you accountable (and will tell you to shut up when it's all about you).

It's key to have true friends and mentors who keep you accountable so you don't always assume your next idea is your best idea ever. Making requests for accountability from your closest friends, advisers, and coaches regarding how you are showing up for people is also critically important—that is, getting some checks and balances on when you are talking too much about your own interests. I think you will agree that your closest friends should always tell you the truth, with love never leaving the room.

There are two things that must be eliminated when dealing with the folks around you in order to see the maximum yield on your relationship capital: complacency and arrogance. If you are too complacent (not engaging or being interested in the other person) or if you are arrogant (being a bit too "interesting" and making it all about you), you need an honest intervention from someone who cares about you. You can't invest in relationship capital if either of those things is getting in the way of how you interact with everyone around you. These two things will stop you in your tracks from creating a bigger future for yourself. And since I can't trust myself to be 100 percent aware all the time if either of those two things are creeping in, I surround myself with people who have permission to let me know immediately and loudly if I am becoming complacent or arrogant. I chose those people because I know they will tell me what I need to hear and that they will communicate it only with love and respect.

Here's the quick prescription for building your relationship capital account, which automatically includes compound interest:

- It's always about what you can contribute first to the other person, not what you can get from them. Find out what that person cares about and invest in that.

- Be appreciative and respectful always . . . I guess that's pretty obvious, but good manners never go out of style.

- Don't come out of nowhere with your communications to anyone. Be consistent, and don't presume to make an "ask" of someone, no matter how small, if you haven't invested in the relationship first.

- Have people around you to let you know when you are being complacent . . . firmly, directly, and in a spirit of love and respect.

- Have people around you that will let you know when you are being arrogant . . . firmly, directly, and in a spirit of love and respect (though a kick in the head might also be in order here).

- Do your homework when entering into any new "investment" (i.e., relationship). You probably ask a ton of questions before investing your money; you should ask just as many (or more) when bringing another person into your world.

A high-value relationship capital account doesn't happen easily or without a lot of time and effort. It must be valued as a privilege and not simply an asset. Cherish it and nurture it as you make additional deposits every day.

THE POWER OF INTENTIONAL DINNERS

Marty loved bringing together experts for meals . . . he created "expert lunches" early in his career to gather the best content for his publications and to make himself smarter. Those lunches evolved into something much more, what he eventually called The Boardroom Dinners. In many industry circles—including direct marketing, publishing, media, health, finance—these became legendary.

While eating dinner seems like a fairly straightforward endeavor, creating dinners over decades that were magical events involved a lot of planning and thinking. Buying dinner for a group of people is easy; making dinner an experience people will never forget takes a little work. Since I would encourage everyone to bring some variation of intentional dinners into their lives, I will share today what makes creating these gatherings so magical . . . and how profound they can be for you, your career, and everyone you feed.

The first dinner took place in Marty's New York City apartment, overlooking Central Park, catered by world-class chefs. Because of the size of his apartment, the dinners were limited to a maximum of 14 people (which is a fine number to make them work well). Marty would host a dinner each month, and it was considered a privilege when anyone in the Boardroom family of writers, sources, clients, and partners received an invitation.

As the company became more mature and the word spread about these special dinners, they only got bigger and more profound. Guests told their friends about the amazing conversations, connections, and projects that were coming out of the dinners, and soon people were reaching out to us for invitations. After Marty gave up the apartment, he began holding the dinners at the world-famous Four Seasons restaurant in New York City, where a seat at one of his "salons" became one of the most coveted invites across multiple industries.

Rick Frishman, an author and friend who attended many of these dinners, profiled them in his book *Networking Magic*, calling them "networking events that pay homage to a master networker and to his amazing passion for the best" and that "it is an honor to be invited." Another regular attendee, marketing consultant Ken Glickman, said that they were "evenings that create a tremendous amount of enthusiasm and positive energy."

Keep in mind, though, that all these extraordinary outcomes won't happen by accident. The more you plan in advance for success, the more success you will have. As you think about creating your own version of intentional dinners, remember the lessons we've talked about in this book regarding the need to love your customers (giving them more than they would ever expect), how to approach your partners (always making them feel like teammates), and the importance of being interested and invested in making people feel special. Dinners like these are a perfect way for you to express these core beliefs.

Be all about intention. Leave nothing to chance. Make your intentional dinner a platform and an individual expression of your own insatiable curiosity and that of your guests. Bring your brilliance, and the brilliance of those you most respect, forward in a bold way. By inviting other people who are as voracious and curious in self-education as yourself, you've created another way to "expand your library."

Making the Invite List

In the early days, Marty hosted the dinners by himself; later on, I had the privilege of co-hosting over 150 dinners with him. If you were an expert who appeared in any of our publications, you were immediately added to the guest list for the future. If you were an expert, author, speaker, or thought leader we met at a conference, or if you were someone we heard in the media, or someone fascinating we read about, your name would also be added to our invite list.

Assembling experts in every industry and vocation, and having them share with each other in their area of expertise, guaranteed that everybody left the room smarter after dinner. Marty's simple summation about the dinners was "There is no better way to spend an evening."

You can do the same thing, adding potential dinner guests as you go (in your current circles), and then adding guests in circles you constantly build as you make deposits into your relationship capital account. Plan them out in advance and give guests a choice of dates, especially if you have a lot of people in your world who live out of town.

Dinner Logistics: Intentionality Matters

Make sure you get biographies or CVs for all the guests in advance. The night before each dinner, read each person's biography carefully, and on the basis of common interest areas and connections you can plainly see (or sometimes just infer), create a seating chart to maximize the experience for every attendee. Seat people near each other who have clear synergies or have the potential to create opportunities together. Sometimes you might just think certain people would find each other fascinating.

I follow this procedure whenever I host a dinner at one of my Titans Mastermind meetings, or any time I host any kind of dinner, which I do often. While the events would probably work even if the seating were left to chance—since all the attendees are incredibly interesting people doing incredibly interesting things—the chances of creating bigger opportunities for guests is exponentially improved with this kind of planning.

The proof is that these dinners create more lasting friendships and profitable projects than any other kind of dinner I've ever attended. As Rich Frishman puts it:

> Since these kinds of dinners place a higher premium on the quality of the guests than on the areas of their expertise, focusing on a diverse range of businesses, professions, and disciplines gathering around the table is the priority. Guests in the past have been spellbound by information disclosed by experts on everything from terrorism to sex therapy. Medical researchers have explained the latest breakthroughs in their fields and a former White House staffer from the Kennedy White House has shared inside stories about the JFK era.

Sometimes randomness can even lead to fireworks, and I recall Marty and I being a little devilish when setting up the table when we did it together. There was the dinner when we had America's leading anti-tobacco physician scheduled to sit next to a well-known and very successful (but chain-smoking) publishing executive . . . and since those were the days when you could smoke cigarettes indoors, it was not surprising that neither guest was all that happy. As I remember, the executive left before dinner and the doctor ended up with an empty seat next to him. Oh well. Another time we sat a well-known physician— very traditional and set in his ways—next to a naturopathic physician. The naturopath promptly began making a case that more physicians needed to learn more about diet and nutrition in medical school, instead of simply learning to dispense prescription drugs for illness as the first line of defense. No one left in a huff that night . . . but the conversation was a lot spicier than the food.

Once you assemble your guests at their assigned seats, explain the purpose of the dinner—to bring together some of the most fascinating people you could find to share unique insights and ideas, have compelling conversations, and enjoy some excellent food at the same time. Or whatever your vision might be.

Prepare an index card from each guest's bio or C.V. and make it your job to introduce each of your special guests, with the intention of having everyone at the table be *interested* in each person rather than allowing each guest to share their own bio, which would only make them *interesting*. And while this is subtle, reading their bios for them rather than having them introduce themselves is far more powerful. It's always better to have others brag about you than to do it yourself.

After reading all the bios, tell everybody that it is time to enjoy their dinner, enjoy their neighbor, and if you want to steal from my playbook, remind them that they are all strategically placed at the table so they will have nothing in common with their dinner mates (jokingly emphasizing how strategically you have actually placed them).

Then let them know that after dinner, you will play "pass the mic," with each guest sharing something in their area of expertise for a few minutes. For those who tell you they are not really experts in anything (which is never true), hold your thumb and forefinger an inch apart and remind them of the Dick Benson premise that "Everyone knows everything about this much." (See below for more on this under "Everyone Belongs.")

If you like, have a few questions prepared for specific attendees if there is a hot topic you would like to discuss with the table.

Dinner Follow-Up

After the dinner conversation is completed and before the guests leave, promise everyone that they will get a list with the contact information of all the attendees. In addition, if any of your guests have a book, an article, or material they want to share with the group, invite them to send that to you so you can include those extras in the "goodie bag" that becomes the follow-up package from the dinner (including the contact info). A bulky package beats a follow-up e-mail every time.

Everyone Belongs

Don't allow anyone to play small at your dinners. As you create bigger and better dinners, someone is bound to look around and wonder if they really belong. I say shut that down immediately, having fallen into the same trap myself. If this does happen, explain why they belong as much as anyone and that you are very excited that they are there, and that you can't wait to hear what they were going to share. If they don't believe you, emphasize to them that everybody is an expert in something, and when you share your expertise and your passion in a way that is totally giving, extraordinary things happen for everyone around you. And that's precisely the reason why dinners like these are so profound in their simplicity.

A small but important point: it's critical that there is no outside noise and that you have complete privacy. And one other crucial detail: the dinner must be at one long table so everyone can see everyone else at all times. Always close the table, with the hosts (or host and a VIP) at the head and tail. It gives the room a feeling of much more community when it's closed. I don't recommend more than 30 at one of these events, and I have found that 15 to 20 is an ideal number.

One of the most incredible experiences of my career was when I had 67 people at a VIP dinner at the Titans of Direct Response event—yes, at one long table. At the other end of the table from me was marketing icon and Titans keynote speaker Dan Kennedy. I would have needed a bullhorn to get his attention, but, thank goodness, we had a microphone system when we played "pass the mic." We didn't get to everyone around the table that night, but we did teach everyone how to set up an intentional dinner as a tribute to Marty, who invented them.

Frishman sums it up perfectly:

> Start with the best people you can reach. Invite your most interesting, enjoyable, entertaining friends and contacts. Invite people you've heard about but don't know. Invite people whom you've wanted to meet. Select guests who are experts in fields that interest you and in areas that you know nothing about. It doesn't have to be all talk. If you know musicians, poets, or entertainers, then ask them to your gathering to liven up and diversify the mix.
>
> Work on a scale that you can afford. Although good food certainly helps, great people should be your top priority. So when you're starting out, think first about the quality of your guests, about attracting the very best people. And if the food is a way to attract heavy hitters, do whatever you can, within your means, to get them to the table. Then get them talking.
>
> Prepare and ask questions that will make your guests expound. Once they're talking, sit back and let the magic work.

You'll be amazed at what can happen when you add intentionality and structure to something as simple as a dinner.

A SIMPLER (BUT EQUALLY POWERFUL) VERSION OF INTENTIONAL DINNERS

Even if the idea of organizing one of these dinners seems a bit overwhelming or you are not comfortable doing something quite that large, there is another format I love (since I never want you to waste an opportunity to learn and grow with every meal . . . and I am not talking about your waistline).

Two amazing entrepreneurs I am lucky enough to consider great friends, Michael Fishman and Ramit Sethi, invented their own version of an intentional dinner format that I will call "The Six-Person Anytime/Anywhere Dinner." This works best when you have a planning partner (as Michael and Ramit had in each other). Each person invites two superstars in their world that the partner has not met before or doesn't know well. You end up with six people in a single conversation for the entire dinner. It's okay in this format for each person to do their own intro (with prompts from the hosts). My favorite prompts are:

- What is your superpower?
- What is your biggest success?
- What is your biggest failure?
- If you could have dinner with anyone in history (besides the other five people at this table!) who would it be, and why?

Of course, you will have many more questions of your own as people start talking.

Imperative for The Six-Person Anytime/Anywhere Dinner is a round table and a quiet spot in a restaurant (if you can't do it in a private room). These smaller dinners are so easy to do, and you can do them as often as you like. For example, whenever I attend a large event or seminar and I did not have time to plan anything in advance, I always look for five other people that I know I can learn from and create a Six-Person Dinner on the fly.

I think you can see that something as simple yet profound as these intentional dinners can be a pretty hefty deposit into your relationship capital account on a regular, consistent basis.

I'll spend the rest of this chapter discussing five additional concepts that will contribute to investing in your own relationship capital. I think each of these can be adapted with all you do in business—and in your personal life, too.

1. EMBRACE COMPETITION AS COEXISTENCE

When we approach business with a spirit of generosity and humility, everyone we come into contact with has to up their game. It's good for us individually, and it's good for business. This is one of the reasons I have a portrait of legendary New York Yankees pitcher Mariano Rivera in my office, even though I'm a die-hard Mets fan. (Those of you who are not from New York may not know that Yankees fans and Mets fans are super competitive with each other and it's understood that you must choose whether to be a fan of one or the other but never both.)

While I never really root for the Yankees, Rivera is still my favorite player of all time because he embodied this philosophy of competitive coexistence. He is the best closer the game has ever seen. (A closer is the pitcher responsible for getting the last three batters out when your team is ahead—and they are the hardest three outs, since getting them means you win and not getting them means you lose.) What is fascinating about Rivera is that he was the best at this high-pressure job in the history of the game, yet he only had one pitch (most pitchers have an arsenal of different pitches, like a fastball, a curveball, a changeup, etc.). The one pitch Rivera had—called a cut fastball—was lethal. It looked good enough to hit until the last second, then it dropped down drastically as a batter tried to hit it. The result was usually Rivera 1, batter 0. Much of the time, he was unhittable.

What is extraordinary, however, is that he was an open book about his superpower of throwing this unhittable pitch with every player and coach that came to him for help—whether they were on his team or not. Instead of guarding his incredible ability and refusing to share it, he openly shared how to throw it to anyone who asked. He knew that his role wasn't just to win games, but to make everyone, and the sport, better. A rising tide lifts all boats. While I can't prove this, I also think he knew that no one could really throw the pitch as well as he did (even with personal instruction from him); and if for some reason they did learn how to do it better, he'd have a worthy competitor to surpass instead of just being the best with no real competition.

It's the same in business. If you share your secret sauce, and you're generous with your time and insights, everyone in your industry will have to raise their standards. Sharing your best stuff freely will inevitably help your customers trust you more and make your competitors respect you more. And an added bonus is that your ego will be kept in check—always a good thing.

Copywriting great Gary Bencivenga was Rivera-like in terms of teaching his most valuable writing secrets. And since he still had a formidable track record of getting winners against all the top copywriters he ever competed with, I know that embracing this concept only made him better.

I don't mean to depress you with another take on this, but whether you like it or not, a hundred years from now (no matter how young you are today), we will all be in the ground with lots of dirt on top of us. Taking your best work and best ideas to the grave might be okay for you, but it's not for me. I only say this to put competition into perspective. Facing down your own mortality has a way of helping you stay calm and let go of having to constantly keep what you think are secrets to yourself.

2. DON'T MAKE YOUR LAWYER RICH

Some of my best friends are attorneys. I also know many recovering attorneys who I like a lot too. However, even though we all need legal advice from time to time, I will submit to you that there are better ways to do business than living lawsuit to lawsuit and always thinking "adversarial" rather than "peaceful coexistence."

The story that follows proves that it's a lot harder to build relationship capital when you immediately think "problem first" rather than "potential opportunity first." And it's also a lot harder if you are one of those people who will die on a sword over "the principle of the thing." If you tend to hold on to things at all costs to prove a point, I encourage you to read on, and if you don't, read on anyway, because I think this story will reinforce how we should always try to turn lemons into lemonade as our *first* course of action.

When I hosted the Titans of Direct Response event in 2014, one of the first things I needed to do was to create a logo—so I went to an online design site and held a contest. I ended up with something I loved, with colors and a font that fit the magnitude of the event, and a titan's shield that was powerful yet subtle.

Using the event as a springboard, I branded everything I have done since under Titans: Titans Mastermind, Titans Master Class, Titans DVDs, and Titans Marketing (which I was even able to trademark). After launching Titans Marketing about a year after the 2014 event, a friend e-mailed me to say that there was an up-and-coming online marketing company calling themselves Titans of Marketing.

Despite having a trademark, I don't *own* the word "titan," and the term gets around: it's been used by NFL teams past and present, by various gurus in other industries, and even by a company that places advertising at bus stops in New York City. But Titans of Marketing? That sounded too close for comfort. So I went to their website, and while they were not competing directly with me, what was shocking was their logo—the colors and font were identical to mine, but instead of the shield, there was a Spartan helmet. What was also strange was that the helmet logo was from a design given to me during my own design contest, which I rejected in favor of the shield. What to do?

My attorney suggested we send a cease and desist letter, which I considered . . . but not for very long. Others suggested I sue them outright (and not all those folks were lawyers, mind you). Still others told me to forget about them, saying that anyone who would show such little imagination and ingenuity would not stand the test of time and they would be out of business before we knew it.

I decided not to take any legal action, which was easy, based on all the lessons I had learned up until that point regarding the waste of time and money a lawsuit entails. After 30-plus years of watching people rip off promotions, copy, and titles (and more) from right under our noses and the noses of friends and colleagues alike, I knew that chasing every little infraction by taking some kind of legal action was only a distraction and would not be a good use of my energy or time.

And of course, pursuing stuff like this is a great a way to add to the billable hours of your friendly attorney, often with little or no return on that money. When legal situations arose throughout my career, I did a simple calculation in my mind of not only the money going out to an attorney but the opportunity cost and money lost by not staying focused on marketing. I remember a comment from Marty once when we were dealing with a legal situation that involved a rip-off: "I don't want lawyers running our business. I just want reasonable and intelligent lawyers helping us do the right thing. And suing will never be our first option."

For a while I decided to just forget about those "other Titans," until one day I discovered that one of the partners in that business had sent me a friend request on Facebook (which I hadn't gotten around to accepting yet)—and he had even liked a post of mine.

I decided to reach out to him directly. No lawyer required. I privately messaged him on Facebook, asking him why he would be so lazy with the naming of his company, and especially with the development of his typeface and logo. I wrote the note assuming he had heard of my epic event, and that he wanted to cash in on the tsunami that was the Titans brand in direct marketing. Well, he clearly was not aware of my press clippings . . . he didn't even know who I was or what I was talking about. I got a good lesson in getting over myself. But that's not the biggest lesson from this story.

Once we connected and I showed him what I was talking about—my logo and branding next to his—he was shocked.

Together we figured out what happened, and both of us learned two very valuable lessons.

Lesson #1 (Micro)

When you go to a public site to get work from designers who are not getting paid top dollar, don't assume they are being 100 percent original. It became clear to us that that someone took a good design that failed to win a previous contest (mine) and figured they could recycle it for another contest without changing very much. Of course, "stealing is a felony; stealing smart is an art." I guess this example was neither a felony nor art. It was just opportunistic on the designer's part . . . and the Titans of Marketing were simply caught in the crossfire. I didn't need to accuse anyone of anything.

Lesson #2 (Macro)

Jumping to conclusions—and jumping to legal action without all the facts—is a waste of time and money. When I discovered the truth, I felt there was now lemonade to be made from lemons. I scheduled a call to learn more about these competitive Titans, their business, their overall mission, and their future plans as coexisting Titans.

What I found were two young, ambitious entrepreneurs—full of enthusiasm for marketing and the direct response business we all love—actually, the kind of marketers I regularly seek to attract to my tribe. On the call, they volunteered to change their name before I even asked, saying they would be going in a completely new direction with their branding and their logo. They seemed inspired to raise the bar higher for their business after the call, and I was inspired to help them.

I offered my consulting services at no charge to create their new brand, and I began asking more about what they offered to their clients and how we might even work together. It turned out that their skill set had tremendous value to various clients and mastermind members I was serving at the time. And while I didn't ask them for anything specific in return, they offered to sell, as an affiliate partner, the $2,000 product from the Titans of Direct Response event I had created (a package of DVDs, interviews, and swipe files that were sold to those who were unable to attend). And of course I offered them an affiliate commission for every one they sold.

These guys went from being the jerks ripping me off to my newest affiliate partner. This felt much better than paying legal fees, and I'm sure they would agree that the last thing they would have wanted was the stress and cost of legal action from me.

And the story goes on . . . I spoke at a large online marketing conference some years later, and one of the partners from the former Titans of Marketing was sitting in the front row while I was on stage. After the event, he was one of the first people to post on Facebook saying nice things about me (and no, it had nothing to do with the affiliate commissions I had paid him in the past). He went from potential adversary to friend for life.

This is not an isolated incident. I have had many experiences over my career that speak to this theme. Many don't involve legal issues or lawyers, but they all work on the premise that assuming the worst of people as your first reaction is *not* a winning formula for a peaceful life. Or for a relationship capital account you can access at any point in your career.

I even had a dose of inspiration from my mentor on this topic on one of the saddest days of my life. Marty was on his deathbed, and I couldn't believe it when he asked what I was working on. The man was unstoppable, right to the end. I told him about a few tricky deals that were going on at the company, and through a difficult breath he just said, "Be fair."

Obviously Marty had taught me that lesson over the previous 30 years too, and it stays with me every day. Don't always think in terms of getting the advantage, whether it's your partners, employees, consultants, or competitors—they all deserve respect and fair treatment, even on the days when it's the last thing you feel like giving them. Keep litigious thinking out of

all you do. Of course, sometimes you may actually need a lawyer
. . . but above all, be fair.

3. REMEMBER THAT SOMEONE IS ALWAYS WATCHING

On January 1, 2000, my clock and computer continued to
work (despite the fear that the world would end with the coming
of the new millennium) . . . and later that month, I traveled to
Los Angeles for Jay Abraham's "all superstar event" dedicated
to some new marketing medium called the Internet. Jay—along
with fellow direct response rock stars Audri and Jim Lanford—
created an event like no other at the time. They called it the Billion Dollar Internet Strategy Setting Summit. Not a big promise
at all, right?

Despite the hyperbole, it sounded interesting. And after all,
it was Jay. Only someone with his experience could legitimately
put a billion-dollar claim on an unproven medium . . . and he
delivered a massive amount of value. I learned a ton at the event
and made some lifelong friends there as well, many of whom
became important people that I've followed and learned from
over the years, including Audri and Jim Lanford, Paul Hartunian,
Dana Blankenhorn, Jim Sterne, Corey Rudl, and of course, Jay
Abraham. And unbeknownst to me, there were people watching me back then who I wasn't even aware of—future superstars
who became life changing for me much later.

Thirteen years later, a LinkedIn request hit my inbox out of
the blue from a guy by the name of Jeff Walker. I had heard of
Jeff and admired him, but I had no idea that he was at that event
back in 2000. If you don't know Jeff by name, you may know his
Product Launch Formula process—which has been responsible
for close to a billion dollars' worth of online sales of products
and services to date (I guess it proves that Jay knew what he was
talking about when he named the seminar).

Jeff is a marketing genius and one of the real good guys in
this business. He's got a heart of gold to go along with being
a marketing badass (and to me, "badass" is at the top of the

marketing food chain). But if not for the Abraham-Lanford event (and my philosophy of responding to LinkedIn requests), Jeff would have remained just one more amazing person I looked up to in this fantastic industry.

My response to the LinkedIn request from Jeff was "Is this *the* Jeff Walker?" And to my surprise, I received a response back from Jeff saying he had followed my career for many years and he was a fan. Who knew? I surely didn't. I had known of him for a long time, but at the time of his LinkedIn request, I can't say we had ever truly connected . . . so when I asked him how he knew me, he told me this story.

He had scraped and clawed his way to Los Angeles to attend Jay's event in 2000 (with no idea how he was going to afford it) to learn for himself how to create a billion-dollar Internet strategy. He said he watched me moderate a roundtable discussion on something at that event and had been impressed. He couldn't believe how much I was sharing without any expectation of anything in return, since I was a paying attendee and not technically a speaker. I had no recollection of this at all . . . but it wasn't simply dumb luck that I was on my best behavior when Jeff was observing me. Consistency, congruency, integrity, being yourself at all times, always showing up with your best, no matter the situation—those qualities win every time. And as this crazy situation shows, you never know who's watching and what opportunities might turn up for you when you are playing a long game.

This reconnection to Jeff on LinkedIn led to an invitation to his Platinum Plus mastermind group in January of 2013, where I met and interacted with 30 of the most successful folks in Jeff's tribe. I fell in love with all of them. They all just gave and gave . . . and still give and give. Jeff attracts the best of the best marketers with the biggest hearts. In addition, despite most of them being a lot younger than me, they knew as much (or more) about direct response marketing (and how it drives all marketing, regardless of channel) as I did. I probably had 20 more years of experience than most of them, but even so, I was by no means the smartest person in the room—so I knew I was in the right room.

My experience with Jeff's mastermind made me join the group as a paying member, and I have never looked back. Being a member has been equivalent to studying for my Ph.D. in online marketing (and entrepreneurship). I should have my degree in a few decades. Not only have many of the members of that mastermind been guest speakers at my own mastermind group, I have done a considerable amount of business with others—and it's where I got to know Reid Tracy at a much deeper level, which led to this book being published by Hay House. All that from just being a nice guy and sharing at a roundtable, not knowing everyone who was there but knowing that everyone who was there mattered.

And I'm so glad that the world didn't end on December 31, 1999.

4. SEND CHRISTMAS CARDS IN JULY

When the doorbell rang early one December morning, I was reluctant to answer. But I could see a guy through the window wearing a brown suit (not one of my favorite fashion colors), and when I made out the UPS logo on his shirt and saw his matching brown truck in my driveway, I ran to open the door. Whatever he had for me was going to be better than any e-mail or PDF I was reading or downloading. Packages are welcome on my doorstep all year round—how about for you?

Then later in the day, I waited in a very long line at the post office behind a guy with a shoebox full of Christmas cards stamped and ready to go. I thought it was kind of early for that, being the week after Thanksgiving, but I admired his preparation. And it got me thinking.

If you are one of those people who sends cards to everyone important in your life sometime before Christmas, do you also stay in touch all year round? Kudos to you if you do that, since I believe that true contribution and connection with the most important people in your life is not a one-time-a-year thing; and I also believe it's much more powerful when we go beyond just sending cards.

I am not anti-Christmas or anti–New Year, so please don't call me a grinch, but I would like you to consider a different take on all of this. Thinking you have deepened your relationships with everyone in your address book simply by sending a card might be worth reconsidering. It's not the worst thing you can do, but there are additional meaningful things you may want to consider.

How many of the cards that you receive during the holidays are memorable? Do you save them? Do they enhance your life beyond that moment? The beauty of thinking about everyone in your life all year round and not having to look for an excuse (or holiday) to connect is that it truly builds relationship capital. And I will add that the lumpier the packages you send, the better—but anything is better than nothing. E-mail is nice . . . a physical card is better . . . and something that barely fits in the mailbox is best.

Here's a quick story to illustrate why "lumpy direct mail" is also not just for folks over 50. I was with a client a few years ago and everyone around the table was younger than me (this happens more often these days . . . which I love). I asked the youngest person at the table (she was in her mid-20s), "Do you own a mailbox?" Thank goodness she said yes, because I was afraid my next question was going to be "Do you know what a mailbox is?"

Then I asked, "When you go to your mailbox, if there is something in it that is thicker, bulkier, and not in a traditional envelope (and addressed by hand), would you open that first when you get back inside?" She said she actually opens stuff like that *before* she gets inside, way before checking her other mail . . . and way, way before she checks her e-mail or phone. Remember, your least crowded inbox is not in your computer.

This focus group of one told me it's possible that sending three-dimensional packages to the people we love most might not have a minimum age requirement. I have since checked this out with other 20-somethings and my research has proved the theory that they also like big packages in their mailboxes. Lumpy packages have stuck out in crowded mailboxes for decades. They stick out even more now in less crowded mailboxes. They're fun for all ages in all seasons. And they are especially powerful when personalized.

In addition, assuming that your customer doesn't live in an area where parcels are routinely stolen, your package and the message will actually get delivered. With impact. And keep in mind that the United States Postal Service is often kinder and gentler than whoever is responsible for delivering your e-mail, and they will not label your physical mail as "spam"—it will almost always get delivered.

As you have learned, list segmentation rules . . . whether it's a huge subscriber list or buyers list or a list of business VIPs or just friends and family. Sending thoughtful gifts and small, targeted mailings is just another form of segmented, personalized direct mail that anyone can use effectively.

The Power of Regifting (To Get You Started)

Believe it or not, you can make a huge impact without paying anything *except* the postage . . . and if you think you look like a cheapskate when you regift, think again. Let me give you some examples that might inspire you to think of ways to deepen your contributions to the VIPs in your life without ever going to a store or logging onto Amazon. Hopefully you will see in the examples below that it is always the thought that counts and that the gift can simply be part of the guaranteed delivery system of the thought. Think "presence" over "presents" . . . but do both with your gifting and regifting.

Reading is fundamental.

Every book you receive as a gift that you own already is thoughtfulness ready for a mini direct mail campaign. When I receive a duplicate book, I immediately think, *Who in my life would this help, enhance, or create value for?* It's the note with the book that shows how much you care and how much you were thinking about them . . . and if you need to admit it's a "regift," feel free.

Sugar is sweet but not for me.

I often receive a lot of food that I don't eat or can't eat (e.g., sweets). I recently received something delicious from an exotic place, which was very thoughtful—I still sent a thank-you note. Unfortunately, the delicacies in question were not on my diet. But I remembered a good friend of mine had just vacationed in the same exotic place, so I sent them to him with a special note saying how much he meant to me.

Promote the heroes in your life.

When I was hosting one of my first mastermind meetings, I presented two (clean and new) T-shirts I'd received for supporting a wonderful volunteer organization to two of the members who sat on the hot seat during the meeting. They were asking for feedback and advice from the group, specifically about how they could add more charitable giving into their business models. These "regifts" were presented in public and in person (I saved on postage too!) . . . and I included personal notes so I could tell each of them how much I admired their missions and commitment to giving.

The endorphin rush.

Walking to the table in my office where I pile up my gift packages every day for different people in my life may not register as exercise on my Fitbit, but every package makes someone else bigger and stronger, with care and intention. And there is no bigger achievement for me each day than figuring out how I can touch someone with something special just for them. The reason I needed to hire an assistant who could come to my house once a week (no virtual assistant in the Philippines for me) was precisely to take those packages to the post office. I love this kind of "direct mail"—but I don't love standing in line at the post office.

Nothing is a throwaway.

This is not about "one person's garbage is another person's treasure". . . and of course, giving your unwanted goods and clothes to charity is always a good thing to do. But at least once a day, if I have not created a package for someone, I walk around my office or check my bookshelves or go to my storage closet and see what reminds me of who. As the great Jay Abraham taught me (and what this last chapter is all about), "Your relationship capital is the most valuable asset in your portfolio." And one huge way to achieve "compound interest" on that account is to touch everyone in your life in the most meaningful ways and do it whenever the mood hits you—or whenever you've got some "junk" lying around.

5. STAY HUMBLE, EVEN WHEN YOU THINK YOU'VE GOT IT MADE

When Gary Bencivenga (the aforementioned Mariano Rivera of copywriting) retired, he hosted an event called the Bencivenga 100. It was a two-day farewell tour for the world's top copywriter, sharing everything he had learned along the way. It was $5,000 per seat and attended by a who's who of direct marketing and copywriting. It was truly incredible—one of those events that, years later, everyone says they went to, even if that's not quite true. It's sort of like those epic sports events that everyone says they went to, which makes you wonder how 500,000 people could fit into a 50,000-seat stadium.

The first day of the Bencivenga 100 was on May 20. I remember because it was my birthday. I hate my birthday but I love baseball, and it was my lucky day: my beloved Mets were playing the hated Yankees . . . and I had a ticket. I was sitting in the upper deck directly behind home plate, and for the first time in my life, after attending hundreds of live baseball games, I caught a foul ball, hit by the best Mets player at the time, Mike Piazza. I was thrilled. But at the same time, I categorize things like souvenir baseballs the same way I categorize mugs and cute little boxes from faraway lands. Put simply, they are just dust catchers. So . . . what to do with the baseball?

I came up with a killer idea. The next day, at day two of the Bencivenga 100, I took the baseball through the crowd during breaks and got every copywriter I knew to sign it. It was an all-star team of copywriters who were attending, including Gary Halbert, John Carlton, Parris Lampropoulos, David Deutsch, Jim Punkre, Richard Armstrong, Clayton Makepeace . . . and I know if I keep going, I will just insult everyone I don't name. Suffice it to say that anyone who was anyone in direct response copywriting was at the event, and I got all of them to sign the baseball. I was then privileged to have the opportunity to present the baseball to Gary after the afternoon break in front of the entire crowd.

But here's the hard lesson I learned from it later on:

A few years after the event, a copywriter I had never heard of sent me a LinkedIn request. Per my LinkedIn procedure, I checked out his profile and sent a personal e-mail with my usual goal of creating potential synergies right at the beginning of our relationship. He sent me a beautiful response, telling me how much he admired Boardroom, and that he had followed my career for many years. He then said he was actually at the Bencivenga 100 event (and he wasn't bluffing), and that when I was walking around the room on day two collecting those autographs for Gary's baseball, "you made eye contact with me, sized me up, and then just kept on walking."

I will never forget how that hit me right in the gut . . . I must have seemed like such a jerk. Fortunately for me, he wasn't bitter or angry. He admitted that he was a rookie in the business at the time, and that getting to that event had been a launching pad for his career. But it made me think about all the people we meet (or go out of our way *not* to meet) every day. We make judgments that some people are more "useful" to us than others.

But it's important for all of us to realize that everyone we come into contact with has a story, a contribution, and the ability to add value to our lives and the lives of others. And this is even truer as we attain more fame and fortune ourselves. It's so easy to get lost in the echo chamber of success, of people fawning over you and nodding along to everything you say like you can do no wrong. Keeping both feet firmly on the ground is critical to maintaining your good reputation and to thinking clearly. That's why I'm a broken record on having people around you who will tell you the honest truth and save you from your own ego.

I thought a lot about that copywriter at the Bencivenga 100. Surrounded by hall of famers, he chose not to be intimidated, seeing the opportunity right in front of him and how far he had come, instead of how far he still had to go. That's the kind of person I want around me . . . and I could have had him (and many others like him) as part of my universe much earlier if I had been more attentive and more humble and had asked more questions along the way. Well, better late than never. It's never too late to make up for a lost contribution.

If you're ever on the receiving end of this kind of interaction, let me add this from Nelson Mandela's 1994 inaugural speech, a quote that I believe originally came from Marianne Williamson: "Our deepest fear is not that we are inadequate; our deepest fear is that we are powerful beyond measure." Have no fear . . . you are not inadequate.

And don't think that even today I am never in a situation like that young copywriter was at the Bencivenga 100. I never hold it against someone for not noticing me, because it's up to me to get noticed. Some people (like me at that event) can just be a little slow to notice your greatness. Keep holding up your end of the bargain (i.e., being powerful beyond measure), and put in the hard work, because remember, you never know when someone else has their eye on you.

KEY TAKEAWAYS

Success in business is not just about the numbers. It's also the result of surrounding yourself with remarkable people who lift you up—and being that kind of person for others. The more proactively you build your connections with other great people, the more growth you will see, both personally and professionally.

- Be a strategic contributor, and remember that personal connection in business trumps just about every other strategy for professional growth.

- Don't connect superficially, or simply "network"— always put your best effort into your interactions with people, whether they are new relationships or longstanding ones.

- There is a compound interest that develops on your relationship capital. The value of your relationships increases over time, in terms of the fulfillment you get from them as well as the potential for personal and business growth and opportunity. Relationship capital is an investment for a lifetime.

- Be proactive in building interesting relationships: intentional dinners are a fun and effective way of doing this. When creating your intentional dinners, make your invite list carefully, plan the logistics and seating thoroughly, and make sure there is a way for guests to connect and follow up with each other after the event.

- Beyond intentional dinners, there are five simple ways to invest in your relationship capital:

  1. Embrace competition as coexistence.
  2. Don't make your lawyer rich.
  3. Remember that someone is always watching.
  4. Send Christmas cards in July.
  5. Stay humble, even when you think you've got it made.

■ ■ ■

As we come to the end of this book, I'm reminded of a wonderful proverb: "We make a living by what we get, but we make a life by what we give." As an entrepreneur and marketer, you have an incredible opportunity to contribute your unique genius to the world.

Remember, your list, the people on the receiving end of your business, is the most important asset you will ever have.

- Treat those people with the care and respect they deserve.

- Make them great offers that will truly serve them.

- Invest in the world-class creative that will communicate those offers in ways that will resonate with them—as individuals—as much as possible.

- Run your campaigns by the numbers, measuring everything.

- Be committed to the fundamentals of direct response, never being afraid to dig deep into the original source material, where it all came from—it will only make you a better marketer in the future.

- Always keep RFM and LTV top of mind.

- Protect your business by diversifying and using multiple channels; invest heavily in your customer support and fulfillment; and always overdeliver.

- And finally, be in the game for the long run and play fair. You'll sleep better, and you will be richer for it in every way.

FURTHER READING

DIRECT MARKETING (ONLINE AND OFFLINE)

Brunson, Russell. *Expert Secrets: The Underground Playbook for Creating a Mass Movement of People Who Will Pay for Your Advice*. New York: Morgan James Publishing, 2017.

Brunson, Russell. *DotCom Secrets: The Underground Playbook for Growing Your Company Online*. New York: Morgan James Publishing, 2015.

Caples, John. *Tested Advertising Methods*. 4th ed. Englewood Cliffs, NJ: Prentice-Hall Career & Personal Development, 1982.

Dworman, Steven. *$12 Billion of Inside Marketing Secrets Discovered Through Direct Response Television Sales: And how you can profitably apply them to your business*. Beverly Hills, CA: SDE, Inc., 2004.

Godin, Seth. *Permission Marketing: Turning Strangers into Friends and Friends into Customers*. New York: Simon & Schuster, 1999.

Hatch, Denny. *Method Marketing: How to Make a Fortune by Getting Inside the Heads of Your Customers*. Chicago: Bonus Books Inc., 1999.

Hatch, Denny, and Don Jackson. *2,239 Tested Secrets for Direct Marketing Success: The Pros Tell You Their Time-Proven Secrets*. Chicago: NTC Business Books, 1998.

Levesque, Ryan. *Ask. The counterintuitive online formula to discover exactly what your customers want to buy...create a mass of raving fans...and take any business to the next level*. Nashville: Dunham Books, 2015.

Libey, Donald R., and Christopher Pickering. *Libey and Pickering on RFM and Beyond: Wisdom, Analytics and Tactics for Improving Multichannel Profitability*. Expanded 2nd edition. West Des Moines, IA: Merit Direct Press, 2005.

Marshall, Perry. *80/20 Sales and Marketing: The Definitive Guide to Working Less and Making More.* Irvine, CA: Entrepreneur Press, 2013.

Polish, Joe. *Joe's Marketing Book.* Tempe, AZ: privately printed, 2016.

Reeves, Rosser. *Reality in Advertising.* New York: Alfred A. Knopf, 1961.

Ries, Al, and Jack Trout. *The 22 Immutable Laws of Marketing: Violate Them at Your Own Risk!* New York: HarperCollins Publishers, 1993.

Simpson, Craig, and Brian Kurtz. *The Advertising Solution: Influence Prospects, Multiply Sales, and Promote Your Brand.* Irvine, CA: Entrepreneur Press, 2016.

Kennedy, Dan S. *The Ultimate Marketing Plan: Target Your Audience! Get Out Your Message! Build Your Brand!* Avon, MA: Adams Business, 2011.

Skrob, Robert. *Retention Point: The Single Biggest Secret to Membership and Subscription Growth for Associations, SAAS, Publishers, Digital Access, Subscription ... Membership and Subscription-Based Businesses.* Tallahassee, FL: Membership Services, Inc., 2018.

Stone, Bob, and Ron Jacobs. *Successful Direct Marketing Methods: Interactive, Database, and Customer Marketing for the Multichannel Communications Age,* 8th ed. New York: The McGraw-Hill Companies, Inc., 2008.

Throckmorton, Joan. *Winning Direct Response Advertising: How to Recognize It, Evaluate It, Inspire It, Create It.* Englewood Cliffs, NJ: Prentice-Hall Inc., 1986.

Walker, Jeff. *Launch: An Internet Millionaire's Secret Formula to Sell Almost Anything Online, Build A Business You Love, And Live The Life Of Your Dreams.* New York: Morgan James Publishing, 2014.

COPYWRITING AND CREATIVE

Accountable Advertising, Inc. "Gary Bencivenga's Marketing Bullets," Marketing Bullets Archives. 2018. https://marketingbullets.com/archive.

Bird, Drayton. *How to Write Sales Letters That Sell: Learn the Secrets of Successful Direct Mail,* 2nd ed. London: Kogan Page, 2002.

Bly, Robert. *The Copywriter's Handbook: A Step-by-Step Guide to Writing Copy That Sells.* New York: Dodd, Mead & Company, 1985.

Carlton, John. *Kick-Ass Copywriting Secrets of a Marketing Rebel.* Reno, NV: Carlton Ink, 2002.

Carlton, John. *The Entrepreneur's Guide To Getting Your Shit Together.* Scotts Valley, CA: CreateSpace Independent Publishing Platform, 2013.

Collier, Robert. *The Robert Collier Letter Book.* East Setauket, NY: Robert Collier Publications, 1937 (revised 1950, 1978).

Deutsch, David, *Think inside the Box*. Delray Beach, FL: Early to Rise, 2006.

Edwards, Ray. *How to Write Copy That Sells: The Step-By-Step System for More Sales, to More Customers, More Often*. New York: Morgan James Publishing, 2016.

Ford, Mark Morgan, and Will Newman. *Persuasion: The Subtle Art of Getting What You Want*. Delray Beach, FL: American Writers & Artists, Inc., 2014.

Forde, John, and Michael Masterson. *Great Leads: The Six Easiest Ways to Start Any Sales Message*. Delray Beach, FL: American Writers & Artists, Inc., 2011.

Halbert, Bond. *The Halbert Copywriting Method Part III: The Simple, Fast & Easy Editing Formula That Forces Buyers to Read Every Word Of Your Ads!* Scotts Valley, CA: CreateSpace Independent Publishing Platform, 2016.

Halbert, Gary. *The Boron Letters*. Los Angeles: Bond Halbert Publishing, 2013.

Halbert, Gary. "The Gary Halbert Letter," The Gary Halbert Letter. 2003. www.thegaryhalbertletter.com.

Handley, Ann. *Everybody Writes: Your Go-To Guide to Creating Ridiculously Good Content*. Hoboken, NJ: John Wiley & Sons, Inc., 2014.

Hanly, Laura. *Content That Converts: How to Build a Profitable and Predictable B2B Content Marketing Strategy*. Lisbon: Hanly Creative, 2017.

Hatch, Denny. *Write Everything Right!: Let the world's highest-paid writers show you the secrets of making readers love your: e-mails, letters, memos, blog, ... website and yes, especially your résumé!* Philadelphia: Direct Marketing IQ, 2014.

Hopkins, Claude. *My Life in Advertising*. Chicago: NTC Business Books, 1966.

Hopkins, Claude. *Scientific Advertising*. Chicago: NTC Business Books, 1966.

Kennedy, Dan. *The Ultimate Sales Letter: Attract New Customers. Boost Your Sales*. 4th ed. Avon, MA: Adams Business, 2011.

Makepeace, Clayton. "The Total Package: Business-Building Secrets for Growth-Obsessed Companies," Makepeace Total Package. http://www.makepeacetotalpackage.com.

Miller, Donald. *Building a StoryBrand: Clarify Your Message So Customers Will Listen*. Nashville: HarperCollins Leadership, 2017.

Nicholas, Ted. *Magic Words That Bring You Riches*. London: Ted Nicholas, Chesham House, 1995.

Ogilvy, David. *Confessions of an Advertising Man*. Harpenden, Herts, UK: Southbank Publishing, 1963.

Ogilvy, David. *Ogilvy on Advertising*. New York: Random House, 1983.

Pressfield, Steven. *The War of Art: Break Through the Blocks and Win Your Inner Creative Battles.* New York: Black Irish Entertainment LLC, 2002. Paperback edition.

Schwab, Victor O. *How to Write a Good Advertisement: A Short Course in Copywriting.* New York: Harper & Row, 1962.

Schwartz, Eugene, M. *Breakthrough Advertising.* Westport, CT: Titans Marketing, 2017. Original copyright 1966 by Barbara Schwartz. *(Author's note: This classic could easily be in the Direct Marketing section or the Market Psychology section, since this is the one book that transcends everything we do in marketing. I put it in with Copywriting and Creative as a tribute to Gene Schwartz, possibly the greatest copywriter of all time.)*

Schwartz, Eugene, M. *The Brilliance Breakthrough: How to Talk and Write So That People Will Never Forget You.* Westport, CT: Titans Marketing, 2017. Original copyright 1994 by Eugene M. Schwartz.

Sugarman, Joe. *Advertising Secrets of the Written Word: The Ultimate Resource on How to Write Powerful Advertising Copy from One of America's Top Copywriters and Mail Order Entrepreneurs.* Las Vegas: DelStar Publishing, Inc., 1998.

Sugarman, Joe. *The Adweek Copywriting Handbook: The Ultimate Guide to Writing Powerful Advertising and Marketing Copy from One of America's Top Copywriters.* Hoboken, NJ: John Wiley & Sons, Inc., 2007.

Sugarman, Joe. *Triggers: 30 Sales Tools You Can Use to Control the Mind of Your Prospect to Motivate, Influence and Persuade.* Las Vegas, NV: DelStar Books, 2014.

Zinsser, William. *On Writing Well: The Classic Guide to Writing Nonfiction.* 7th ed., revised and updated. New York: HarperCollins Publishers, 2006. First published 1976.

BUSINESS GROWTH

Abraham, Jay. *Getting Everything You Can Out of All You've Got: 21 Ways You Can Out-Think, Out-Perform, and Out-Earn the Competition.* New York: Truman Talley Books / St. Martin's Press, 2000.

Agugliaro, Mike. *Nine Pillars 2.0: The Game-Changing Formula to Create Massive Transformation in Your Business and Life.* New Jersey: privately printed, 2017.

Bettger, Frank. *How I Raised Myself from Failure to Success in Selling.* New York: Prentice Hall Press, 1947.

Chowdhury, Subir. *The Ice Cream Maker: An Inspiring Tale About Making Quality the Key Ingredient in Everything You Do.* New York: Currency / Doubleday, 2005.

Edelston, Martin, and Marion Buhagiar. *"I" Power: The Secrets of Great Business in Bad Times.* Fort Lee, NJ: Barricade Books, 1992.

Fields, Jonathan. *Uncertainty: Turning Fear and Doubt into Fuel for Brilliance.* New York: Penguin Group, 2011.

Frishman, Rick, and Jill Lublin. *Networking Magic: How to Find Connections that Transform Your Life.* 2nd edition, updated. New York: Morgan James Publishing, 2014.

Gladwell, Malcolm. *Outliers: The Story of Success.* New York: Hachette Book Group, 2008.

Harnish, Verne. *Mastering the Rockefeller Habits: What You Must Do to Increase the Value of Your Growing Firm.* New York: SelectBooks, Inc., 2006. Paperback edition.

Harnish, Verne. *Scaling Up: How a Few Companies Make It...and Why the Rest Don't.* Mastering the Rockefeller habits 2.0. Ashburn, VA: Gazelles Inc., 2014.

Keller, Gary W., and Jay Papasan. *The ONE Thing: The Surprisingly Simple Truth Behind Extraordinary Results.* Austin, TX: Bard Press; 2013.

Kennedy, Dan. *No B.S. Sales Success in the New Economy.* Irvine, CA: Entrepreneur Press, 2010.

Kim, W. Chan, and Renee Mauborgne. *Blue Ocean Strategy: How to Create Uncontested Market Space and Make the Competition Irrelevant,* Expanded edition. Boston: Harvard Business Review Press, 2015.

Koenigs, Mike. *Publish And Profit: A 5-Step System For Attracting Paying Coaching and Consulting Clients, Traffic and Leads, Product Sales and Speaking Engagements.* San Diego: privately printed, 2012.

Lee, Ryan. *Passion to Profits.* Connecticut: privately printed, 2011.

Long, David. *Built to Lead: 7 Management R.E.W.A.R.D.S Principles for Becoming a Top 10% Manager.* Las Vegas: Next Century Publishing, 2014.

Masterson, Michael. *Ready, Fire, Aim: Zero to $100 Million in No Time Flat.* Hoboken, NJ: John Wiley & Sons, Inc., 2008.

McCarthy, Ken. *The System Club Letters: 57 Big Ideas to Transform Your Business and Your Life.* Tivoli, NY: privately printed, 2013.

McKeown, Greg. *Essentialism: The Disciplined Pursuit of Less.* New York: Crown Business, 2014.

Newport, Cal. *Deep Work: Rules for Focused Success in a Distracted World.* New York: Grand Central Publishing, 2016.

Sullivan, Dan. *The Dan Sullivan Question.* Toronto and Chicago: The Strategic Coach, 2009.

Tribby, MaryEllen. *Reinventing the Entrepreneur: Turning Your Dream Business into a Reality.* Hoboken, NJ: John Wiley & Sons, Inc., 2013.

Vaynerchuk, Gary. *Jab, Jab, Jab, Right Hook: How to Tell Your Story in a Noisy Social World*. New York: HarperCollins Publishers, 2013.

Wickman, Gino, and Mark C. Winters. *Rocket Fuel: The One Essential Combination That Will Get You More of What You Want from Your Business*. Dallas: BenBella Books, Inc., 2015.

DIRECT MAIL

Benson, Richard. *Secrets of Successful Direct Mail*. New York: The McGraw-Hill Companies, Inc., 1987.
(Author's note: See page 251 for a sample.)

Burnett, Ed. *Complete Direct Mail List Handbook: Everything You Need to Know About Lists and How to Use Them for Greater Profit*. Englewood Cliffs, NJ: Prentice Hall, 1988.

Grossman, Gordon. *Confessions of a Direct Mail Guy*. Westport, CT: Titans Marketing (original copyright Gordon W. Grossman), 2006.

Harper, Rose. *Mailing List Strategies: A Guide to Direct Mail Success*. New York: The McGraw-Hill Companies, Inc., 1986.

Hatch, Denison. *Million Dollar Mailings: The Art and Science of Creating Money-Making Direct Mail, Including Secrets of Using Direct Mail to Make Money on the Internet*. Chicago: Bonus Books, 2001. Originally published in 1992 by Denison Hatch.

Hodgson, Richard S., *Direct Mail and Mail Order Handbook*. 3rd edition. Chicago: The Dartnell Corporation, 1988.

Kennedy, Dan, and Craig Simpson. *The Direct Mail Solution: A Business Owner's Guide to Building a Lead-Generating, Sales-Driving, Money-Making Direct-Mail Campaign*. Irvine, CA: Entrepreneur Press, 2014.

Schwartz, Eugene M. *Mail Order: How to Get Your Share of the Hidden Profits That Exist in Your Business*. Westport, CT: Titans Marketing, 1982. (Original copyright Boardroom Reports, Inc.)

MARKET PSYCHOLOGY AND INSPIRATION

Anderson, Hans Christian. *The Emperor's New Clothes*. Boston: Houghton Mifflin Company, 1949.

Andrews, Andy. *How Do You Kill 11 Million People?: Why the Truth Matters More Than You Think*. Nashville: Thomas Nelson, 2011.

Ariely, Dan. *Predictably Irrational, Revised and Expanded Edition: The Hidden Forces That Shape Our Decisions.* New York: Harper Perennial, 2010. Originally published in 2008 by HarperCollins.

Bach, David. *Debt Free For Life: The Finish Rich Plan for Financial Freedom.* New York: Crown Business, 2010.

Bach, David. *The Automatic Millionaire, Expanded and Updated: A Powerful One-Step Plan to Live and Finish Rich.* New York: Crown Business, 2016. Originally published in 2003 by Broadway Books.

Burchard, Brendon. *High Performance Habits: How Extraordinary People Become That Way.* Carlsbad, CA: Hay House, Inc., 2017.

Burg, Bob, and John David Mann. *The Go-Giver, Expanded Edition: A Little Story About a Powerful Business Idea.* New York: Penguin Random House LLC, 2015. Originally published in 2007 by Penguin Random House LLC.

Cairns, Julie Ann. *The Abundance Code: How to Bust the 7 Money Myths for a Rich Life Now.* Carlsbad, CA: Hay House, Inc., 2015.

Carnegie, Dale. *How to Win Friends & Influence People.* New York: Pocket Books, 1936.

Carty, Thomas. *Backwards, in High Heels: Faith Whittlesey, Reagan's Madam Ambassador in Switzerland and the West Wing.* Oxford: Casemate Publishers, 2012

Cialdini, Robert. *Influence: The Psychology of Persuasion, Revised Edition.* New York: William Morrow and Company, 1993. Originally published in 1984 by William Morrow and Company.

Cialdini, Robert. *Pre-Suasion: A Revolutionary Way to Influence and Persuade.* New York. Simon & Schuster Paperbacks, 2016.

Coelho, Paulo. *The Alchemist.* New York: HarperCollins Publishers, 1993.

Grant, Adam. *Give and Take: Why Helping Others Drives Our Success.* New York: Penguin Group, 2013.

Graziosi, Dean. *Millionaire Success Habits: The Gateway to Health & Prosperity.* Expanded edition. Carlsbad, CA: Hay House, Inc., 2019.

Hallowell, Edward M., and John J. Ratey. *Driven to Distraction: Recognizing and Coping with Attention Deficit Disorder from Childhood through Adulthood.* New York: Anchor, 2011. Originally published in 1994 by Pantheon Books.

Hallowell, Edward M. *Success Strategies for the Crazy Busy.* Audiobook edition. Chicago: Nightingale-Conant, 2014.

Hemphill, Barbara. *LESS CLUTTER More Life: A Life's Teachings.* Pasadena, CA: True Roses, Inc., 2014.

Hogshead, Sally. *Fascinate, Revised and Updated: How to Make Your Brand Impossible to Resist.* New York: HarperCollins, 2016.

Hyman, Mark. *The Blood Sugar Solution: The UltraHealthy Program for Losing Weight, Preventing Disease, and Feeling Great Now!* New York: Little, Brown and Company, 2012.

Ikonn, Alex, and UJ Ramdas. *The Five-Minute Journal: A Happier You in 5 Minutes a Day.* Toronto: Intelligent Change, 2016.

Keppe, Norberto. *The Origin of Illness: Psychological, Physical and Social.* Englewood Cliffs, NJ: Campbell Hall Press, 2000.

Klaff, Oren. *Pitch Anything: An Innovative Method for Presenting, Persuading, and Winning the Deal.* New York: The McGraw-Hill Companies, 2011.

Maltz, Maxwell. *Psycho-Cybernetics: Updated and Expanded.* New York: Perigee, 2015.

Meisel, Ari, and Nick Sonnenberg. *Idea to Execution: How to Optimize, Automate, and Outsource Everything in Your Business.* Austin, TX: Lioncrest Publishing, 2016.

Meisel, Ari. *The Art of Less Doing: One Entrepreneur's Formula for a Beautiful Life.* Austin, TX: Lioncrest Publishing, 2016.

Pausch, Randy. *The Last Lecture.* London: Hodder & Stoughton, 2008.

Rand, Ayn. *The Fountainhead.* With an afterword by Leonard Peikoff. New York: The Bobbs-Merrill Company, 1943. Renewed copyright in 1971 by Ayn Rand.

Rivera, Mariano, and Wayne Coffey. *The Closer.* New York: Back Bay Books / Little, Brown and Company, 2014.

Sethi, Ramit. *I Will Teach You To Be Rich.* New York: Workman Publishing, 2009.

Silver, Yanik. *Evolved Enterprise: An Illustrated Guide to Re-think, Re-image & Re-invent Your Business to Deliver Meaningful Impact & Event Greater Profits.* Washington, D.C.: Ideapress Publishing, 2015.

Silverstein, Shel. *The Giving Tree.* New York: Harper & Row, 1964.

Seuss, Dr. *Oh, The Places You'll Go!.* New York: Random House, 1960.

Stephenson, Sean. *Get Off Your "But": How to End Self-Sabotage and Stand Up for Yourself.* San Francisco: Jossey-Bass, 2009.

Voss, Chris. *Never Split the Difference: Negotiating As If Your Life Depended on It.* New York: HarperCollins, 2016.

Weintraub, Jerry. *When I Stop Talking, You'll Know I'm Dead: Useful Stories from a Persuasive Man.* New York: Twelve, 2010.

BENSON'S RULES OF THUMB

Author's note: I thought it would be extremely useful and insightful to include Dick Benson's 31 "Rules of Thumb" that open his classic book, *Secrets of Successful Direct Mail,* as an addendum to the reading list I have created for *Overdeliver.* Please remember that Dick wrote these rules pre-Internet, yet every one of them has an application to online media.

"In defense of these prejudices: I have a lot of scar tissue backing up these principles. I offer them to you with this qualifier: They work for me."

—DICK BENSON

1. A two-time buyer is twice as likely to buy as a one-time buyer. Most of the experts I know who issue catalogs, handle circulation for publications, or raise funds by mail know this to be true.

2. The same product sold at different prices will result in the same net income per thousand mailed.

3. Sweepstakes will improve results by 50 percent or more.

4. A credit or bill-me offer will improve results by 50 percent or more.

5. Tokens or stickers always improve results.

6. Memberships renew better than plain subscriptions by 10 percent or more.

7. "Department store" pricing always pays except for membership offers.

8. You can never sell two things at once.

9. Self-mailers almost never work.

10. The more believable a special offer, the more likely its success.

11. The addition of installment payments for an item over $15 will increase results by 15 percent.

12. Dollar for dollar, premiums are better incentives than cash discounts.

13. Adding elements to a mailing package, even though obviously adding cost, is more likely to pay out than cheapening the package.

14. For magazines a "soft" offer ("Try a complimentary copy at our risk") is better than a hard offer (cash or "bill me").

15. A Yes-No option will increase orders.

16. "FREE" is a magic word.

17. Two premiums are frequently better than one.

18. Long copy is better than short copy.

19. Personalized letters work better to house lists (those who have bought or subscribed before) than to "cold" lists.

20. Brochures and letters should stand alone and each of them should contain all the information.

21. Direct mail should be scrupulously honest.

22. Subscriptions sold at half-price for at least eight months will convert at renewal time just as strongly as subscriptions sold for a full year at full price.

23. Lists are the most important ingredient to the success of a promotional mailing.

24. The offer is the second most important ingredient of direct mail.

25. Letters should look and feel like letters.

26. An exclusive reduced price to a house list will more than pay its way.

27. To predict final results from a promotion, you can assume you will always receive as many more orders as you've received in the past week. This projection will generally be valid beginning with the second week's orders and continuing thereafter.

28. A follow-up mailing dropped two weeks after the first mailing will pull 50 percent of the original response.

29. An incentive to pay cash when you offer both cash and credit options reduces net response.

30. Test-mailing packages are best when they come from independent creative sources.

31. Offers of subscriptions using two terms (i.e., 8 months, 16 months) will pull more money . . . but 10 percent fewer orders.

Nothing works all the time, but ignore any of these rules at your own peril.

INDEX

A

Abraham, Jay, xxiv, 98, 103–104, 231, 237
Abundance mind-set
    customer service and generosity, 176
    100:0 concept and, 11
Accountability, 216
Advertising, direct marketing vs., xxii
Advertising Solution, The (Kurtz), 19
Affiliate deals, 70
À la carte buying of marketing services, 152–155
Anecdotal evidence, following, 41–46
Arrogance, avoiding, 216
Assets, assessing, 103–108
Attribution, 159–161
Audience. *See* List management
Auerbacher, Adolph, 41, 44–45

B

Bach, David, 192
Barrier to switch, 174, 186–188
Behavior. *See also* Customers
    Breakthrough Advertising (Schwartz) on, 21–23, 31
    human behavior and effect on marketing, 20–22
    tracking of, 69–70

transaction data, 78–79
Bencivenga, Gary
    Bencivenga 100, 237–239
    bookalog by, 94–97, 99
    on controls, 8–9
    expertise shared by, 226
    humility of, 127–128
Benson, Dick
    on "bogey," 38
    on expertise, 221
    on list management importance, xxiv–xxv
    multichannel marketing and, 153, 155
    reliance on smart people by, 5
    "Rules of Thumb," 251–253
    Secrets of Successful Direct Mail, 195
    on testing methodology, 111
Best practices
    care and concern for customers, 52
    consequential thinking in messaging, 51
    copy and creative resources, 49–50
    copywriting perfection, 50
    customer feedback, 50
    customers' care for your business, 52
    discipline of, 46–49
    language usage, 53
    logic line, 51–52
    strategic use of content, 49
Betuel, Eric, 108

Billion Dollar Internet Strategy Setting Summit (2000), 231
Bill-me-later offers, 60–62, 95
BL/P. *See Bottom Line/Personal* (Boardroom)
Boardroom Dinners (intentional dinners) model, 217–225
Boardroom Inc. *See also Bottom Line/Personal* (Boardroom)
  The Book of Inside Information, 100
  The Bottom Line Yearbook, 108
  The Encyclopedia of Estate Planning, 24
  growth of, xvii
  Healing Unlimited, 100
  Health Confidential, 93
  How to Do Everything Right, 98–99
  launch of, 91
  legacy of copywriters of, 130
  The Little Black Book of Secrets, 96
  Tax Hotline, 131
  The 30-Day Diabetes Cure, 89–90
  trade books repositioned as direct mail by, 99–103
Boardroom Reports (Boardroom)
  launch of, 60–62, 91–92
  niche markets of, 66–68
  rebranding of, 92–93
"Bogey," 38
Bookalogs, 94–97, 99
Book of Inside Information, The (Boardroom), 42–43, 100
Boswell, Thomas, 169–170
Bottom Line/Personal (Boardroom)
  Boardroom Reports rebranded as, 92
  customer focus of, 67–68
  infomercials by, 42–49
  LTV of customers of, 37–39, 195–199
  offers and, 92, 94–95, 98
Bottom Line/Tomorrow (Boardroom), 24
Bottom Line Yearbook, The (Boardroom), 108
Branding strategy
  aggression vs. brand congruency, 45
  fundamentals of personal brand, xxvii
  offers and, 91–93
Breakthrough Advertising (Schwartz)
  handwritten letter sent with, 120–121
  on human behavior, 21–23, 31
  republishing of, by Kurtz, xx, 21–22

C

Campaign. *See* Offers
Caples, John, 126
Cards, for relationship capital, 212, 233–237
Carlton, John, 118, 191
Change, expecting, 40
Change of address files (COA), 73–74
Characteristics of world-class copywriters
  curiosity, 121–122
  humility, 127–128
  hunger, 119–121
  importance of copywriting and, 129–130 (*See also* Copywriting)
  passion, 124–126
  portfolio of work and sharing success, 128–129
  smarts, 122–123
  understanding of direct marketing principles, 126
Collier, Robert, 126
Compensation, royalties as, 28
Competition
  as coexistence, xix, 225–226
  studying controls of competitors, 32
Compiled lists, 68–70
Complacency, avoiding, 216
Concept tests (Q tests), 87–91
Congruent marketing, 200–204
Connection ("Vitamin C"), 209–213
Consequential thinking in messaging, 51
Contact strategy, 76–77
Content. *See also* Copywriting
  assessing assets for offers, 106–107
  strategic use of, 49
Controls. *See also* Measurability
  beating, 14, 48, 96, 98, 108
  creativity of, 23–24, 28
  defined, 3
  gaining new controls, 8–9

studying controls of competitors, 32

Conversion, 162–163

Copywriting, 117–146. *See also* Creative
characteristics of world-class copy
writers, 119–129
copy and creative resources for,
49–50
copywriters as key to marketing,
129–131
creativity of, 23–26
importance of, 117–119
language usage, 53, 139–141
perfection of, 50
relationship between message and
list for, 139–141
research for, 133–137
revisiting discarded ideas for,
137–138
segment psychology for, 142–145
support for, 131–133
tailoring, 141–142

Core Principles
creativity (#3), 23–26
marketing as psychology (#1), 20–23
original source material and prior
success (#5), 30–32
shortcuts (#2), 22–23
swipe files (#4), 26–29

Creative
congruent marketing and, 200
creativity (Core Principle #3), 23–26
creativity of offers, 113–114
defined, 117
tailoring of, 141–142

Curiosity, of copywriters, 121–122

Customers. *See also* Customer service
and fulfillment; Lifetime value (LTV);
Multichannel marketing; Relationship
capital
buying behavior of, 21–23, 31,
69–70, 78–79
feedback by, 50, 67–68
multibuyers, 72–74
renewals by, 195–197

Customer service and fulfillment,
169–190
barrier to switch and, 174, 186–188
baseball analogy to, 169–174
for customer retention, 174–178
distractions from, 179–186
"marketing by walking around,"
175–176
secret shoppers' insight for, 178–179

D

Database. *See* List management

Data cards, 63–64

Decision-making, "moose on the table"
and, 201

Deutsch, Dan, 6

Differentiation, 211–212

Direct mail
creative copywriting for, 23–26
expense of postage for, 33–34, 48
list management for, online
marketing, 34
"lumpy direct mail," 234–235
online marketing vs., 34–37
swipe files for, 26–29

Direct marketing, 33–55
best practices for, 49–53
defined, xxii
direct mail vs., xxvi
discipline for, 46–49
following marketing trends and, 41–46
fundamental lessons of, xxiii–xxviii
lifetime value (LTV) and, 37–41
list management for direct mail vs.
online marketing and, 34
measurability of, xxii–xxiii
understanding of, by copywriters,
126 (*See also* Copywriting)

Discarded ideas, revisiting, 137–138

Discipline
following best practices for, 49–52
value of, 46–49

Distractions, dealing with, 179–186

Downs, Hugh, 46

Dworman, Steve, 45

E

Edelston, Marty. *See also* Boardroom Inc.
  on avoiding legal problems, 228
  Boardroom Dinners (intentional dinners) of, 217–225
  Boardroom Reports growth and, xvii
  Boardroom Reports launch by, 60–62
  celebratory gifts by, 24
  characterization of, 135
  on consequential thinking, 51
  on copywriting, 120
  curiosity of, 130
  Four Pillars of Being Extraordinary of, 2–3, 7–8
  as "giver," 12–13
  legacy of, 170, 214
  on logic line, 51–52
  "nice notes" by, 212
  on teaching for success, xx
E-mail
  cost of, 36
  for customer relationship, xxv–xxvi
Employees, happiness of, 174
Encyclopedia of Estate Planning, The (Boardroom Reports), 24
End users. *See* Customers
Ethics, xxiv
Expertise
  Boardroom Dinners (intentional dinners) model for, 217–225
  as fundamental lesson of direct marketing, xxvii
  reliance on smart people for, 5–7
  sharing, with competition, 226

F

Facebook, 30–31
Farber, Barry, 45–46
Financial issues
  compensation with royalties, 28
  discipline and, 46–53
  of mailing, 33–34
  marketing trends and, 41–46
  measuring LTV, 37–39
  monetary, defined, 74–75 (*See also* Recency, frequency, and monetary (RFM) scores)
  recency, frequency, and monetary (RFM) scores, 35–37
  tracking performance, 39–41
Fishman, Michael, 224
Five-minute favor concept, 12
41/39/20 formula, 58–60, 83
Four Pillars of Being Extraordinary
  Edelston and, 2–3
  helping others first (Pillar 4), 7–8
  outworking everyone else (Pillar 1), 3
  possessing insatiable curiosity (Pillar 2), 4–5
  surrounding yourself with smart people (Pillar 3), 5–7
Frequency, defined, 72–74. *See also* Recency, frequency, and monetary (RFM) scores
Frishman, Rick, 218, 220, 223
Fundamental lessons of direct marketing
  credibility and transparency, xxvi
  of direct marketing measurability, xxvi
  ethics, xxiv
  expertise, xxvii
  involvement, xxiii
  relationship management vs. customer importance, xxv–xxvi
  time needed for list management, xxiv–xxv
  using multiple channels for marketing, xxviii

G

Gifts, for relationship capital, 233–237
Give and Take (Grant), 11
Givers, Takers & Matchers concept, 11–13, 209
Glickman, Ken, 218
Grace issues, 60
Grammar, language usage and, 53
Grant, Adam, 11
Grossman, Gordon, 36, 100–101, 110, 112

Guthy, Bill, 43
Guthy-Renker, 43, 160–161

H
Halbert, Gary, 6, 119–121, 123, 125–126
Hallowell, Ned, 209–210
Handwriting, impact of, 120
Hay House, 39
Healing Unlimited (Boardroom), 100
Health Confidential (Boardroom), 93
Helping others first (Pillar 4), 7–8
Hiring practices, 131, 134, 152–155
Hopkins, Claude, 31, 175
Horizontal vertical niche, defined, 84
How Life Imitates the World Series
(Boswell), 169–170
How to Do Everything Right (Board-
room), 98–99
Humility
of copywriters, 127–128
for relationship capital, 237–239
Hunger, of copywriters, 119–121
Hurricane Hugo, effect on marketing,
183–184

I
Infiniti, 187–188
Infomercials
advent of, 41–46
discipline needed for, 46–49
Intentional dinners (Boardroom Dinners), 217–225

J
Jayme, Bill, 23–26
Johnson, Arthur, 45–46, 121–122

K
Kennedy, Dan, 29, 50, 147, 223
Kissinger, Henry, 132
Kurtz, Brian. *See also* Boardroom Inc.
blog of, 213
Breakthrough Advertising (Schwartz),
republished version, 21–22
briankurtz.me, xxviii

L
Lampropoulos, Parris, 4, 122, 131
Learning from others, 208–209
Legal problems, avoiding, 226–231
Lifetime value (LTV), 191–205
congruent marketing for, 200–204
importance of, 37–41
as key metric, 192–195
multichannel marketing and,
156–159
offers and, 97
renewals and profit, 195–197
targeting customers and, 191–192
up-front marketing expenses and,
197–200
LinkedIn, 209–210, 238
List management
assessing assets for offers, 105–106
compiled lists vs. response lists,
68–70
congruent marketing and, 201–204
devoting time to, xxiv–xxv
for direct mail vs. online marketing,
34
list, defined, 57–58
list as donation, example, 183–184
list building and, 64–65
list history and, 134
list managers and list brokers, xvii–xx
relationship between message and list
for copywriting, 139–141
segmentation and list selection,
191–192
time needed for list management,
xxiv–xxv
"tribe," 36
understanding market for offers,
84–86 (*See also* Offers)
Little Black Book of Secrets, The (Boardroom), 96
Logic line, 51–52
LTV. *See* Lifetime value (LTV)
"Lumpy direct mail," 234–235

M

Magalogs, 27, 35–36
Marketing as psychology (Core
  Principle #1), 20–23
"Marketing by walking around,"
  175–176
Marketing channels. *See* Multichannel
  marketing
Marshall, Perry, 19, 50
Martin, Mel, 25
Measurability
  of copywriting success, 158–159
  importance of, for direct marketing,
    xxii–xxiii
  LTV as key metric, 192–195
  LTV calculations and up-front
    marketing expenses, 197–200
  of multichannel marketing, 155–156
  regression modelling for, 30–31
  of statistical significance, 109–112
  tracking performance, 39–41
Meredith Corporation, 41
Messaging
  aggression vs. brand congruency, 45
  consequential thinking in messaging, 51
  relationship between message and
    list for copywriting, 139–141
Monetary, defined, 74–75
"Moose on the table," 201
Multibuyers, 72–74
Multichannel marketing, 147–167
  attribution and, 159–161
  conversion and, 162–163
  as fundamental lesson of direct
    marketing, xxviii
  importance of using multiple
    channels, 147–150
  LTV of customers and, 156–159
  measuring, 155–156
  one-stop shopping dangers, 152–155
  online to offline to online (O to O
    to O) for, 163–165
  researching channel of choice for
    customers, 150–152
  targeting for market and, 60
  television for, 41–49

N

Networking, 207–208. *See also* Relation-
  ship capital
Networking Magic (Frishman), 218
"Nice notes," 212
Niche marketing, 66–68, 84

O

Offers, 83–115
  assessing assets for, 103–108
  bill-me-later offers, 60–62, 95
  branding strategy and, 91–93
  campaign structure and, 94–99
  creativity of, 113–114
  finding niches for, 84
  41/39/20 formula and, 58–60, 83
  measuring statistical significance of,
    109–112
  premiums with, 108–109
  pyramiding, 112–113
  Q tests and, 87–91
  repositioning older products as, 99–103
  understanding market for, 84–86
Ogilvy, David, 20–21, 122, 140
1 + 1 = 64 concept, xx
100:0 concept, 9–11
Online marketing. *See also* Financial issues
  direct mail vs., 34–37
  list management for, direct mail vs., 34
  recency, frequency, and monetary
    (RFM) scores for, 75–77
  testing for, 48
Online to offline to online (O to O to
  O), 163–165
Open Church movement, 27
Operation Desert Shield, effect on marketing, 182–183
Original source material, 17–32
  basing work on fundamentals of, 17–20
  creativity (Core Principle #3), 23–26
  marketing as psychology (Core
    Principle #1), 20–22
  prior success of (Core Principle #5),
    30–32
  researching, 229–230

shortcuts (Core Principle #2), 22–23
swipe files (Core Principle #4), 26–29
Outworking everyone else (Pillar 1), 3
Overdeliver, 1–15
   controls and, 8–9
   Four Pillars of Being Extraordinary
    for, 2–8
   Givers, Takers & Matchers concept
    for overdelivering, 11–13
   100:0 concept for overdelivering, 9–11
   relationship management vs.
    customer importance, xxv–xxvi, 1–2

P

"Paranoid package" example, 97–99
Passion, of copywriters, 124–126
Personal Power (Robbins), 43
Platinum Plus, 232–233
Portfolio of copywriting work, 128
Possessing insatiable curiosity (Pillar
   2), 4–5
Premiums as offers, 108–109
Promotions, assessing assets for offers,
   107–108
Pyramiding, 112–113

Q

Q tests, 87–91

R

Reader's Digest, 36, 100–101
Reality in Advertising (Reeves), 18–19
Recency, frequency, and monetary
   (RFM) scores, 57–87
   bill-me-later offers and, 60–62
   compiled lists vs. response lists,
    68–70
   defined, 70–71
   frequency, defined, 72–74
   industry niche ("table selection")
    and, 66–68
   list building and, 64–65
   list importance and, 57–58
   monetary, defined, 74–75
   for online marketing, 75–77

recency, defined, 71–72
recency issues and effect on
   customer service, 182–185
regression modelling and
   demographic segmentation, 77–80
   for segmentation, 35–37
   targeting and, 58–60, 63–64
Reconnection with prior contacts, 231–
   233, 237–239
Reeves, Rosser, 18, 19
Regression modelling, 30–31, 77–80
Relationship capital, 207–241
   avoiding legal problems and,
    226–231
   benefits of, 213–214
   cards and gifts for, 212, 233–237
   customer importance vs., xxv–xxvi
   embracing competition as
    coexistence, 225–226
   humility for, 237–239
   intentional dinners (Boardroom
    Dinners) model for, 217–225
   as investment in future, 214–217
   learning from others, 208–209
   making connection with ("Vitamin
    C"), 209–213
   networking and, 207–208
   reconnection with prior contacts
    and, 231–233, 237–239
Religion, power of, 27–29
Renker, Greg, 43, 127–128, 160–161
Repositioning, 99–103
Research
   by copywriters, 133–137
   relationship capital and, 229–230
   researching customers' channel of
    choice, 150–152
Response lists, 68–70
Response rate, to Q Testing, 88–89
Retention of customers, 174–178
Return rates, by customers, 172
RFM. *See* Recency, frequency, and mon-
   etary (RFM) scores
Robbins, Tony, 43
Rodale Press, 101
Royalties, 28

"Rules of Thumb" (Benson), 251–253
Rutz, Jim, 6, 26–29

S

Scarcity mind-set vs. abundance
    mind-set, 11
Schefren, Rich, 199
Schwartz, Eugene (Gene) M.
    Boardroom Reports launch and, 62
    Breakthrough Advertising, xx, 31,
        120–121
    copywriting and, 134–136
    curiosity of, 121
    on language usage, 53, 139–141
    on marketing as psychology, 20,
        22–23
    1 + 1 = 64 concept of, xx
Scientific Advertising (Hopkins), 31
Secret shoppers, 178–179
Secrets of Successful Direct Mail (Benson),
    195
Segmentation
    LTV and list selection, 191–192
    recency, frequency, and monetary
        (RFM) scores, 35–37, 77–80
    segment psychology needed for
        copywriting, 142–145
    targeted list segmentation, 62
    (*See also* Target marketing)
Sethi, Ramit, 224
Shortcuts (Core Principle #2), 22–23
Single channel marketing, dangers of,
    152–155
Smarts, of copywriters, 122–123
Social media
    Facebook, 30–31
    LinkedIn, 209–210, 238
    multichannel marketing and, 150
Spielberg, Steven, 124
Statistical significance, 109–112
Strategic use of content, 49
Success, repeating (Core Principle #5),
    30–32

Success, shared by copywriters, 128–129
Sullivan, Dan, 6, 11, 198
Surrounding yourself with smart people
    (Pillar 3), 5–7
Survey package promotion example,
    94–97, 99
Survey tests (Q tests), 87–91
Swipe files (Core Principle #4)
    assessing assets for offers, 107–108
    overview, 26–29

T

"Table selection," 66–68
Target marketing. *See also* List
    management
    mailing thoughtful cards/gifts to
        subscribers or acquaintances,
        233–235
    recency, frequency, and monetary
        (RFM) scores and, 58–60, 63–64
    targeted list segmentation, 62
Tax Hotline (Boardroom), 131
Television infomercials, 41–49
Third party offers, 37
30-Day Diabetes Cure, The, 89–90
Titans of Direct Response (event), 29,
    127–128, 223, 227
Tracy, Reid, 39
Trade books, repositioned as direct mail,
    99–103
Transaction data, 78–79
"Tribe," 36
Trudeau, Kevin, 44
Trump, Donald, 139–141

U

Ultimate Healing (Boardroom), 46
Unique selling proposition (USP), 18, 19
U.S. Postal Service
    change of address files (COA), 73–74
    zip codes for compiled lists, 69

V

Vertical niche, defined, 84
"Vitamin C" (connection), 209–213

W

Walker, Jeff, 231–233
Wanamaker, John, 155
Williamson, Marianne, 239
*World's Greatest Treasury of Health
    Secrets, The* (Boardroom), 45

Z

Zip codes, 69

ACKNOWLEDGMENTS

We all know we can't do anything in life without a loving and supportive family, and in my case, I've been so lucky to have Robin, Alex, and Madeline as my cheering section. In addition, my sister Ellen and my supportive parents have been there from the start (even though my parents never really understood what I did for a living—my Mom still doesn't—and she thinks I should get an M.B.A.!).

And there are many more people I would like to thank and acknowledge. I stand on the shoulders of so many giants from so many phases of my career.

Someone suggested that this book could be titled *All My Mentors Are Dead*. Sounds a little maudlin, I know, but my philosophy when I was in my 20s and 30s was to have mentors in their 60s and 70s, since they had all the wisdom and I had none. Unfortunately, that means I've already lost way too many of the people who taught me the most.

Leading that list is Marty Edelston, who is all over this book and all over my life. I've been blessed to have had someone who was both a business mentor and almost like a second father to me.

Gene Schwartz, who comes up time and again not only in this book but in everything I do, is a giant of a man to be looked up to, and not just because he was so tall. I also want to thank his wife, Barbara Schwartz, who trusted me to be the shepherd of her beloved husband's work. Without her (and her trusted adviser Steve Scherer), the world would not have complete access to Gene's brilliance as they do now, specifically *Breakthrough Advertising* and *The Brilliance Breakthrough*. And a shout-out to my friend and direct marketer Jim DiCola for partnering with me to bring *The Brilliance Breakthrough: How to Talk and Write So People Will Never Forget You* back from the dead (no more $4,000 copies on Amazon—it is now totally accessible and affordable to everyone in marketing and copywriting). Having that Gene Schwartz lost classic available in addition to *Breakthrough Advertising* is a blessing. Other greats who are no longer with us and who I miss terribly:

Dick Benson, the curmudgeon's curmudgeon to many, but to me he was always "Timid Timothy," as he liked to be called. No one could understand that one . . . but I did.

Rodney Friedman, Benson's partner in some of the most successful direct marketing franchises ever, who left us way too soon.

Lee Epstein, who taught me not just how to give, but to give without an expectation of a return.

Bill Jayme, whose creative contributions were always matched by his huge heart.

Adolph Auerbacher, the man with the best judgment ever.

Jim Rutz, one of the liveliest minds ever to write copy.

Fred Catona, "Mr. Direct Response Radio."

Scott Haines, one of Gary Halbert's prized students, also left us way too soon. As did Audri and Jim Lanford, masters of innovation.

Bob Stone, the man who wrote "The Bible" of Direct Marketing.

Other mentors and friends, mostly retired but not forgotten, include Gordon Grossman, who is quoted a lot in this book and who taught me so much about direct marketing fundamentals and databases; and Denny Hatch, who taught me how to "write everything right" (the title of one of three of his books that are listed in my reading list).

Copywriters have been a big part of my life. While I'm done calling myself a copywriter wannabe, I also know how much I owe to all the great copywriters I have ever worked with wishing I could be as prolific as they are. That's why I will always be a copywriter groupie. So many copywriters made me look so good over so many years (and they were always super generous, saying that I helped *them* look good because I knew something about lists). But my skill was nothing compared to theirs. I want to acknowledge the original Mount Rushmore of Boardroom copywriters—in addition to Gene Schwartz, there was the late Mel Martin, the best copywriter no one ever heard of; the aforementioned Jim Rutz; and of course, Gary Bencivenga, the "Mariano Rivera of copywriting," considered the top copywriter alive today.

Then there's the more modern Mount Rushmore—the copywriters I worked with most in the second half of my career at Boardroom: Eric Betuel, David Deutsch, Arthur Johnson, and Parris Lampropoulos. Four geniuses, and four special friends as well.

Before I go on to talk about all of the other copywriters I have learned so much from—as well as marketers and thought leaders of all kinds who influenced me the most—I have to call out a "moose on the table": I am well aware that to this point, I have not listed any women in my professional acknowledgments . . . yet.

During the early part of my career, there were far fewer women teaching and mentoring—and thank goodness there are so many more today.

I received a lot of flak at the "Titans of Direct Response" event in 2014 for not having any female speakers, and I sporadically receive e-mails in response to my blog posts when I talk about my key mentors from my past (who are mostly male), asking, "Why no women?"

As far as that event, because it was a tribute to Boardroom and Marty Edelston, the sad truth is that when Boardroom was founded in 1972 (and in the years that followed), the builders, consultants, and copywriters from the outside were mostly men. I know some women even boycotted the event, which hurt. I did my best to explain, and I have had to live with this sad fact despite the event being a huge success.

Note: I can tell you, however, that many of the key folks internally at Boardroom during my tenure were women, and most of the senior staff while I was there were female as well. Two extraordinary women, Joan Throckmorton and Rose Harper, helped build and shape Boardroom from the outside, even in the early years, Joan as a copywriter and Rose as a list broker. Since neither one was alive in 2014, I distributed their out-of-print classic books to the most prolific and dynamic women in direct response marketing who were in the audience at "Titans." Their books are included in my reading list despite being out of print. I've got my copies of their books in a prominent spot on my bookshelf.

I do my best to pay it forward (and I will continue to do so) to the women (and men) who have shaped my world and the world of so many other direct response marketers . . . and you will see many amazing women in the rest of these acknowledgments. The change has done us good.

There were many other copywriters (and designers) that made me and everyone else at Boardroom look good for many years, writing control after control. In addition to every copywriter I've mentioned already, there was Marcella Allison, Richard Armstrong, Sol Blumenfeld, Belinda Brewster, Carline Anglade-Cole, Henry Cowen, Rob Davis, Lee Euler, Pat Garrard, Lori Haller, Bill Jayme, Barnaby Kalan, Kent Komae, Clayton Makepeace, Bernie Mazel, Don Pierce, Jim Punkre, Michele Raes, Heikki Ratalahti, Kim Krause Schwalm, Alice Taus, and David Wise. My apologies to anyone I did not mention.

Other copywriters and "teachers of writing copy" I also learned so much from (although I don't recall any of these folks writing a control for Boardroom—which is not my only criteria for greatness!) include Jon Benson, Drayton Bird, Bill Bonner, John Carlton, Craig Clemens, Doug D'Anna, Ray Edwards, Ed Elliott, Mark Ford, John Forde, Marie Forleo, "Doberman Dan" Gallapoo, David Garfinkel, Justin Goff, Bond Halbert, Kevin Halbert, Don Hauptman, "Big Jason" Henderson, Daniel Levis, Ryan Markish, Sam Markowitz, Scott Martin, Ted Nicholas, Caleb O'Dowd, Mike

Palmer, Traian Sava, Joe Schriefer, Ben Settle, Richard Stanton-Jones, Amit Suneja, Mike Ward, and Irving Wunderman.

I also want to thank "copywriter trainers" and coaches Katie Yeakle, Denise Ford, Kevin Rogers, Kira Hug, Rob Marsh, Abbey Woodcock, K. C. Baney, Ramit Sethi, Joanna Wiebe, and anyone else who takes on this noble mission—for all they do to train the next generation of A-list copywriters and for letting me into their respective worlds to teach and be part of that mission.

And even though I didn't know all six legends from my first book, they live on in this book too—in addition to Gene Schwartz, there's John Caples, Robert Collier, Gary Halbert, Claude Hopkins, and David Ogilvy. Of course, I owe an additional debt of gratitude to my co-author of *The Advertising Solution*, Craig Simpson, who could have done the book on his own but brought me in as a partner, which gave me the confidence to write this book. And thanks to Lawrence Bernstein for helping us create a swipe file for the ages (www.TheLegendsBook.com) from those six legends as a companion resource to the book. That was also an inspiration for the creation of www.OverdeliverBook.com, which I hope you will all access as a complement to Overdeliver.

Thanks to all the people who participated in the *Breakthrough Advertising* interviews (not otherwise mentioned in my acknowledgments), which enabled so many additional eternal truths to pass into the next generation, and many of those truths are covered in this book: Bob Bly, Harlan Kilstein, Milt Pierce, Yanik Silver, Joe Vitale.

Since we now can all agree that "lists are 41 percent," and the most important part of every marketing campaign (with apologies to the copywriters!), I will always be indebted to the two men who taught me the list business—Dave Florence and Mike Manzari. And I am also indebted to Richard Viguerie, who was one of my first "professors" of direct mail along with Dick Benson.

I think fondly on those days as a "list manager" and learning the business from Dave, Mike, and Richard, which led me into a world of direct marketing (mostly direct mail and print and eventually online) in the 1980s, 1990s, and early 2000s where I made so many lifelong friends to this day (although we have lost a few along the way). All are (or were) teachers and students of the craft with me every step: Marie Adolphe, Susan Allyn, Tom Amoriello, Karen Arbegast, Simon Aronin, Bill Baird, John Baldwin, Terri Bartlett, Stacy Parks Berver, Jock Bickert, Arthur Blumenfield, Stuart Boysen, JoAnna Brandi, Annette Brodsky, Nora Brophy, Mike Brostoff, Ed Burnett, Cindy Butehorn, Jimmy Calano, Tom Callahan, Brian Carnahan, Jeff Carneal, Cary Castle, Nancy Cathey, Frank Cawood, Sandy Clark, Bob Cohn, Kevin Cordray, Pat Corpora, Tom Corry, Dan Danielson, Bill Denhard, JoAnne Dunn, Mal Dunn, Suzanne Eastman, Robert Englander, Larry Epstein, Barbara Erlandson, John Finn, Kevin Finn, Ed Fones, Carrie French, Joe Furgiuele Hank Garcia, Lois Geller, Jonah Gitlitz, David Gitow, Dick Goldsmith, Deb Goldstein, Dan Gonzalez, Jerry Gould, Fran Green, Denise Greiner, Judy Haselhoef, Peggy Hatch, John Hendrickson, Gary Hennerberg, Gail Henry, Leon Henry, Stuart Hotchkiss, Beth Hurwitz, Charles Inlander, Karen Isenberg, Stuart Jordan, Barbara Kaplowitz, Joel Katz, Graeme Keeping, Dee Kendall, Bob Keppel, Dan Kern, Jackie Kern, Beth Dent Ketzner, Bob King, Liz Kislik, Dave Klein, Jeff Kobil, Ed Krug, Cyndi Lee, Don Libey, Tim Litle, Marc Liu, Michael Loeb, Lorna Lowery, Coleen Malc, Carole Mandel, Lon Mandel, Harriet Maneval, Harvey Markovitz, Bob Marty, Angelo Matera,Linda McAleer, Jeff Meltzer, Steve Millard, Jon Mulford, Joel Nadel, Ted Nicholas, Andrea Nierenberg, Hal Oringer, Charles Pace, John Pahmer, Chris Paradysz, Pierre Passavant, Dave Penzell, Ben Perez, Reed Phillips, Tom Phillips, Jerry Pont, Rick Popowitz, Jim Prendergast, Kathi Ramsdell, Steve Rapella, Donn Rappaport, Tom Reynolds, Tom Rocco, Marji Ross, Mac Ross, Nat Ross, Hank Rossi, Nick Sarantakos, Bruce Seide, Harold Shain, Joe Shain, Mike Shapiro, Ed Sheehan, David Shepard, Christine Slusarek, Laurie Spar, John Squires, Ralph Stevens, John Suhler, Bob Teufel, Jenny Thompson Rich Vergara, Frank Ward, Wallace Ward, Sue Webb, Martin Weiss, Ann Wixon, Chip Wood, Andy Yoelin, Alan Zamchick, Dawn Zier, Caroline Zimmerman.

A special acknowledgment to Steve Dworman, who taught me the direct response television business and, together with the amazing team at Boardroom, created one of the biggest direct marketing success stories of multichannel marketing—ever.

I'd like to acknowledge my accountability group—who I like to call my "$25 group"—the cheapest mastermind around to join, but one that is as rich as any with information and influence—my brothers Michael Fishman, Jim Kwik, and Ryan Lee. And thanks to the unwavering support from two "brothers in arms," guys who always have my back and know this business as well as anyone I have ever met, Alan Kraft and Jim Kabakow.

Thanks to the three people I go to when I need the ultimate in guidance and coaching: Joe Polish, Dan Sullivan, and Jeff Walker.

And there are a whole host of marketing geniuses, thought leaders, entrepreneurs, and pioneers I follow to this day, and will follow to the day I die, beginning with the keynote speakers from the Titans of Direct Response event not yet mentioned elsewhere: Dan Kennedy, Perry Marshall, Joe Sugarman, Ken McCarthy, and Greg Renker.

And so many others who have taught me so much and believed in me over the years, including Mike Agugliaro, Kristen Arnold, Lou Aronica, David Bach, Ellyn Bader, Eric Bakey, Allen Baler, Erin Baler, Craig Ballantyne, Joe Barton, Bari Baumgardner, Lee Bellinger, Susan Berkley, Dan Benamoz, Larry Benet, Dave Berg, Bob Beverley, Josh Bezoni, Paul Bigham, Daniela Birkelbach, Dana Blankenhorn, Chandler Bolt, Chrissy Borchardt, Joshua Boswell, Patrick Bove, Shelley Brander, Rae Brent, Ross Bridgeford, Justin Brooke, Dr. Joy Browne, Russell Brunson, Shaun Buck, Dr. Ruth Buczynski, Erin Burch, Todd Brown, Brendon Burchard, Bob Burg, Michael Cage, Julie Cairns, Jesse Cannone, Mike Capuzzi, Adee Cazayoux, Alex Charfen, Joseph Choi, Rich Christiansen, Robert Cialdini, Lisa Cini, Ian Clark, Mike Cline, Travis Cody, Melinda Cohan, Mike Colella, Paul Colligan, Chad Collins, John Corcoran, Jeff Corriveau, Dave Coyle, JV Crum III, Cedric Crumbly, Fernando Cruz, Phil Cuzzi, Stan Dahl, Stephen Dean, Eelco de Boer, Dave Dee, Ryan Deiss, Gina DeLong, Rachelle Diaz, Mike Disney, Eric Douay, Hugh Downs, Andy Drish, John Lee

Dumas, Mary Jane Dykeman, Bo Eason, Dawn Eason, Yuri Elkaim, Ryan Ellefsen, Roxanne Emmerich, Al Evans, Marc Evans, Marty Fahncke, Michelle Falzon, Summer Felix, Ilan Ferdman, Jonathan Fields, Jim Fitzgerald, Jason Fladlian, Joe Foley, Denise Ford, Nick Fosberg, Tim Francis, Dr. Stephen Franson, Katrin Frößler, Jason Friedman, Rick Frishman, Dylan Frost, Roy Furr, Jayson Gaignard, Thaddeus Gala, John Gallagher, Jason Garber, Randy Garn, Susan Garrett, Arthur Gelber, Kevin Gianni, Ben Glass, Elaine Glass, Ken Glickman, JB Glossinger, Gary Goldstein, David Gonzalez, Denise Gosnell, Bill Gottlieb, Bill Gough, Helmut Graf, Carla Graubard, Steve Gray, Dean Graziosi, Seth Greene, Craig Gross, Aharon Pinchas Grundman, David (Jay) Guigue, Garrett Gunderson, Audrey Hagen, Dr. Ned Hallowell, Derek Halpern, Will Hamilton, Rick Harmon, Verne Harnish, Paul Hartunian, Clay Hebert, Barbara Hemphill, Cameron Herold, Doug Hill, Tracy Hinken, Jess Holland, Shel Horowitz, Martin Howey, Jeremey Hunsicker, Don Hutcheson, Khoa Huynh, Dr. Mark Hyman, Danny Iny, Dean Jackson, Richard James, Debra Jason, Joline Johannes, Jeff Johnson, Shane Johnston, Darcy Juarez, Attila Pongor-Juhasz, Dr. Joel Kahn, Mark Kaplan, Danny Katz, Noah Katz, Brian Kay, Jesse Kay, David Kekich, Frank Kern, Erik Kerr, Rachel Kersten, Sidney Kess, Gail Kingsbury, Mastin Kipp, Esther Pinky Kiss, Mindie Kniss, Mike Koenigs, Jason Korman, Steve Krein, Ken Krell, Dr. Judy Kuriansky, Dan Kuschell, Nicholas Kusmich, Victoria Labalme, Vishen Lakhiani, Tim Larkin, Glen Larson, Sage Lavine, Carey Leader, Ryan Levesque, Senator Joseph Lieberman, Justin Livingston, Steve Loflin, David Long, Pauline Longdon, Michael Lovitch, Rick Lugash, Margaret Lynch, Jeff Madoff, Alice March, Frank Maguire, Michael Maidens, Wendy Makepeace, Alex Mandossian, Steven Mandurano, Brad Martineau, Paul Martinez, Clate Mask, Harry Massey, Kathy Mauck, Dane Maxwell, Shannon McCaffery, Andrew McCall, Richard McFarland, Ryan McGrath, Greg McKeown, Amy Dow McLaren, Stu McLaren, Ari Meisel, Blue Melnick, Ed Mendlowitz, Dan Meredith, Mike Michalowicz, Christian Mickelsen, Sheila Mielcarek, James Mielnik, Donald Miller, Eunice Miller, Richard Miller, Mike Monahan, Jeff Moore, Brian Moran, Tom Morkes,

Ben Morris, Marisa Murgatroyd, Jeff Murphy, Nick Nanton, Praveen Narra, Dr. Michael Neal, Ken Neumann, Sebastien Night, Myles Norin, Bill O'Hanlon, Ed O'Keefe, Dr. Tom Orent, Nick Ortner, Eben Pagan, Dr. Steven Palter, Kathleen Patten, David Paull, Tim Paulson, Molly Pearson, Peter Pearson, Sarah Petty, David Phelps, Kim Walsh-Phillips, Greg Poulos, Annie Hyman Pratt, UJ Ramdas, Phil Randazzo, Hallvard Reiso, Ken Rendell, Norman Rentrop, Eric Rhoads, Mike Rhodes, Lee Richter, Buck Rizvi, Susan RoAne, Ocean Robbins, Robin Robins, Erico Rocha, Dan Roitman, Olivier Roland, Greg Rollett, Zac Romero, Anna Rossi, Lisa Rossi, Richard Rossi, Christopher Ruddy, Ginger Rutz, Myra Salzer, Rich Schefren, Patricia Schramm, Congressman Christopher Shays, Ron Sheetz, Farukh Shroff, Ben Simkin, Sonia Simone, Steve Sims, Steve Sipress, Ryan Skelly, Robert Skrob, Babs Smith, Dr. Michael Solomon, Frank Sonnenberg, Nick Sonnenberg, Paulette Sopoci, Selena Soo, Robert Spector, Jonathan Sprinkles, Casey Stanton, Dr. Mark Stengler, Dr. Sean Stephenson, Sarah Anne Stewart, Marc Stockman, Hillary Styles, Neil Sutton, Ed Swain, Jaime Tardy, Ricardo Teixeira, Rich Thau, David Thompson, Kevin Thompson, Susan Peirce Thompson, Mark Timm, MaryEllen Tribby, Christie Turley, Josh Turner, Zim Ugochukwu, Ron Urbach, Daryl Urbanski, Erin Verbeck, JJ Virgin, Chris Vos, Jon Walker, Shannon Waller, James Wedmore, Dr. Jeremy Weisz, Joel Weldon, Barbara Weltman, Ambassador Faith Whittlesey, Kyle Widner, David Will, Ethan Willis, Ann Wilson, Mark Winters, Stephanie Winston, Dave Woodward, Ian Wyatt, Keith Yackey, Pamela Yellen, Melissa Young, Rob Zadotti. And trying to list everyone means I missed someone . . . thank you to anyone I should have mentioned and didn't.

I'd like to thank everyone I worked with at Boardroom over my 34 years. Any time this book makes it seem like I did anything great by myself, I did not. We hired the best, which made Boardroom an icon in the direct marketing world and a company that attracted the brightest minds in the business. Everyone there did, and still does, incredible work and makes Boardroom the most amazing direct marketing think tank that has ever existed.

Thanks to the people I work with now in Titans Marketing—my assistant, Carla Zwaan, who runs so much of the business day to day, my marketing partner, Chris Mason, and the wonderful Mary Grace "Macy" Mahait who does so much behind the scenes (and on the other side of the world) in the Philippinnes. And I rarely make a move in the business without consulting my "consigliere" Peter Hoppenfeld, who is always there for me too, as are my financial advisors Barry Gothelf and Tom Henske and my IT support genius, Paul Schietinger. A special shout out to Ron Drescher, a "best man" in my life—one who had "toast privileges" at my wedding—and who is also responsible for so much excellent legal work behind the scenes.

Thank you to all my Titans Mastermind and Titans Master Class members mentioned and not mentioned by name above, past, present, and future, as I continue my mission to reach more people with what I have to teach—they make it all worthwhile, and they inspired me to write this book as much as anyone.

I also want to thank the early readers of the manuscript: Jay Abraham, Jim DiCola, Perry Marshall, Rob Hanly, and Robert Skrob.

And a special shout-out to my "Uncle Jay" (Jay Abraham) for writing the foreword and being a guiding light and motivator to me for more than 25 years, and he remains that today.

A big thank-you and acknowledgment to my developmental editor on this book, Laura Gale. I could not have gotten here without her—she had incredible patience when I didn't do my homework and kept me on the straight and narrow to get this book finished.

Thank you to the folks at Morgan James—particularly Karen Anderson and David Hancock—for their support.

Finally, I want to thank Reid Tracy, Patty Gift, Anne Barthel, Mary Norris, Rachel Shields Ebersole, Marlene Robinson, Stacey Smith, Tricia Breidenthal, Lindsay McGinty, Lauren Rosenthal, Catherine Veloskey, Celeste Phillips, Steve Morris, and the rest of the amazing team at Hay House for believing in me and this book.

ABOUT THE AUTHOR

Brian Kurtz has been a serial direct marketer for almost 40 years and never met a medium he didn't like . . . and while he's had much success, he also must admit that trying to sell subscriptions and books on the back of ATM receipts and under yoghurt lids were only a 'good idea at the time'.

As a key business builder at Boardroom Inc. with founder Martin Edelston, Brian worked with, and was mentored by, many of the top marketers and copywriters who have ever lived.

Overdeliver is Brian's second book. His first book, co-authored with Craig Simpson, was *The Advertising Solution* (2016), which profiled and taught core marketing fundamentals from six of the greatest advertising legends ever (www.TheLegendsBook.com).

Today Brian consults and works directly with bleeding-edge direct response marketing companies and entrepreneurs in a wide variety of categories and in all channels through his two mastermind groups, Titans Mastermind and Titans Master Class (and soon to be a third, Titans Xcelerator). He also publishes books and materials for direct response marketers (including owning the exclusive rights to the landmark work by Eugene Schwartz, *Breakthrough Advertising*, with Gene's wife, Barbara).

He writes and speaks regularly at marketing and copywriting events. Find out more about Brian at briankurtz.net and access free resources accompanying this book at www.OverdeliverBook.com.

WWW.OVERDELIVERBOOK.COM

Thank you for purchasing *Overdeliver*!

Consistent with the title, I want to continue to "overdeliver" to you for many years to come.

If you go to www.OverdeliverBook.com, you will be treated to priceless and hard-to-find resources from many of the greatest direct-response marketers and copywriters of all time, most of whom have been profiled in this book.

These are free resources to help you build your business for a lifetime playing the long game.

What I have put together so far (and I will be adding even more to www.OverdeliverBook.com regularly):

- Rare and classic videos from many of the "Titans of Direct Response," many of which I spoke about in *Overdeliver*

- Tips and secrets from top copywriters not available anywhere else

- "The lost chapters" from *Overdeliver* . . . research and writing I have done since this book was completed

- PDFs and access to books that are either out-of-print or will only be available on this site

- Swipe files to study and adapt from all marketing channels to get your messages noticed and remembered, whether you work online, offline or both

- A compilation of the best headlines of all time . . . over 10,000 of them

- And much more as I find best-in-class information and best practices that will help you build your business in the present . . . and into the future.

www.OverdeliverBook.com

In the meantime, keep overdelivering for anyone you serve . . . and go forth and multiply!

Hay House Titles of Related Interest

YOU CAN HEAL YOUR LIFE, the movie,
starring Louise Hay & Friends
(available as an online streaming video)
www.hayhouse.com/louise-movie

THE SHIFT, the movie,
starring Dr Wayne W. Dyer
(available as an online streaming video)
www.hayhouse.com/the-shift-movie

■ ■ ■

HIGH PERFORMANCE HABITS: How Extraordinary People Become That Way, by Brendon Burchard

MILLIONAIRE SUCCESS HABITS: The Gateway to Wealth & Prosperity, by Dean Graziosi

OPPORTUNITY: How to Win in Business & Create a Life You Love, by Eben Pagan

WOMEN ROCKING BUSINESS: The Ultimate Step-by-Step Guidebook to Create a Thriving Life Doing Work You Love, by Sage Lavine

All of the above are available at www.hayhouse.co.uk

■ ■ ■

Hay House Podcasts
Bring Fresh, Free Inspiration Each Week!

Hay House proudly offers a selection of life-changing audio content via our most popular podcasts!

Hay House Meditations Podcast

Features your favorite Hay House authors guiding you through meditations designed to help you relax and rejuvenate. Take their words into your soul and cruise through the week!

Dr. Wayne W. Dyer Podcast

Discover the timeless wisdom of Dr. Wayne W. Dyer, world-renowned spiritual teacher and affectionately known as "the father of motivation." Each week brings some of the best selections from the 10-year span of Dr. Dyer's talk show on Hay House Radio.

Hay House Podcast

Enjoy a selection of insightful and inspiring lectures from Hay House Live events, listen to some of the best moments from previous Hay House Radio episodes, and tune in for exclusive interviews and behind-the-scenes audio segments featuring leading experts in the fields of alternative health, self-development, intuitive medicine, success, and more! Get motivated to live your best life possible by subscribing to the free Hay House Podcast.

Find Hay House podcasts on iTunes, or visit
www.HayHouse.com/podcasts for more info.

CONNECT WITH
HAY HOUSE
ONLINE

🌐 hayhouse.co.uk   **f** @hayhouse

📷 @hayhouseuk   🐦 @hayhouseuk

▶ @hayhouseuk   ♪ @hayhouseuk

Find out all about our latest books & card decks • Be the first to know about exclusive discounts • Interact with our authors in live broadcasts • Celebrate the cycle of the seasons with us • Watch free videos from your favourite authors • Connect with like-minded souls

'*The gateways to wisdom and knowledge are always open.*'

Louise Hay